Global Security Upheaval

Global Security Upheaval

Armed Nonstate Groups Usurping State

Stability Functions

Robert Mandel

Stanford Security Studies, An Imprint of Stanford University Press
Stanford, California

Stanford University Press
Stanford, California

Special discounts for bulk quantities of Stanford Security Studies are available to corporations, professional associations, and other organizations. For details and discount information, contact the special sales department of Stanford University Press. Tel: (650) 736.1782, Fax: (650) 736.1784

Printed in the United States of America on acid-free, archival-quality paper

Library of Congress Cataloging-in-Publication Data

Mandel, Robert
    Global security upheaval : armed nonstate groups usurping state stability functions / Robert Mandel.
        pages cm
    Includes bibliographical references and index.
    ISBN 978-0-8047-8497-9 (cloth : alk. paper)—ISBN 978-0-8047-8498-6 (pbk. : alk. paper)
        1. Security, International.   2. Non-state actors (International relations)   3. Political stability.   I. Title.
    JZ5588.M365 2013
    355′.033—dc23

                                                                        2012038607

Typeset by Newgen in 10/14 Minion

Contents

Illustrations

Figures

Tables

Acknowledgments

THIS STUDY—my eleventh book—is the product of years of deep pondering. It represents the next step in my continuing intellectual journey through the key dimensions of post–Cold War post-9/11 global disorder. The relationship between armed nonstate groups and stability links up with many of today's most pressing global security concerns.

Compared to my previous books, this study dramatically shakes up core security assumptions, and for that reason the scope of this undertaking was huge, requiring familiarity with several disparate bodies of literature. An investigation of this magnitude can rarely be executed successfully without outside help. I wish to thank my two undergraduate student research assistants, Marie Steinrücke and Alexis Frisbie, for considerable help with the case studies and for refinement of some of the general ideas. My conversations with my colleagues at other institutions, especially Phil Williams, Troy Thomas, and Bill Casebeer, were absolutely invaluable. At my own institution, I wish to thank Heather Smith-Cannoy for her constant enthusiastic encouragement on this project. Geoffrey Burn, the security studies editor for Stanford University Press, was once again exceptional in his kindness, humor, compassion, and support throughout this book's rather lengthy review process. Beyond examining the published literature, numerous conversations with several colleagues in government intelligence and defense organizations have significantly contributed to my thinking, and they all deserve thanks. However, I take full responsibility for any egregious errors found in this volume.

This book is dedicated to those academic scholars and government policy makers who are eager and able to question prevailing global security assumptions (rather than to defer and conform to popular schools of thought) and who are open to "outside-the-box" iconoclastic thinking rather than conventional modes of analysis. Despite the illusion of receptivity to unorthodox ways of looking at the world, many positive and negative incentives draw analysts to try to fit into dominant ways of thinking instead of truly questioning what they read and hear regardless of the prestige of the sources; and to stick with narrow and safer topics of inquiry rather than going out on a limb to boldly challenge what has come beforehand. My hat goes off to those who avoid this inertia-laden trap and have the courage to be truly creative in the security realm.

Global Security Upheaval

1 INTRODUCTION

Analytical Focus

THIS STUDY CHALLENGES the prevailing understanding of how security provision works within the contemporary international system. Conventional thinking about international stability rests on five main assumptions: (1) states and intergovernmental organizations are "the dominant locus of authority in global society,"[1] as "territorial state sovereignty is the natural and right form of political organization that delineates and produces world order";[2] (2) armed nonstate groups are illegitimate "spoilers," disrupting security and triggering political disorder and violent conflict;[3] (3) the mass public consistently demands state government protection;[4] (4) private bodies can enhance security only if they do not rely on the threat or use of violence, as with transnational market-based or humanitarian organizations;[5] and (5) if a state is not providing stability, "a strategy of strengthening and expanding governmental capacity would be a sensible response to the governance deficit."[6] Both scholars and policy makers have relied on these tried-and-true premises for centuries.

Since the end of the Cold War in 1989, central state governments have typically been considered the most important or even the sole sources of stability, and subnational and transnational nonstate forces have been identified as a major source of global instability, facilitating ominous disruptive flows of people, goods, and services that have moved readily across international boundaries. Although these claims have some validity, both contentions appear to be too sweeping. In a world where it is possible to identify the devolution of authority from the state to armed nonstate groups,[7] these mainstream security beliefs merit reexamination.

So in contrast, this study calls into question all five commonly held contentions about global stability. A careful assessment of prevailing assumptions and recent real-world trends creates a startling set of counterpropositions: (1) areas exist where it makes little sense to rely on central state governments for stability; (2) attempts to bolster such governments to promote stability often prove to be futile; (3) armed nonstate groups can sometimes provide local stability better than states; (4) power-sharing arrangements between states and armed nonstate groups may sometimes be viable; and (5) these changes in the international setting call for major analytical shifts and significant deviation from standard responses. Figure 1.1 summarizes the differences between conventional and unconventional thinking about stability promotion. These differences reveal a drastic rather than an incremental shift in thinking about global security, one that creates challenges for policy that call for nothing less than a new security framework promoting global order.

Figure 1.1. Conventional and unconventional security orientations

Conventional security mode

Territorial state sovereignty is the natural and right form of political organization that delineates and produces world order.

Armed nonstate groups are illegitimate "spoilers," disrupting security and triggering political disorder and violent conflict.

The mass public consistently demands protection specifically from the central state government.

Private bodies enhance security only if they do not rely on the threat or use of violence, as with market-based or humanitarian groups.

If a state does not provide stability, strengthening and expanding government capacity is a sensible response to the governance deficit.

Unconventional security mode

Areas exist where it makes little sense to rely on central state governments for stability.

Attempts to bolster such governments to promote stability have often proven to be futile.

Armed nonstate groups can sometimes provide local stability better than states.

Power-sharing arrangements between states and armed nonstate groups may sometimes be viable.

Recent changes in the international setting call for major analytical shifts and significant deviation from standard responses.

CENTRAL THRUST

This study's central thrust is to analyze conceptually and empirically the ongoing global shift in security governance from public to private hands. It focuses on when this shift is most and least conducive to stability, when armed nonstate groups are most and least effective in promoting stability, and when power sharing between central state governments and armed nonstate groups makes the most and least sense. Thus this investigation emphasizes a fluid "emergent actor" approach rather than a reification of the state system,[8] addressing a crucial security gap in understanding the opportunities and dangers posed by nontraditional coercive sources of authority in international relations.

The two pivotal focal points in this study are stability and armed nonstate groups. When considering stability, the study concentrates on the role of armed nonstate groups; and when considering these groups, it concentrates on their impact on stability. This investigation deemphasizes other nonstate stability sources, including noncoercive subnational and transnational groups; and other outcomes, including justice and human rights. Throughout, there is awareness that the relationship between the study's two main concepts is both two-way and dynamically interactive—besides the impact of armed nonstate groups on stability, the presence or absence of stability may affect the likelihood of emergence and strength of armed nonstate groups.

The United States National Intelligence Council, the American intelligence community's center for long-range strategic thinking, has recognized the centrality of both armed nonstate groups and stability. Armed nonstate groups, whose importance the National Intelligence Council noted because of their growing power in the increasingly multipolar global system,[9] are important because, conceptually, anarchy permits coercive forces other than states to assume some security governance functions; and, empirically, several recent armed nonstate group control attempts have challenged states as the exclusive source of international stability. Within the post–Cold War setting, prevailing security conditions have been conducive to the reemergence of these groups and to their filling existing authority voids. Stability, whose importance the National Intelligence Council underscored through the creation since 2004 of an Instability Watch List,[10] is important because (1) conceptually, stability is widely considered a central facet of local, national, regional, and global security; (2) empirically, the current scope and direction of worldwide instability are truly ominous; and (3) empirically, the United States in its foreign military policy has recently begun using the phrase "stability operations"[11] to describe a key component of its strategy—post-combat goals of "winning the peace" and engaging in successful post-conflict reconstruction, or of minimizing the disruptive impacts of failing states and ungoverned areas. Within a chaotic world containing multiple competing core values, stability merits attention as a necessary but not sufficient security prerequisite, for stability is perhaps the only common security goal transcending profound cultural differences. Examining the emerging relationship between armed nonstate groups and stability brings into question crucial related notions, such as "good" security governance, sovereignty, and legitimacy.

This study's central thrust links up with important broader security issues. These include:

1. changes in security governance, incorporating the contraction of state and expansion of nonstate security functions

2. diversity in both form and function of customary authority structures across countries

3. transformation of the notions of sovereignty and legitimacy in the current global security setting

4. differing conceptions of stability, leading to contrasting and potentially contradictory policies toward armed nonstate groups

5. backfire effects of security governance initiatives on stability, emerging when inappropriate actions are undertaken toward armed nonstate groups

6. proliferating marginalized areas without effective security governance in today's world

7. state reluctance to negotiate or share power with armed nonstate groups

8. difficulties encountered by international law and international organizations in recognizing armed nonstate groups playing a role in security governance

9. acceptance by affected populations of coercive rule if protection and basic survival needs are effectively provided for

10. greater savviness by armed nonstate groups than states in coping with imminent global instability challenges

11. differentiation advantages in policies toward cooperative and uncooperative armed nonstate groups

12. accountability losses resulting from increasingly intertwined nontransparent relationships between public and private authority structures, and among the armed nonstate groups themselves

Key questions emerge about when armed nonstate groups work in a top-down versus bottom-up manner, operate comfortably within and outside of prevailing security norms, and trigger opposition, nonresponse, or cooperation from or collusion with states.

This study thus connects what goes on within states to what goes on across states, explores the changing web of linkages between state and nonstate parties, and emphasizes the growing role of subnational and transnational forces in international relations. The analysis emphasizes wherever possible how the impacts of armed nonstate groups on stability are both causes and consequences of other more widely studied global security transformations. In the end, any attempt to alter the role of armed nonstate groups in affecting stability would require both a fuller understanding of these relationships and an ability and willingness to address and transform key security parameters intertwined with these changes. Such willingness may on occasion necessitate compromising the principles embedded in enlightened liberal democratic values situated in an open globalized world.

Examining patterns of armed nonstate groups' impact on stability provides a unique lens through which to analyze today's global security dilemmas. One could grapple with fundamental security questions in international relations about the impact posed by (1) armed nonstate groups compared to central state governments; (2) armed nonstate groups compared to transnational organizations not relying on coercion, such as private multinational corporations and private humanitarian organizations; and (3) state and nonstate stability challenges in the current international system compared with state and nonstate stability challenges in previous global settings (including during the Cold War). This special lens also permits analysis of the preparedness of targets coping with armed nonstate groups compared with targets coping with other kinds of security concerns. Placing this study's central thrust in the broader context of threat, vulnerability, and preparedness seems helpful in understanding how the impact of armed nonstate groups on stability presents similar and different challenges compared with other security concerns.

This analysis is explicitly from a security perspective, because armed nonstate groups appear to have their most direct influence in the security realm, and because these security impacts seem to be more important and have more far-reaching consequences than any other type of impact. Given the frequency and severity of instability in recent decades, leader and mass public fears have intensified about the loss of protection and the potential coercive destruction of the political regime, civil society norms, and persons and property. The disruptions generating these fears involve pernicious implications that merit both increased understanding and improved management. Despite this study's security focus, there is a concerted effort to integrate insights from any relevant work dealing with the topic from the widest range of different analytical angles.

Several elements of this study make it unique. First, it represents the first major study to look comprehensively at the potential of armed nonstate groups to promote stability and improve security governance. From a scholarly standpoint, most international relations security literature is still state-centric and does not focus on the significant "coercive transition"[12] occurring globally. From a policy standpoint, states and international organizations are still wary of any form of support or acceptance of security control by armed nonstate groups. Second, this study is the first systematic conditional analysis of when and how armed nonstate groups are most and least likely to enhance stability, in the context of assessing the comparative advantages of the full range of potential stability enhancers. Third, this is the first comparative assessment of armed nonstate groups exclusively focused on their stability impact, and the first conceptual examination of global stability that highlights the ways in which coercive private forces can sometimes be viable alternatives to states. Fourth, this is the first study to include policy recommendations for simultaneously facilitating cooperative armed nonstate groups and impeding uncooperative armed nonstate groups. Fifth, this study is the first to analyze the ongoing security governance transformation in supply-demand terms. Sixth, it is the first study to examine in detail the ties between this security transformation and clashing societal values. Finally, this study is the first exploration of exactly when and how power sharing can occur between central state governments and armed nonstate groups, and when and how such cooperative arrangements are most and least likely to promote stability.

INVESTIGATOR MODE

A crucial premise endorsed by this study is that the impact of armed nonstate groups on stability is neither random nor haphazard, and has significant enduring patterns meriting investigation. Exploring these patterns should allow deeper understanding of the roots of armed nonstate group behavior and stability on the local, national, and global levels; improved comprehension of the short-term and long-term impacts of armed nonstate groups on stability; better anticipation of what these groups might do in response to differing opportunities and roadblocks they encounter and how resulting stability challenges might transform in the future; and sounder ideas about effective management of armed nonstate groups and effective promotion of global stability. Although the primary thrust of the book is more explanatory than predictive or prescriptive, it does offer future projections and policy guidelines about armed nonstate groups and stability.

This book utilizes comparative case study analysis to explore the security transformation and the impact of armed nonstate groups on stability. Although a burgeoning set of local, national, and transnational armed nonstate groups exist, and there are many instances where these groups have attempted some form of security control, this study emphasizes major cases that had significant repercussions on stability, with attention to whether these impacts have been positive or negative. For each of the twelve cases included in the study, security importance trumped other considerations, including the amount of research material available.

Four obstacles impede rigorous research on this topic: (1) the prevalence of biases about armed nonstate groups; (2) the absence of hard data and the associated impediments to valid generalizable research findings; (3) the challenge in finding a meaningful and relevant definition of stability; and (4) the difficulty of isolating armed nonstate group control attempts from those of the rest of society.

First, many researchers seem to operate with a foregone conclusion that armed nonstate groups are always dangerous, eager to promote violence, devoid of legitimacy, and utterly destabilizing. Second, there are no reliable aggregate data—qualitative or quantitative—on global armed nonstate group behavior, owing heavily to secrecy: accounts are often tainted with subjectivity, with little cross-checking because there is no systematic way of verifying claims. Much literature contains colorful, idiosyncratic illustrations of how a particular armed nonstate group operates in a particular situation, but it is difficult to tell how representative these are of broader patterns. The reality that both law enforcement groups and armed nonstate group members often closely guard data relevant to armed nonstate group control attempts creates a huge investigative roadblock.[13] Third, no universally accepted yardstick exists for stability, with differences often reflecting clashing cultural values, and consensus within states—in the eyes of either the central state government or the mass public—varying markedly. Some metrics directly contradict others, and even when they do not, the result can be dangerously conflicting policies for stability promotion among neighboring countries. Fourth, it is hard to differentiate among the roles of the different shady and not-so-shady players involved in armed nonstate group activities and to distinguish these from activities undertaken routinely by the rest of society. Moreover, "the identities of terrorists, guerrilla movements, drug traffickers, and arms smugglers are becoming more slippery," with considerable "identity mutation" apparent.[14]

To overcome research bias regarding armed nonstate groups, this study is committed to minimizing stereotyping of armed nonstate groups, to qualifying its arguments about these groups' activities, and to avoiding any fixed, universal deterministic assumptions about these groups or their relationship to stability. This investigation probes dispassionately into optimal stability-promoting security governance without prejudice about what type of parties—state or nonstate—are the providers. Perhaps most important, from the outset this inquiry has been as open to seeing cases where armed nonstate groups wreak havoc and chaos as it has been to seeing cases where they have stabilizing effects on the affected population.

To maximize the validity and generalizability of its findings, this investigation covers the widest range of both successful and unsuccessful—and constructive and destructive—efforts to achieve security control by armed nonstate groups. To increase the credibility of findings and to address the absence of hard data, this study utilizes diverse independent sources in investigating each case, highlighting controversies and differences of opinion for any firm conclusions reached. Furthermore, because many conventional assumptions about armed nonstate groups' impact on stability seem wrongheaded or ill advised, with many political leaders possessing conflicting contentions about how to deal with armed nonstate groups and undertaking policy responses that fail to achieve stated goals, this study recognizes its responsibility to look at the widest range of evidence to be able to improve the understanding of patterns across the differing cases and thus of the coherence of resulting policies. Failing to consider a broad enough range of cases, so as to be able to identify predictable patterns of resulting stability impacts by armed nonstate groups, could inadvertently reduce the possibility of developing globally applicable policies to manage the embedded security dangers.

To address the challenge of finding a relevant and meaningful definition of stability, this study derives—from a comprehensive review of the different stability metrics and the underlying stability controversies they highlight—four essential stability functions. The selection of these four functions as relevant and meaningful across the board is carefully justified, and they are applied consistently and evenhandedly to all cases to determine stability outcomes of armed nonstate group control attempts. Even though no definition of stability is perfect, it seemed imperative for this study to settle on a single, overarching operational definition.

To remedy the ambiguity surrounding armed nonstate groups and their activities—and to overcome the obstacle of isolating armed nonstate groups and activities from those involving the rest of society—this study's cases identify those areas where the dividing line between licit and illicit, covert and overt, legitimate and illegitimate, and officially sanctioned and unsanctioned is the murkiest. The cases acknowledge both the constant morphing of armed nonstate groups and the significant state of flux in the relationships between armed nonstate groups and states, and between armed nonstate groups and stability. Although the domestic and global boundaries between public and private governance, and between formal and informal rule, are blurring,[15] it is still possible to detect and isolate distinctive patterns relevant to this study's central thrust.

The study's scope is global, given that armed nonstate groups operate throughout the world. This means is that, although attention is paid to both local and global stability, there is no special focus on armed nonstate groups or on stability in any particular country or region, or in any one set of narrow security interests—including those of the United States. Many analysts assume that armed nonstate groups are a developing-country issue, not touching advanced industrial societies, but this study challenges that premise through its case studies. Moreover, there is neither a summary of trends by country or region nor a comparative analysis across countries or regions, for patterns uncovered transcend national borders and do not reveal cross-regional differences. The expansion of armed nonstate group control attempts to include different parts of the world and forms of illicit behavior has made encompassing an international scope—incorporating both advanced industrial societies and the developing world—essential for capturing the full range of security implications.

Because of the major impact of the end of the Cold War upon (1) the dramatic unleashing of armed nonstate groups, (2) the increased volatility of the global security context, and (3) the intensified security-policy maker needs for assistance in facilitating or impeding armed nonstate control attempts, this study's time span is the post–Cold War global security environment. There is a significant difference in the parameters surrounding armed nonstate group activities between the bipolar superpower-dominated Cold War and the increasingly multipolar post–Cold War eras. Many of the armed nonstate groups explored have transformed dramatically to adapt to the changing opportunities present within the contemporary global security environment. The decades since the fall of the Berlin Wall allow reflection on how the emerging patterns have changed since the early 1990s, and especially after September 11, 2001 (referred to as 9/11). Most important, this analysis emphasizes how the impact of armed nonstate groups on stability is likely to transform in the future, given twenty-first-century changes in the global security context.

Because of the wide range of armed nonstate group control attempts and a desire to be comprehensively inclusive of their stability implications, this study's span of concern incorporates both human security and state security impacts. More narrow and traditional conceptions of stability focus on perpetuation of the political regime in power, and so from that perspective it might seem as if a focus on stability would tilt this analysis toward state rather than human security. However, as will be discussed in Chapter 2, this study develops and utilizes a much broader notion of essential stability functions that squarely emphasize protecting the people and providing for basic survival needs, fully incorporating the range of human security impacts as well as more traditional central state government security concerns.

BOOK ORGANIZATION

This volume provides a step-by-step exploration of the nature and desirability of the global security upheaval taking place, chronicling the dramatic shift in security governance—for better or for worse—from public to private hands. This study presents the controversies surrounding armed nonstate groups and stability, the transformation of global security control, case analyses revealing empirical evidence surrounding armed nonstate group security control attempts, analysis of these case study patterns, complexities surrounding private coercive stability promotion, and policy guidelines pertaining to the impact of armed nonstate groups on stability. Each chapter builds on the discoveries and findings of the preceding chapters, allowing comparison and integration of key insights. Wherever possible, the study endeavors to avoid leaving the reader with sweeping generalizations and instead to uncover specific conditions under which the patterns identified and the conclusions reached are most and least likely to occur.

Because of the scope of the topic covered and the complexity of relationships discussed, two mechanisms are frequently employed for clarification. First, each chapter uses figures to highlight key conceptual points, allowing readers to gain a quick understanding of a section's main thrust and to compare at a glance multifaceted findings across topics and sections. Second, the book contains extensive cross-referencing, allowing readers who want more background on a topic to easily find the appropriate discussion in another section.

This introductory chapter explains and defends the study's central thrust. Then Chapters 2 and 3 explain the study's two central emphases—stability and armed nonstate groups. Chapter 2 analyzes common instability metrics, underlying stability management controversies, the essential stability functions, and the modern stability conundrum. Chapter 3 presents the major state and nonstate sources of stability, armed nonstate groups' essential qualities, the major types of armed nonstate groups, and the major types of armed nonstate group control attempts. So as to provide an interpretive context for what follows, Chapter 4 details the transformation of global security control through exploring the changing supply of and demand for global security and the global shift in security governance.

Chapter 5 presents detailed case analyses that focus on major incidents of armed nonstate groups attempting to achieve security control. That chapter explores the general background, armed nonstate group efforts, and stability impacts in twelve cases—Chechens in Russia, Executive Outcomes in Sierra Leone, Revolutionary Armed Forces of Colombia (FARC) in Colombia, gangs in Somalia, Hezbollah in Lebanon, Irish Republican Army in the United Kingdom, Islamic Army of Aden in Yemen, Lord's Resistance Army in Uganda, Mara Salvatrucha in the United States, posses in Jamaica, Taliban in Afghanistan, and Yakuza in Japan. Chapter 6 then analyzes the general patterns evident from these cases, including the overarching findings about the relative success of armed nonstate groups and of armed nonstate group security control attempts, the conditions under which armed nonstate groups are most likely to enhance stability, and additional lessons from the case studies. Chapter 7 explains the complexities surrounding this form of private coercive stability promotion, incorporating dilemmas surrounding the clash of conflicting societal values, tensions between coercive force and stability, private coercive stability promotion challenges and risks, and needed rethinking of how to frame stability promotion. Chapter 8 concludes with a discussion of policy guidelines that include identifying what to do and not do in order to promote stability; specific strategies to facilitate cooperative armed nonstate groups in order to maximize their contributions to stability; and specific strategies to impede uncooperative armed nonstate groups in order to minimize their disruptions to stability.

TARGET AUDIENCE

This study takes a fresh, integrative, conceptual look at armed nonstate groups' potential as stability enhancers. As such, it does not provide an encyclopedic empirical review of existing knowledge pertaining to armed nonstate groups and stability, but rather it generates new, balanced insights about when it would be most beneficial or most detrimental to incorporate armed nonstate groups in power-sharing arrangements with central state governments to promote stability in contemporary international relations. The emphasis is thus on probing unconventional conceptual analysis, not on providing exhaustive factual detail.

This study explicitly attempts to avoid making judgments about the universal desirability of armed nonstate groups' impacts on stability. Instead, the goal is to identify the controversies, costs, and benefits surrounding these impacts, so that readers can think about them in the context of their own beliefs. This analysis takes into account widely differing political, cultural, and economic values; and the work's aspiration is to have its conclusions apply to issues related to sovereignty and the evolution of the state system, military strategy and stability operations, and counterinsurgency movements and the spread of global violence well into the future as the identified trends develop.

The ideal reader would be a person who is an independent critical thinker, who loves being exposed to conceptual wrinkles involving opposing viewpoints, and who appreciates the opportunity to draw his or her own conclusions. In contrast, a reader who craves definitive, sweeping conclusions spelled out and ready to consume might become frustrated. The measure of success of this study is its ability to get readers of all types to rethink and question their assumptions about states, armed nonstate groups, and stability, and be stimulated into new thinking about how to promote durable authority under global anarchy.

Because many readers may find the central thrust of this book to be counterintuitive if not objectionable, the arguments presented attempt to acknowledge and take into account opposing "devil's advocate" positions. That should encourage readers to decide for themselves whether to accept the dominant global security paradigm or be open to the kind of alternative approach presented in this study. One way or another, they should end up taking a different look at common international security assumptions.

Despite its iconoclastic nature, the intended audience for this book is wide. Students and academic scholars of international relations should find it intelligible, and its writing is designed to communicate to those outside the ivory tower, such as researchers in think tanks and analysts in government security agencies. Expressing ideas in such a way as to promote dialogue among these different constituencies should help with both understanding contrasting perspectives and discovering creative solutions to the security challenges identified. Toward this end, there is a concerted effort to avoid obscure jargon and mysterious acronyms.

2 THE NATURE OF STABILITY

ALTHOUGH STABILITY IS ONE of the most widely pursued security goals, understanding its dynamics requires careful scrutiny. To set the stage for evaluating armed nonstate groups' impact on stability, the analysis sorts through the thicket of conceptual confusion by (1) delineating the common instability metrics, (2) analyzing the underlying stability management controversies, (3) presenting the essential stability functions, and (4) introducing the modern stability conundrum, including uncertainties affecting stability attainment and the causes and consequences of instability.

COMMON INSTABILITY METRICS

The first step toward finding a meaningful definition of stability is to review existing instability metrics. Instability scholarship falls into several categories: direct instability studies, broad studies incorporating instability as one element, state fragility studies, state sovereignty studies, state weakness studies, and global peace studies. The indicators of instability suggested by these studies fall into five general categories: political illegitimacy, rights-depriving discrimination, social ineptitude, economic ineffectiveness, and conflict-conducive atmosphere.

Direct instability studies use three interrelated metrics. The first comes from the Central Intelligence Agency Directorate of Intelligence's Political Instability Task Force (PITF), which predicts political instability and covers the period 1955–2010.[1] The instability indicators of this metric are regime type, infant mortality, conflict-ridden neighborhood, and state-led discrimination.

The second metric is based on the University of Maryland Center for International Development and Conflict Management's Peace and Conflict Instability Ledger, which ranks 163 countries (based on the PITF) by their estimated risk of instability from 2010 to 2012.[2] The instability indicators of this metric are institutional inconsistency (not uniformly autocratic or democratic), economic closure (not integrated with the global economy), high infant mortality rates, militarization, and neighborhood security (neighboring states with armed conflict).

The third metric is derived from the United States Agency for International Development Office of Conflict Management and Mitigation's alert list in 2010, which ranks more than 160 countries (based on the Peace and Conflict Instability Ledger) according to the future risk of political instability and violent conflict.[3] The instability indicators of this metric are the probability that a state will experience a coup d'état, civil war, government collapse, or other central government disruption, driven by state economic, political, social, and security attributes.

Broad studies incorporating instability as one element employ two metrics. The first comes from the World Bank's Worldwide Governance Indicators Project, which reports good governance indicators for 212 countries and territories from 1996 to 2008, incorporating political stability as one of six dimensions.[4] The instability indicators of this metric are "perceptions of the likelihood that the government will be destabilized or overthrown by unconstitutional or violent means, including politically-motivated violence and terrorism."[5]

The second metric is derived from the Country Indicators for Foreign Policy Project (sponsored by the Canadian International Development Agency), which incorporates governance and political instability as one of its nine dimensions.[6] The instability indicators of this metric are lack of representative and accountable institutions for channeling grievances; the presence of transitional states or immature democracies at higher risk for violent change; denial of civil and political liberties, rights of assembly and association, and freedom of the press; and endemic corruption of political elites.

State fragility studies, whose focus is "now recognized as a source of our nation's most pressing security threats,"[7] involve two metrics. The first is *Foreign Policy* and the Fund for Peace's Failed States Index, which ranks 177 countries worldwide according to their level of fragility.[8] This metric has the following instability indicators:

1. mounting demographics pressures
2. massive movement of refugees or internally displaced persons, creating complex humanitarian emergencies
3. a legacy of vengeance-seeking group grievance or group paranoia
4. chronic and sustained human flight
5. uneven economic development along group lines
6. sharp and/or severe economic decline
7. criminalization and/or delegitimization of the state
8. progressive deterioration of public services
9. suspension or arbitrary application of the rule of law and widespread violation of human rights
10. a security apparatus operating as a "state within a state"
11. a rise of factionalized elites
12. intervention of other states or external political actors

The second metric is based on the United Kingdom's Department for International Development measures of instability in the form of fragility.[9] The instability indicators of this metric are the level of state will and capacity for safety and security, effective political power, economic management, and administrative capacity to deliver services.

State sovereignty studies utilize two metrics. The first is a state sovereignty index reflecting the "sovereignty gap"—"the disjunction between the de jure assumption that all states are 'sovereign' regardless of their performance in practice and the de facto reality that many are malfunctioning or collapsed states incapable of providing their citizens with even the most basic services."[10] The instability indicators of this metric are how far short a state falls in performing these core government functions:

1. rule of law
2. legitimate monopoly on the means of violence
3. administrative control
4. sound management of public finances
5. investment in human capital
6. creation of citizen rights through social policy
7. provision of infrastructure services
8. formation of a market
9. management of public assets
10. effective public borrowing

The second metric is derived from a sovereignty-oriented stability study that claims an equivalence between state sovereignty and overall country stability, where "the very emergence of the modern nation-state is associated with the suppression of brigands, private armies, and other autonomous military formations by the central government."[11] The instability indicators of this metric focus on state capacity to protect its citizenry from internal attack and external disorder.

State weakness studies also employ two metrics. The first comes from The Brookings Institution Center for Global Development's Index of State Weakness, which ranks 141 developing countries.[12] The instability indicators of this metric are state provision of a stable economy to its citizens, facilitating sustainable and equitable growth; the quality and legitimacy of state political institutions; state provision of physical security to its citizens; and state provision of basic goods and services to its citizens (including nutrition, health, education, and access to clean water and sanitation).

The second metric is based on the Harvard University Belfer Center Program on Intrastate Conflict, Conflict Prevention, and Conflict Resolution's measurement in 2004 of state weakness or failure in "effective delivery of the most crucial political goods."[13] The instability indicators of this metric are human security, adjudicating disputes, participation in the political process, and health, education, transportation, communication, and economic services.

Finally, global peace studies use three metrics. The first is derived from the Institute for Peace and Economics' Global Peace Index.[14] The instability indicators of this metric are:

1. a well-functioning government
2. a sound business environment
3. respect for human rights and tolerance
4. good relations with neighboring states
5. high levels of freedom of information
6. acceptance of others
7. high participation rates in primary and secondary education
8. low levels of corruption
9. equitable sharing of resources

The second metric is based on the Center for Systemic Peace's measurement of peace.[15] The instability indicators of this metric are absence of adverse regime change, nonexistence of warfare or genocide, peaceful resolution of disagreements, conflict containment, deterrence or prevention of violence and coercive disruption from internal or external sources, and limitation of casualties.

The third metric comes from the National Defense University Center for Technology and National Security Policy's peace indicators.[16] The instability indicators of this metric are security, social and economic well-being, justice and reconciliation, and governance and participation.

UNDERLYING STABILITY MANAGEMENT CONTROVERSIES

The instability indicators from inside and outside of government cluster into four areas: security authority, public welfare, internal harmony, and external autonomy. They are summarized in Figure 2.1.

Methodological uncertainties surround the minimum duration (transitory versus durable) and minimum continuity threshold necessary for stability; and the relative impact on stability from the frequency and magnitude of disruptions. Ongoing disagreements often indirectly limit expectations surrounding stability just in trying to restore a society to pre-crisis or pre-war conditions—involving "achieving short-term priorities, such as reestablishing a modicum of security, restoring traditional elites, and providing vital services in whatever ways those were delivered previously"—rather than achieving any meaningful improvements in long-term order.[17] Advanced industrial societies and developing countries often have different notions of stability and stability management, which creates political, economic, and cultural challenges to resolving these controversies.

Security Authority Controversies

Each of the four areas of instability indicators brings its own questions and controversies.

Beginning with security authority, analysts ask: Does a state government have to be capable and willing to fulfill all the requirements of sovereignty to be stable? Those who focus on central government stability tend to answer this question positively, while those who focus on societal stability tend to answer negatively. Traditionally, sovereignty has been defined as "juridical sovereignty," where there is legally sanctioned national government control of territory and what transpires within states. Because the formal notion of juridical sovereignty applies poorly in practice to many weak states, the term has expanded to focus more on "empirical sovereignty," where there is a more flexible determination

Figure 2.1. Stability management controversies

Security authority

Does a state government have to be capable and willing to fulfill all the requirements of sovereignty to be stable?

Can a state be stable if its government lacks exclusive territorial control and shares power with nonstate groups?

Is preservation of a state's political regime and prevention of its overthrow what matters most for stability?

Can a failed or failing state be stable?

Public welfare

Does a system of authority within a state have to embody some minimum level of legitimacy in order to be stable?

Does a state have to conform to "enlightened" global norms incorporating democracy and civil society to be stable?

Does a state have to provide for basic needs to its citizenry to be stable?

Can a state incorporating severe human exploitation, inequality, or injustice be stable?

Internal harmony

Does a state have to experience the absence of violent conflict to be stable?

Does a state have to embody a consistent pattern of peaceful resolution of internal disagreements to be stable?

Does a state's society have to be nonmilitarized to be stable?

Does a state need to possess an internal consensus about a distinctive national identity to be stable?

External autonomy

Does a state have to experience the absence of external coercive intervention to be stable?

Does a state need to be able to make security decisions completely on its own to be stable?

Does a state have to exhibit low or reciprocal external security dependence to be stable?

Does a state need to be located within a region devoid of highly contagious turmoil to be stable?

of effective governance over a particular set of people.[18] This broader concept assumes an expanded role for self-determination of peoples covering both state and nonstate sources of security governance; and the possession by both states and nonstate groups of their own ethical standards and code of honor restraining their behavior.

Second, can a state be stable if a central state government lacks exclusive territorial control and shares power with nonstate groups? Those who focus on state sovereignty may demand exclusive territorial control, not just a monopoly on the legitimate use of force,[19] and may oppose nonstate provision of core state functions because it "leads to a higher cost structure and the creation of financially unsustainable and unaccountable practices" and negatively impacts "the legitimacy and sovereignty of the state."[20] In contrast, opponents may downplay sovereign territorial control and accept informal nonstate control possession of a closed political community.[21] This acceptance may result from not only more openness to nonstate stability providers,[22] but also to greater recognition that nonstate groups have been gradually supplanting central state government authority in many parts of the world.[23]

Third, is preservation of a state's political regime, proliferation of its formal institutions and infrastructure, and prevention of its overthrow essential for a state to be stable? Those emphasizing state stability may require a focus on regime perpetuation and bureaucratic institutionalization, associated with the scope of governance,[24] and on government regime hegemony. Others disagree with this state-centric view by placing a different weight on structure, process, and leadership versus outcome as key determinants of stability.

Fourth, can failed or failing states exhibit stability? Those focusing on government stability tend to answer this question negatively, while those focusing on societal stability tend to identify situations where, even with a functional government vacuum, countries may exhibit stability resulting from nonstate group action or cohesive communities providing order. Some believe that failed or failing states typify the worst possible stability predicament, while others believe that the government plight is not the key to stability.

Public Welfare Controversies

Regarding public welfare, analysts ask: Does a system of authority have to embody some minimum level of legitimacy to be stable? Traditionally, political legitimacy has been defined as "the compatibility of the results of governmental output with the value patterns of the relevant system."[25] It involves maintenance of fairness and justice, following due process, adherence to an explicit set of moral and legal principles, and compliance with the popular will in determining leadership and making decisions.[26] Because, like traditional sovereignty, this formal legitimacy notion applies poorly in practice to many weak states, functional legitimacy has expanded to focus on a more flexible interpretation of acceptable governance, downplaying the ways in which a ruling authority gains power. It operates according to accepted rules and standards, or conforms to the general will of the people. This broader concept of legitimacy assumes an expanded role for consequentialist utilitarian measures gauging the extent to which rulers are willing and able to provide valuable services to their citizens: "rather than drawing its legitimacy from a social contract between citizens and governments," many countries today "rely on a combination of tribal and religious authorities as well as economic incentives to establish their legitimacy."[27] Legitimacy as an absolute prerequisite for stability may thus depend on using formal versus functional legitimacy and on the importance placed on accepted versus effective authority.

Second, does a state have to conform to "enlightened" global norms incorporating a particular form of government—such as democracy—or a particular form of society—such as civil society—to be stable? Those who focus on global stability might stress the need to conform with—or at least be compatible with—dominant global values, believing that consistency with global norms is essential for stability because of the need to fit in well with existing levels of globalization and international interdependence; while those who focus on local or national stability might disagree. As to having an optimal form of government or society in mind, this orientation would sharply restrict one's openness to many stabilizing arrangements, particularly since at least one study has found that "the most stable regimes are full autocracies."[28]

Third, does a state need to have explicit enunciated goals, principles, and strategies, rather than simply the desire to maintain power or to oppose adversaries, to be stable? Those advocating stability with normatively desirable political and social forms tend to answer negatively, while those without these ideal forms in mind tend to answer positively.

Fourth, does a state have to provide basic needs to its citizenry to be stable? Those focusing on state stability tend to answer this question negatively, while those emphasizing societal stability tend to answer positively. Although countries define basic needs differently, the underlying distinction revolves around whether the plight of the mass public is deemed central or peripheral to stability, and whether ruling authorities are deemed responsible for addressing shortfalls in basic needs.

Fifth, can states tolerating or promoting severe exploitation, inequality, or injustice be stable? If so, such states may violate a widely accepted premise that stability requires public consent via persuasion, trust, or apathy;[29] and, if not, such states may have to possess a well-defined and fairly formulated and implemented system of law. Some aspects of this issue, such as exploitation or injustice, seem more controllable (though less objectively measurable) through political action than others, such as socioeconomic inequality. Those emphasizing state stability might answer this question positively, while those emphasizing social stability might respond negatively.

Internal Harmony Controversies

Turning to internal harmony, analysts ask: Does a state have to experience the absence of domestic violent conflict to be stable? The answer may depend on the scope and intensity of the conflict: some assume that only large-scale internal violent conflict, with considerable casualties, creates instability; whereas others deem even low-level violence to be destabilizing. Furthermore, for some analysts, government-versus-citizenry conflict is more destabilizing than violent conflicts strictly among governing factions or nonstate groups.

Second, does a state have to embody consistent peaceful resolution of disagreements between the ruling authority and the people, as well as among domestic groups, to be stable? This question considers the manner of resolving conflicts versus conflict itself. If cultural norms suggest resolving disagreements nonviolently, and/or a functioning judicial system exists for dispute management, then a state might seem to be more stable than if neither is the case. However, some analysts do not consider these issues to be central to the determination of stability.

Third, does a state's society have to be nonmilitarized to be stable? Many observers assume that the presence of large numbers of armaments, coercive personnel, and people with military or police training will increase the potential for violence and instability, while others assume that these elements are not a pivotal influence or could be just as important in enforcing order as stimulating violent disorder. Opposite assumptions are made about the psychological impact of visible instruments of force present within a country.

Fourth, does a state need to possess internal consensus about a distinctive national identity, readily distinguishable from that of others, to be stable? Some analysts argue that possessing a distinctive national identity can cause high national morale and stabilizing unity and pride within a country, while others see the same type of identity triggering virulent nationalism and destabilizing external aggression. A key to this debate is whether one assumes that the development of a distinctive national identity necessarily triggers intolerance within a society and across societies.

External Autonomy Controversies

In addressing external autonomy, analysts ask: Does a state have to experience the absence of external coercive intervention to be stable? Some observers see external coercive intervention as almost always constituting a disruption to stability and highlighting state ineptitude, while others believe that such intervention can enhance stability in a situation where chaotic anarchy might otherwise reign. A key difference revolves around an underlying premise that external intervention is stabilizing only if it is unambiguously noncoercive, if it is explicitly requested by the recipient, or if its exclusive credible aim is to restore order. Second, does a state need to be able to make decisions completely on its own to be stable? Disagreement exists between those who feel that self-sufficiency in making security policy leads to stability and those who believe that burden sharing and joint decision making lead to stability. Part of the issue is whether a state chooses to invite outside influence into its security decision making versus finding itself subjected to unrequested (and sometimes undesired) outside influence from other countries.

Third, does a state have to exhibit low or reciprocal external security dependence to be stable? This issue harkens back to a long-standing debate about whether external dependence is a sign of strength or weakness. Within a globalized society characterized by high levels of skewed interdependence, it might seem unrealistic to posit low or reciprocal interdependence as a prerequisite for stability. At the same time, too high a level of dependence on outside states can make vulnerability to crucial disruptions more likely and thus can sometimes promote instability.

Fourth, does a state need to be located within a region devoid of contagious turmoil or intense antagonisms affecting the country to be stable? Some analysts consider the condition of the geographical area around a state to be pivotal in determining that country's stability, while others look almost exclusively at what goes on within the given state. The basis for this difference is the extent to which observers think that a country's stability is impervious (high external autonomy) versus vulnerable (low external autonomy) to intentional or unintentional spread of chaos from nearby areas.

ESSENTIAL STABILITY FUNCTIONS

This study, taking into account the conceptual controversies surrounding security authority, public welfare, internal harmony, and external autonomy, introduces a new framework for assessing stability from a security perspective.

The purpose of this framework is to gauge and compare how well potential stability enhancers perform in attaining stability goals. Other stability studies compare societies' vulnerability to instability in order to formulate early warning systems or to forecast instability or predict state failure. In contrast, this study pinpoints what functions an ideal stable society would deliver, so that deviations from this ideal can be unambiguously gauged.

Stability, by definition, entails the facilitation of order through predictable continuity, both in people's lives and in governing authority. Comparing how well potential stability enhancers perform requires examining the ratio of significant disruptions that interfere with stability to a country's successful management of such disruptions. Thus a country could be deemed stable if it had few disruptions and a low capacity to manage them, or if it had many disruptions and a high capacity to manage them. The best situation would involve few significant disruptions, high predictable continuity in people's lives and in governing authority, and high capacity by the authority to manage the disruptions.

This study identifies four essential stability functions, which highlight critical dimensions of state security, human security, domestic security, and international security: to provide (1) predictable order through authority, reflected through the prevention or restraint of governance disruption by promoting rules and order with continuity in security authority; (2) a public welfare safety net, reflected through the prevention or restraint of societal disruption by providing for basic survival needs to the affected population; (3) nonviolent resolution of disputes, reflected through the prevention or restraint of internal disruption by ceasing violent conflict or perpetuating peace; and (4) insulation from outside coercive interference, reflected through the prevention or restraint of external disruption by precluding unwanted forceful foreign intervention. Figure 2.2 displays these essential stability functions.

The rationale for identifying these stability functions is multifaceted. First, they are designed to allow for any type of authority—not just state governments—to promote stability, and thus do not require that state governments have total control over their countries or that private groups be excluded. Second, as mentioned in Chapter 1, they are designed to encompass human security concerns as well as state security concerns, for a country's overall stability is increasingly perceived as needing to incorporate the safety of affected people rather than just the preservation of the state regime.[30] Third, they are designed to be applicable across situations and societies, regardless of the stability provider, the stability predicament, or the stability promotion mode. Fourth,

Figure 2.2. Essential stability functions

PREDICTABLE ORDER THROUGH AUTHORITY

State security

Prevention or restraint of governance disruption by promoting law and order with continuity in ruling authority

---

PUBLIC WELFARE SAFETY NET

Human security

Prevention or restraint of societal disruption by providing for basic survival needs for the affected population

---

NONVIOLENT RESOLUTION OF INTERNAL DISPUTES

Domestic security

Prevention or restraint of internal disruption by ceasing violent conflict or perpetuating peace

---

INSULATION FROM OUTSIDE COERCIVE INTERFERENCE

International security

Prevention or restraint of external disruption by precluding unwanted forceful foreign intervention

---

they are designed to cover outcomes across the entire stability–instability continuum, not just extreme order or chaos. Fifth, they are designed to avoid biases about particular optimal political, economic, or cultural structures.

These essential stability functions do not pretend to incorporate all possible stability elements, as they explicitly ignore how the rulers came into power or govern; whether particular political leaders or political beliefs are maintained; whether the affected economy is robust; how much societal infrastructure is present; and how effective any ruling authority is in providing any non-security-related functions or services.

The first stability function of providing predictable order through authority involves promoting rules and order, with continuity in ruling authority encompassing a predictable pattern of political rule without specifying whether a state regime is failed or failing; the authority system incorporates state or nonstate groups; the ruling authority is highly institutionalized; the ruling authority possesses traditional attributes of sovereignty and/or legitimacy; or the ruling authority has absolute territorial control. The underlying assumption is that no single kind of rule is stabilizing in all circumstances. This stability function links with the conceptual controversies surrounding security authority.

The second stability function of providing a public welfare safety net involves attending to basic survival needs to the affected population, encompassing a predictable pattern of attentiveness to the welfare of individual citizens without specifying anything about who is delivering essential goods and services to the affected people; whether the party providing for the basic needs has internal or external legitimacy; the exact nature of the affected population's basic survival needs; the level of similarity or difference in those needs across countries; whether the provision for the basic needs conforms to global "enlightened" norms, including whether any level of democracy or civil society is involved; or whether provision for the basic survival needs incorporates certain political rights, economic prosperity, or social equality within the affected area. Focusing on basic survival needs—rather than other kinds of needs, wants, or "rights" of the affected population—minimizes concerns about areas warranting protection and cross-cultural differences in their definition. Within every society, survival is a primary security goal. This stability function links with the conceptual controversies surrounding public welfare.

The third stability function of providing nonviolent resolution of disputes involves ceasing internal violent conflict or perpetuating internal peace, encompassing a predictable pattern of peaceful resolution of national disagreements without specifying anything about the source of and motive for conflicts, including whether sound justifications exist for their initiation; the involvement of state or nonstate groups in conflict resolution; the extent of central state government capacity to put down insurrections; the level of militarization of the citizenry within the affected society; or the level of internal consensus about a distinctive national identity readily distinguishable from that of other countries. Thus there is no evaluation of the types of conflict that are most tolerable, productive, or justified, or of the types of conflict management that would be most effective, with the result being to maximize diversity in modes of stability promotion. This stability function links with the conceptual controversies surrounding internal harmony.

The final stability function—insulation from outside coercive interference—involves precluding unwanted foreign intervention, encompassing a predictable pattern keeping unwanted outsiders away without specifying anything about the exact level of deterrence or containment of coercive disruption from external sources; a state's ability to make security decisions on its own without outside pressure; the level of threat from external state versus nonstate sources; the level of external security dependence; or the level of contagion by disruptive forces from neighboring countries with significant turmoil or intense hostility or antagonism. From an international perspective, the basic ability to formulate and execute one's own policies is at stake, forestalling external dangers stemming from sources such as failing neighboring countries, unwanted refugee flows, incoming fatal disease, or nearby bases for terrorists or other disruptive groups.[31] The motives for the outside intervention are sidestepped because their justification could be viewed from differing cultural perspectives. There is no underlying sweeping assumption that foreign coercive intervention is inherently stabilizing or destabilizing: for example, in the context of the American pursuit of stability operations abroad, coercive intervention could have the potential to be stabilizing if invited by recipient states. This stability function links with the conceptual controversies surrounding external autonomy.

THE MODERN STABILITY CONUNDRUM

In the twenty-first century, global stability prospects appear dim: there is "a great arc of instability stretching from Sub-Saharan Africa through North Africa, into the Middle East, the Balkans, the Caucasus, and South and Central Asia, and parts of Southeast Asia."[32] Today "forty to sixty states, home to nearly two billion people, are either sliding backward and teetering on the brink of implosion or have already collapsed."[33] Indeed, "the risks of instability and conflict have increased significantly in the regions of the world where these dangers were already high": "new armed conflicts have outnumbered those that have terminated, driving up estimated risks of instability in many regions of the world where neighborhood security has now worsened."[34] Because of these developments, instability may become the new global norm.

Uncertainties Affecting Stability Attainment

The modern stability conundrum reveals four basic sources of confusion, summarized in Figure 2.3, linked to public-private authority differences: (1) stability provider ambivalence, questioning how to judge who has the right to use physical coercion in pursuit of stability; (2) stability system selectivity, questioning how to gauge the breadth necessary for a functional stability system; (3) stability promotion incompatibility, questioning how to evaluate mismatches between potential stability enhancers and instability predicaments;

and (4) stability success ambiguity, questioning how to interpret achievement of effective long-term stability. Different societies, with different capacities to cope with stability challenges, value and aspire for different types and levels of stability. Moreover, thanks to technological advances in transportation and communication, intensifying globalization, increasingly porous borders, and unprecedented cross-boundary movement of people, goods, services, and

Figure 2.3. Modern stability conundrum

Stability provider ambivalence

Not everyone wants the central government to provide security, and security may be a service to be bought and sold.

Selecting stability providers based on effectiveness may clash with prevailing international system norms.

Accepted means of enhancing stability have been ineffective, and largely unaccepted means seem more promising.

Stability system selectivity

Privatizing protection might make it more selectively available and less of a "public good" freely available to all citizens.

Private stability favors some participants over others.

Even public security can produce differential protection in a society, especially for ethnic, religious, or racial groups.

Stability enhancement incompatibility

Private groups minimally threatening the state are not necessarily those maximizing effective stability.

Areas controlled by private groups are not necessarily those with the greatest need for alternative sources of order.

State regimes most receptive to private power sharing are not necessarily those with the most neglected populations.

Stability success ambiguity

Is stability providers' success due more to their actual coercive power or to their perceived legitimacy?

Does private protection success increase mass dissatisfaction with the social contract between the rulers and the ruled?

Is sympathy/respect or fear/terror by the mass public a better motivator for successful attainment of stability?

ideas, each country's security predicament seems increasingly difficult to in-sulate from potentially destabilizing internal or external intervention, about which these societies have sharply differing norms.

The subject of stability provider ambivalence raises the question, "who has, or should have, the legitimate authority to use physical coercion in pursuit of security?"[35] As will be illustrated through the case studies in Chapter 5, not all people expect or want a central state government to fulfill this task, and the privatized free-market mentality embedded in globalization suggests that security might well be treated as a service to be bought and sold on the open market so as to cater to diverse popular preferences. In comparing possible sources of stability, the answer to this question rests both on which are most ef-fective and which fit most comfortably within prevailing local cultural norms, even when these differ from international system values. A key paradox can emerge: the most accepted means of enhancing stability—the application of power by states—has often been demonstrably ineffective in quelling many of today's unconventional threats, and the least accepted means of enhancing stability—the use of force by armed nonstate groups—may show some promise but is relatively untested and is currently outside of prevailing global security governance norms. Moreover, part of this crucial line of inquiry is establish-ing who has the right—states' military/police forces, states' civilian agencies, intergovernmental organizations, armed nonstate groups, private humanitar-ian organizations, or multinational corporations—to determine the answer to this fundamental question. Should private coercive groups be able to decide for themselves when to participate in stability promotion, or should they wait un-til states or intergovernmental organizations recognize their conditional value and invite them in to help manage chaos? No consensus has emerged on who has the right to make this decision, just as today consensus is eroding about the state's right to have a monopoly on the use of force. The security implications would surely differ substantially depending on who makes this crucial decision.

Moving to stability system selectivity, we need to ask: Does a functional sta-bility system have to be universal and all-inclusive within each country? Because state-provided security and defense is usually conceptualized as a "public good" with nonexclusive benefits freely and equally available to all citizens, it might seem as if any form of security privatization would make protection more se-lectively available. Indeed, one major potential disadvantage of private stability provision is the favoring of some participants over others,[36] being available only to a special few based on patron-client relationships[37] or on who can afford it.

Some analysts conclude that "armed actors who answer to private contractors can never serve the entire public."[38] However, this argument ignores the historical pattern of uneven distribution of stability benefits provided by public state sources: "ever since the beginning of the nation-state system, even with completely public security there have been significant differentials in the levels of protection different segments of a society receive, and in many societies certain groups—such as undesired ethnic, religious, or racial minorities or illegal immigrants—have been deemed to be completely outside the protective umbrella of government security."[39] As a result, while in theory private security is less of a public good and is more likely to be exclusionary than public security, in practice the outcome is muddier. Although a private approach could leave unprotected anarchic areas, in those areas receiving protection it preserves the ability of people—who otherwise might lack viable security options—to feel secure and operate within a setting of defined order. Security privatization in the pursuit of stability thus may increase and decrease global anarchy at the same time, depending on whether one is taking into account the perspective of people located inside or outside the private protected zones.[40]

In examining stability promotion incompatibility, analysts ask: How does one evaluate mismatches between potential stability enhancers and dire instability predicaments? Private coercive groups that minimally threaten the state do not necessarily maximally enhance the potential for stability. For example, an armed nonstate group may pose no danger and create no atmosphere of fear precisely because it is weak and ineffective and can do little to change the local security predicament. As well, areas experiencing private security control are not necessarily those with the greatest need for alternative sources of order and for nonstate security governance. For example, some types of armed nonstate groups, such as certain transnational criminal organizations, purposely locate within states with a stable business climate to promote their profitable illicit operations. Lastly, states whose central governments are most receptive to sharing power with private groups are not necessarily those where the affected population feels the most security neglect. For example, government officials' motives for accepting assistance from armed nonstate groups could reflect corruption or a desire to escape direct responsibility for failure. Because the primary motivation of private groups may not be to fulfill the security needs of the affected population, these groups' capabilities and the needs of a country will not match up perfectly in all cases. It therefore may prove difficult to avoid mismatches between the right private group and the right stability need.

In discussing stability success ambiguity, we need to ask: How does one interpret the achievement of effective long-term stability? There is confusion about whether the success of stability providers is due more to their actual coercive power or to their perceived legitimacy, as well as about whether a coercively based stability system without external legitimacy is problematic in the long run. Moreover, there is confusion about whether sympathy/respect versus fear/terror by the mass public is a better motivator for successful long-term compliance to a stable system. From a legitimacy standpoint, rule based on loyalty, sympathy, and respect seems preferable, but for private coercive groups such positive attributes can associate with a particular leader rather than institutionalized structures or carefully considered political processes. As a result, it may be hard to justify sweeping preferences for one type of motivation over another. In addition, uncertainty surrounds whether success in private protection associating with heightened mass awareness of surrounding instability serves to significantly increase mass dissatisfaction with the social contract between the rulers and the ruled, as well as whether such dissatisfaction generates dangerous security implications. In other words, if the public prefers nonstate over state stability enhancers, is there a problem? Overall, mushiness surrounds the exact model for achieving successful long-term stability.

Causes and Consequences of Instability

The primary causes and consequences of instability, important as a context for evaluating armed nonstate groups' influence on stability, are detailed in Figure 2.4. In general, instability may result when unruly elements fostering turmoil overwhelm a ruling authority's capabilities to restrain or mitigate them;[41] or when an authority has not engendered fear of punishment or respect for its legitimacy. In a political context, instability may result from political repression,[42] political injustice, or the lust for power, where individuals or groups see power benefits from instability.[43] Economic causes of instability include rapid or massive upward or downward economic change, "such as sudden jumps in inflation, excessive government debts, poor economic performance";[44] or severe or unexpected deficiencies in the provision of basic services.[45] Military causes of instability could be excessive military spending[46] or societal militarization. Cultural causes of instability may be factionalism or heterogeneity or tensions among ethnic, racial, or religious groups.[47] Finally, environmental causes of instability include population pressures or competition over natural resources.[48]

Figure 2.4. Causes and consequences of instability

CAUSES OF INSTABILITY

General causes

Instability may result when unruly elements fostering turmoil overwhelm the affected authority's capabilities to restrain or mitigate them.

Instability may result from the absence of (1) fear of punishment from an authority or (2) respect for the legitimacy of an authority.

Political causes

Instability may result from political repression or a sense of political injustice.

Instability may result from the lust for power, where individuals or groups see power benefits from instability.

Economic causes

Instability may result from rapid or significant upward or downward economic change.

Instability may result from severe or unexpected deficiencies in provision of basic services.

Military causes

Instability may result from excessive military spending or militarization of a society.

Cultural causes

Instability may result from ethnic, racial, or religious heterogeneity, tensions among internal groups, or factionalism.

Environmental causes

Instability may result from population pressures or competition over natural resources.

CONSEQUENCES OF INSTABILITY

Cycle of turmoil

Instability can descend into a seemingly endless self-perpetuating cycle that leads to more instability and conflict.

Regional conflict contagion

Instability may spread across countries because instability, insecurity, and terror are now easier than ever to export.

Loss of accountability

Instability can decrease accountability for actions taken because of confusion about security management responsibility.

(*continued*)

Figure 2.4. *(continued)*

> *Changing violence sensitivity*
>
> Instability can raise violence intolerance in developed states and raise violence tolerance in developing states.
>
> *Rising internal discontent*
>
> Instability can increase alienation, cynicism, and anger among disgruntled members of the mass public about the value of the state.
>
> *Diminishing external influence*
>
> Instability can reduce a state's ability to employ international diplomacy to transform in desired ways the behavior of other countries.

Turning to consequences: Instability can descend into a seemingly endless self-perpetuating cycle of turmoil: "the more instability there is in a country, the less foreign or domestic investment it will attract, and the less investment, the less growth, which leads to more instability";[49] and "the creation and acceleration of a vicious circle which results in the creation of contending centers of power, the multiplication of increasingly contradictory and ineffective decision-making processes, the loss of trust between citizens and state, the delegitimization of institutions, the disenfranchisement of the citizenry, and ultimately the resort to violence."[50] Unstable states can manifest "the dark side of globalization, and pose a very difficult kind of national security challenge."[51] Indeed, motivating recent American and international attention to unstable states "is the conviction that such countries enable transnational terrorist networks."[52]

As well, instability may cause regional conflict contagion, because "the rapid pace of globalization and technological change mean that instability, insecurity and terror are now more easily exported than ever before."[53] Instability also can reduce accountability for actions taken—and escalate scapegoating and finger-pointing—due to confusion about responsibilities for triggering turmoil and for restoring order. Instability can change violence sensitivity, associating in advanced industrial societies with heightened sensitivity to violence with lower thresholds of acceptable bloodshed, and in developing countries with decreased shock value of frequent unnatural deaths, leading to tolerance of continuing carnage. Instability raises internal discontent, and can lead to growing alienation, cynicism, and anger among disgruntled members of the mass public about the value of the central government caused by a perceived violation of the social contract between the rulers and the ruled. Lastly, instability may diminish a state's external influence, reducing its ability to employ international diplomacy successfully to transform the behavior of other countries in desired ways.

Armed nonstate groups, to be discussed in detail in Chapter 3, can themselves be a cause of instability, and they can redirect the consequences of instability in either positive or negative ways. Like central state governments, these private groups can undertake actions that may either trigger/escalate turmoil or manage/restrain turmoil. The primary difference between states and armed nonstate groups, in terms of instability causes and consequences, is the perceived legitimacy of their actions. In most instances, however, neither party represents the root cause nor the principal security consequence controller regarding stability.

CONCLUDING THOUGHTS

A conceptual complacency has pervaded much analysis of stability, assuming that everyone understands and agrees with its meaning. Stability is but one component of overall security and of "good" security governance, commonly defined as the extent to which a country's rulers provide its citizens with security. Beyond stability, the traditional characteristics of strong, secure states more broadly incorporate "high levels of legitimacy and authority, adequate levels of provision of collective goods, sound economic management, the primacy of the collective, and a high degree of inclusiveness."[54]

For this reason, despite its prevalence in security doctrine, does stability deserve to be the exclusive security outcome this study considers? At least a few analysts doubt that the pursuit of stability should dominate American foreign security policy—a respected *Washington Post* defense columnist argues that achieving stability is not and should not be the primary goal:

> After all, we didn't invade Iraq to provide stability, but to force change. Likewise in Afghanistan. And once we were there, we didn't aim for stability, but to encourage democracy, which (the thought is not original with me) in a region like the Middle East generally undermines stability. I mean, if all we wanted was stability, why not find a strongman and leave?[55]

Stability not only does not encompass all valuable security outcomes, but also has a distinct status quo orientation. This orientation "often leads to the establishment and strengthening of semiauthoritarian structures" which could be undesirable[56] especially when there is a need to uproot a dismal governance predicament prior to stabilizing a better one afterward. Furthermore, it may not always be possible to pursue long-term durable stability within a country in such a way that promotes both domestic and international acceptance, and simultaneously serves national interests by enhancing national power. Stability promotion incorporating significant changes deemed "progressive" usually encounters strong resistance from local citizens even if it ultimately improves their lot. Some analysts doubt both the feasibility and the desirability of stability promotion in today's anarchic world, and the most cynical of them doubt the potential for any value neutrality in pursuing stability.

Nonetheless, within a multivalued globe where predictable continuity may be essential to world order, stability still makes sense as the primary security goal. Even with all of stability's different interpretations, there are few if any other security goals that have so much support as making sense in today's world as a means of improving dimensions of people's lives that they deem most important. Emphasizing other objectives that leave countries sliding toward unpredictable violent disorder is not an attractive alternative.

If pursuit of stability remains the dominant security goal, one of the most pressing needs is to develop more valid and reliable measures of effectiveness in achieving designated essential stability functions. The disagreements about the meaning of stability—evidenced by the variety of instability indicators and the deep stability controversies—have impeded the ability of potential stability enhancers to undertake effective action. In particular, the difficulty in precisely defining stability operations has impeded American government efforts, exemplified by a 2007 U.S. Government Accountability Office report pointing out significant "confusion over how to define stability operations": "this lack of a clear and consistent definition of stability operations has caused confusion across the department about how to identify activities that are considered stability operations, and commanders have difficulty identifying what the end state is for which they need to plan . . . without clear guidance on how and when combatant commanders are to develop stability operations capability requirements, the combatant commanders and the military services may not be able to effectively identify and prioritize needed capabilities."[57] This deficiency urgently needs to be addressed, for without such measures it would be difficult if not impossible to make progress in promoting stability internationally.

Even if approached properly, with sound interpretation and yardsticks for success, there are no guarantees that the pursuit of stability will lead to significant improvement in target areas of the essential stability functions, either for existing authority structures or for the mass population. Within today's largely anarchic global security environment, ominous pitfalls and roadblocks lurk around every corner. Recent history is full of examples of well-intentioned efforts to promote stability in countries around the world that have gone haywire, had little positive impact, or completely backfired.

Given the scope and severity of the challenges faced in establishing stability, this chapter's analysis suggests that the chances for success may be highest if there is diversification of the sources of stability promotion, utilizing multiple different parties rather than a single facilitating party. The need to diversify responsibility for attaining success relates to the inability of any single type of stability enhancer to meet all four of the essential stability functions: not only should the military not be solely responsible for positive outcomes, but also the central state government should not bear this responsibility alone, with use of nonstate sources of stability and power sharing between public governmental and more local private organizations considered. In parallel fashion, this chapter's insights suggest the need for more tolerance of different outcomes across stabilization efforts, avoiding demanding a specific ideal end state such as poverty reduction, the spread of Western democracy, the spread of a particular form of civil society, or adherence to global cultural norms. This change involves openness to multiple stable outcomes, reflecting greater flexibility about the political ideologies, institutional forms, and values involved in stability promotion.

3 THE NATURE OF ARMED NONSTATE GROUPS

TO MEANINGFULLY EVALUATE the impact of armed nonstate groups on stability, this study first places armed nonstate groups in the context of other potential sources of stability in international relations, highlighting the comparative advantages of each. Then the discussion identifies the essential qualities of armed nonstate groups as a whole, including their orientation toward violence. Last, there is a detailed analysis of the differences among the principal types of armed nonstate groups and their security control attempts.

MAJOR STATE AND NONSTATE POTENTIAL SOURCES OF STABILITY

Several different parties in international relations have the potential to affect local, national, regional, and global stability, and comparing them is important so as to place the stability-enhancing capabilities and limitations of armed nonstate groups in perspective. The major categories of parties are national government military and police units, national government civilian agencies, intergovernmental organizations, private armed nonstate groups, private subnational and transnational humanitarian organizations (including groups promoting civil society), and private multinational corporations. Significant differences are evident across these parties in terms of their basic interest, primary goal, organizational structure, relationship with the state, mode of operation, speed of operation, support base, and political legitimacy. Table 3.1 summarizes these differences, recognizing that exceptions and minor variations exist from the broad patterns identified across the parties potentially involved in stability promotion.

Table 3.1. State and nonstate sources of stability

	Public sources				Private sources		
	Government military/ police	Government civilian agencies	Intergovernmental organizations	Armed nonstate groups	Humanitarian organizations	Multinational corporations
Basic interest	National political interest	National political interest	Collective global political interest	Self-interest in grabbing a piece of the pie	Social welfare	Economic profit
Primary goal	Securing law and order	Developing political infrastructure	Maintaining international order	Attaining power and control	Nurturing civil society	Stimulating growth and prosperity
Organizational structure	Hierarchical	Hierarchical	Nonhierarchical	Nonhierarchical	Nonhierarchical	Less hierarchical
Relationship with state	Unequivocally support the state	Unequivocally support the state	Representative of all member states	Mixed	Mixed	Mixed
Mode of operation	Coercive via threat of force	Coercive via legal penalties	Noncoercive voluntary compliance	Mix of coercive and noncoercive tactics	Noncoercive voluntary compliance	Coercive via economic and legal penalties
Speed of operation	Fast	Slow	Very slow	Very fast	Mixed	Mixed
Support base	Local	Local	Global	Local, regional, and global	Local, regional, and global	Global
Political legitimacy	High locally Low globally	High locally Mixed globally	Low locally High globally	Low locally Low globally	High locally High globally	Mixed locally Mixed globally

Differences among Potential Stability Enhancers

The differences in potential stability enhancers' interests and goals highlight their distinctive aspirations. Regarding basic interest, government military and police units and government civilian agencies operate according to national political interests, intergovernmental organizations operate according to collective political interests, armed nonstate groups operate according to self-interest in grabbing a piece of the pie, humanitarian organizations have social welfare justifications, and multinational corporations have economic profit rationales. As to the primary goal, government military and police units seek to secure law and order, government civilian agencies seek to develop political infrastructure, intergovernmental organizations seek to maintain international order, armed nonstate groups seek to attain power and control, humanitarian organizations seek to nurture civil society, and multinational corporations seek to stimulate economic growth and prosperity.

The differences in potential stability enhancers' organizational structure and relationship with the state associate with their level of formality and compliance. Regarding organizational structure, government military and police units and civilian agencies are hierarchical, whereas intergovernmental organizations, armed nonstate groups, humanitarian organizations, and multinational corporations tend to be less hierarchical. As to relationship with the state, government military and police units and civilian agencies, being part of the central state regime, unequivocally support the state, while intergovernmental organizations represent all member states, and armed nonstate groups, humanitarian organizations and multinational corporations have mixed relationships under differing circumstances with the state.

The differences in potential stability enhancers' mode and speed of operation reflect their levels of adaptability and credibility. Regarding mode of operation, government military and police units utilize coercive measures via threat and application of force, government civilian agencies utilize coercive measures via legal penalties, intergovernmental organizations rely on noncoercive voluntary cooperation, armed nonstate groups utilize a mixture of coercive and noncoercive tactics, humanitarian organizations rely on noncoercive voluntary cooperation, and multinational corporations utilize coercive measures via economic incentives and disincentives and legal penalties. As to speed of operation, government military and police units seem relatively fast, with democratic systems slower than centralized systems; government civilian agencies seem slow because of bureaucratic inertia; intergovernmental organizations are exceedingly slow to act because of their complex, multifaceted, cross-national coordination and agreement; armed nonstate groups are exceedingly fast, lacking unwieldy bureaucratic infrastructure; and humanitarian organizations and multinational corporations operate at varying speeds, with particular sensitivity to obstacles surrounding national sovereignty concerns.

The differences in potential stability enhancers' type of support base and political legitimacy indicate the extent to which their activities draw praise or criticism from outside observers. Regarding support base, government military and police units and civilian agencies are both local (national); intergovernmental organizations are global; armed nonstate groups and humanitarian organizations are local, regional, and global; and multinational corporations are global. As to political legitimacy, government military and police units are generally high locally and low globally (if they attempt to exert authority in other societies), government civilian agencies are high locally and mixed globally, intergovernmental organizations are low locally and high globally, armed nonstate groups are low locally and low globally, humanitarian organizations are high locally and high globally, and multinational corporations are usually mixed both locally and globally.

Comparative Advantages of Potential Stability Enhancers

Each type of potential stability enhancer possesses different comparative advantages, summarized in Figure 3.1. Many observers presume a fixed hierarchy of desirability for potential stability enhancers, with public stability enhancers at the top and private stability enhancers at the bottom: specifically, government officials are at the top, noncoercive nongovernmental organizations in the middle, and armed nonstate groups at the bottom. Subsequent discussion will demonstrate the arbitrariness of this hierarchy.

A more nuanced analysis reveals a complex web of advantages among these potential sources of stability. Regarding public stability enhancers: (1) For government military or police forces, the primary comparative advantage appears to be enhancing top-down state government security by promoting control and law and order through assistance in training or strengthening coercive security personnel within the affected society; (2) for civilian government agencies, the primary comparative advantage appears to be enhancing top-down state government security by helping with the construction of political infrastructure within the affected society; and (3) for intergovernmental organizations, the primary comparative advantage appears to be enhancing top-down human

Figure 3.1. Comparative advantages of stability enhancers

COMPARATIVE ADVANTAGES OF PUBLIC STABILITY ENHANCERS

Public government military or police forces

Enhancing top-down state government security through strengthening coercive security personnel, restraining turmoil

Public government civilian agencies

Enhancing top-down state government security through enhancing political infrastructure within the affected society

Public intergovernmental organizations

Enhancing top-down human security through incorporating cross-national assistance and values within the affected area

COMPARATIVE ADVANTAGES OF PRIVATE STABILITY ENHANCERS

Private armed nonstate groups

Enhancing bottom-up human security through helping to provide essential survival needs to the affected population

Private humanitarian organizations

Enhancing bottom-up human security through helping to develop civil society within the affected area

Private multinational corporations

Enhancing bottom-up human security through helping to inject an economic stimulus within the affected area

security through help to incorporate cross-national assistance and values within the affected area. Regarding private stability enhancers: (1) For private armed nonstate groups, the primary comparative advantage appears to be enhancing bottom-up human security by providing for the affected population's essential needs; (2) for private subnational or transnational humanitarian organizations, the primary comparative advantage appears to be enhancing bottom-up human security by fostering the development of civil society within the affected area; and (3) for private multinational corporations, the primary comparative advantage appears to be enhancing bottom-up human security by injecting an economic stimulus within the affected area. It becomes evident from this assessment that no one type of stability enhancer alone possesses the kind of advantages to be able to handle the wide range of instability sources in today's world.

ESSENTIAL QUALITIES OF ARMED NONSTATE GROUPS

The scope of armed nonstate groups has been growing in recent decades. There are now an estimated 2 million gang members worldwide, and within Central America this membership may be larger than government military or police forces.[1] Because such membership is often a carefully guarded secret, neither government officials nor the mass public is aware of the full scope of armed nonstate group operations. To the extent such awareness exists, responses are often clouded because these groups frequently mix their activities with those deemed legitimate and illegitimate by outside observers. Figure 3.2 delineates what armed nonstate groups are and are not, as well as controversies surrounding their definition.

Controversies Surrounding Armed Nonstate Groups

Armed nonstate groups are defined in this study as private, relatively autonomous organizations (not under complete and direct state control) with significant and sustained coercive capabilities for organized violence.[2] This definition contrasts with that of the state—formal political institutions possessing the power to control a fixed bounded territory through enforcement[3]—and excludes critical, normally noncoercive private groups, such as multinational corporations, religious movements, and humanitarian organizations. Armed nonstate groups are "(1) willing and capable to use violence for pursuing their objectives and (2) not integrated into formalized state institutions such as regular armies, presidential guards, police or special forces."[4]

Contrary to popular belief, armed nonstate groups are not active only in the poorest, most politically unstable, and least democratic countries; and they are not invariably bent on disrupting the status quo.[5] These groups often have transnational ties, prefer unconventional decentralized network structure over hierarchical organization, and vary in their territorial or nonterritorial aspirations and in their change or status quo orientations.[6] While the formation of armed nonstate groups tends to take place in a local area, "they are always to some degree internationalized," with outside state governments often involved in their web of relationships.[7] For an armed nonstate group, there are parallels between its governance and its command, control, and communication

Figure 3.2. Essential qualities of armed nonstate groups

What armed nonstate groups are

They are private, relatively autonomous organizations with significant coercive capabilities for organized violence.

They are willing and capable of using violence to pursue their ends and are not integrated into formal state institutions.

They do not wear military uniforms or follow military rules of engagement but mobilize quickly with versatile tactics.

What armed nonstate groups are not

They exclude noncoercive private multinational corporations, religious movements, and humanitarian organizations.

They lack states' formal political institutions possessing the power to control a fixed bounded territory.

They are not recognized by international law as legitimate potential sources of security governance.

Controversies surrounding the definition of armed nonstate groups

Are these really organized groups, as they often are not unitary or stable and have internal splits?

Are they really private nonstate groups, as many have collusive relationships with central state governments?

What is the minimum level of military preparedness for them to possess to be considered "armed"?

Are they rational parties pursuing strategic goals, or are they primitive, barbaric, and inconsistent?

---

structure; and between its political organization and its military organization.[8] Armed nonstate groups face an authority handicap compared with state governments—they are illegitimate under international legal norms,[9] although "groups that suffer excessive violence from repressive regimes seemingly do not suffer noticeably from legitimacy deficits."[10]

Isolating armed nonstate groups is controversial, as definitions "differ between international lawyers, social scientists from different disciplines, and practitioners from international governmental and nongovernmental organizations."[11] First, disputes exist over whether they are really organized groups, as often they are not cohesive,[12] unitary, or stable, with key leadership divisions, leader-follower splits, and follower-follower splits.[13] Second, debates abound over whether these are really private nonstate groups, as they have complex and collusive relationships with central state governments and "are deeply entangled with state power and state agents in complex ways,"[14] making it often difficult to determine the degree to which they are disconnected from national political regimes. Third, uncertainty surrounds whether these are really coercively capable groups, for some lack the military preparedness implied by "armed," because coercive action has substantial prerequisites to be viable; nonetheless, for many groups, "although nonstate armed groups may not wear uniforms or drill in formation, they do maintain the ability to mobilize rapidly for war and adapt their traditional tactics to fight modern foes."[15] Fourth, ambiguity surrounds whether these groups are rational parties pursuing strategic goals,[16] as often they are labeled as primitive, barbaric, emotional, and inconsistent. However, even with internal splits, power variation, state collusion, and occasional aimlessness, most exhibit more than enough coherence to be treated as isolatable armed nonstate groups. Convincing evidence exists that "nonstate movements act strategically and adapt their behavior in response to state policies."[17]

Violence and Armed Nonstate Groups

Violence persists in today's global security setting, despite the diminution of aggregate levels compared to the bloodiest periods of world history. The intensity of global violence, defined broadly as "the deliberate infliction of harm,"[18] is staggering: violence is "part of daily life in the sprawling megacities"[19] around the world; and "since World War II, each decade marked at least ten million people or more dead due to conflict."[20] The impact of the consistently high scope and severity of violence (outside of formal interstate wars) in recent decades contradicts the expectations of civilized progress associated with enlightened liberal Western values.

Much of today's violence involves armed nonstate groups and is in the form of "nonstate wars," occurring when a state has limited or nonexistent capacity to impose order.[21] Regardless of whether they initiate it, these groups often find themselves engaged in violent fighting: "conflicts fought without the involvement of governments—among militias, rival guerilla groups, clans, warlords, or communal groups—are now more numerous than state-based conflicts."[22] In these struggles, armed nonstate groups utilize many different modes of violence, "such as terrorism, suicide bombing, insurgency, and rioting,"[23] along with "pillage, robbery, vandalism, arson, forcible displacement, kidnapping, hostage taking, detention, beating torture, mutilation, rape, and desecration of dead bodies."[24] Although violence initiated by state authorities is often sanctioned and tolerated, "organized violence by nonsovereign actors is seen as illegitimate and transgressive."[25] Indeed, "usurping that unique role as a legitimate user of violence—an action that at least the members and sympathizers of VNSA [violent nonstate actors] see as justifiable and is tolerated by a significant portion of the rest of the world—puts them squarely at odds with the classical state system."[26] In violent conflicts involving armed nonstate groups, mass populations may suffer tremendously: campaigns of often brutal violence are carried out against civilians, and in this irregular violent conflict that "presupposes a relative absence of formal structures" there is often "a breakdown in military discipline," "thus turning war into a cover for decentralized looting, banditry, and all kinds of violence against civilians."[27] During recent decades, violence may have become crueler, with today 75 percent of those killed in wars of all kinds being civilians,[28] with many of the victims being women, children, and medical personnel.[29]

Armed nonstate groups generally have access to the same types of conventional weaponry that states do, and often their weapons come from local sources, sometimes with the complicity of the state.[30] Nonetheless, armed nonstate groups do not require a huge stockpile of arms to make a significant impact on a society, as they often operate through illicit patronage networks incorporating such tactics as monetary payoffs or exemptions to law enforcement.[31] Armed nonstate groups have "launched violent challenges to the state, attacking representatives of state power, state symbols, and state institutions, but typically seeking to avoid direct combat with state armies."[32] Over time, however, armed nonstate groups have become more capable and deadlier. Moreover, "with states losing their ability to use technology to dominate warfare," many of "the most important violent technologies no longer are state-generated" and instead "are the inventions and adaptations of terrorists and insurgents": in the end, "the nature of warfare and military technology is being transformed, as states give up their ability to use their most destructive military technology, and nonstate actors gain greater freedom to use their own."[33] Many armed nonstate groups use force more defensively than offensively, rely heavily on asymmetric warfare,[34] and treat combatants and noncombatants as largely indistinguishable. Thus the greatest coercive differences between states and armed nonstate groups lie not in their weaponry or use of force, but rather in the legitimacy of their actions.

Armed nonstate groups are not always composed of sinister individuals with dastardly motivations and goals, and they are not all bloodthirsty savages—parallel to uncontrolled barbarian hordes attacking the Roman Empire—reveling in death and destruction for their own sake. To many observers, this "medieval savagery" is the dominant image: "undisciplined armed men, marauding soldiers, troops living off the land, and criminal elements prey on the population with complete impunity."[35] Instead, the emerging reality is that armed nonstate groups are becoming increasingly complex[36] and in many ways difficult to understand: they "propagate a multi-faceted, global enterprise where violence is no longer the only product, and in fact, it may not be the most important to group survival; in addition to upholding the time-honored tradition of blowing things up, VNSA [violent nonstate actors] now run clinics and schools, produce and ship drugs, operate charities, and host game shows."[37] In fact, some evidence exists that in many circumstances "violence may be a suboptimal strategy for nonstate actors,"[38] who can feel that they are an integral part of local society. Armed nonstate groups' willingness to die for a cause shows both their strong belief and persistence in pursuing particular ends, and "many of them are concerned about their public image, their moral authority (vis-à-vis their enemies), and their sources of legitimacy."[39] So classifying armed nonstate groups as inherently ignoble appears to be overly sweeping.

In attempts to judge the acceptability of armed nonstate groups' violent activities, one's moral compass can end up being confused. Given that many such groups operate across national boundaries using a "when in Rome, do as the Romans do" mentality, cross-national differences in cultural norms often prevent definitive moral judgments. Because illicit networks are tightly intertwined with both legitimate private-sector activities and the political system in the public sector, globally "there is an enormous gray area between legal and illegal transactions, a gray area that the illicit traders have turned to great advantage."[40] Interdependencies between "dirty" and "clean" markets have become increasingly significant:[41] armed nonstate groups have recently partnered with "governments, financial institutions, mining companies and traders, security companies, mercenaries, and even non-governmental organizations."[42] Indeed, armed nonstate group members "can acquire, sometimes as a result of a definite 'public relations' strategy, a degree of public legitimacy, whether this is through fostering a myth of community spirit (as witnessed by the Yakuza's prompt dispatch of aid to the survivors of the 1995 Kobe earthquake) or by posing as champions of national or cultural identity (whether in Kosovo,

Chechnya, or Kurdistan)."[43] Despite this slippery slope, central state governments for their own purposes often attempt to reinforce and amplify negative public images of armed nonstate groups, engendering suspicion and disapproval toward them by giving them derogatory, violent labels that do not capture the wide range of their motivations, goals, and activities.

MAJOR TYPES OF ARMED NONSTATE GROUPS

The current international system encompasses multiple armed nonstate groups using a wide range of methods and strategies to achieve their goals. These groups include militant religious movements, unruly ethnopolitical groups, criminal organizations, militias, ecoterrorists and antiglobalizationists, warlords, and rebels or insurgents.[44] Today, "there is a truly alarming variety of armed groups active in the world today, which dramatically increases the difficulty of understanding their motivations, methods, and goals."[45] Because this variety is growing rather than shrinking, there is a pressing need to differentiate among them when dealing with their stability implications, particularly in terms of their motives, tactics, power levels, and security impacts.[46]

This study focuses on the five principal "ideal types" of armed nonstate groups capable of engaging in global privatized violence: criminals, mercenaries, rebels/insurgents, terrorists, and warlords.[47] Transnational criminal organizations are private groups that undertake illicit profit-seeking activities across national boundaries. Mercenaries are individuals paid to engage in military activities within and across countries around the world, and they include more formal private military companies. Transnational terrorists are private groups operating across national boundaries using violence or threat of violence to pursue political ends. Insurgents or rebels are private groups within a country using violence or threat of violence to try to overthrow the government. Warlords are private military leaders exercising key influence within a country outside of its central state government's control.

For some analysts, it is controversial to include mercenaries (incorporating private security companies) into this list because (1) mercenaries are legal groups, (2) they often work for states, and (3) unlike many other armed nonstate groups, mercenaries rarely contribute to the root causes of instability. However, in today's world, virtually all the major types of armed nonstate groups exhibit some or all of these ambiguities. For example, warlords in Somalia are as "legal" as any other authority is within a situation of ineffective central government authority; Hezbollah is an organization deemed by the United States to be a terrorist group, yet it has legitimate political party seats in Lebanon; and it is hard to label transnational criminal organizations like the Yakuza in Japan as contributing to instability because they often masquerade as legitimate commercial enterprises wanting a stable business climate, and because they have maintained close ties to establishment government and police officials. In reality, all five types of armed nonstate groups are involved in some sort of shady relationship to legitimate recognized sources of authority and stability.

Armed nonstate groups' relationships and strategies continue to evolve in response to changing vulnerabilities and counterpressures, and so particular behavior can vary markedly:

> In many cases these groups are challenging the state; in others they are cooperating and colluding with state structures; in some, the state is a passive bystander while they fight one another. In several instances they are both fighting one another and confronting state structures that seek either to destroy them or to bring them under control.[48]

However, it is relatively clear in this adaptive evolution that the downturn in the global economy since 2008 has served the interests of many armed nonstate groups. The bright prospects for transnational criminal organization exemplify this trend:

> The global economic crisis has been a boon for transnational criminals. Thanks to the weak economy, cash-rich criminal organizations can acquire financially distressed but potentially valuable companies at bargain prices. Fiscal austerity is forcing governments everywhere to cut the budgets of law enforcement agencies and court systems. Millions of people have been laid off and thus are more easily tempted to break the law. . . . Across the globe, criminals have penetrated governments to an unprecedented degree. The reverse has also happened: rather than stamping out powerful gangs, some governments have instead taken over their illegal operations.[49]

So for the foreseeable future, the international environment will likely remain conducive to armed nonstate group operation.

Despite this atmosphere of opportunity, stable patterns persist among the different armed nonstate groups. Table 3.2 compares the five types of armed nonstate groups in the early twenty-first century, revealing each one's basic orientation, primary motivation, organizational style, relationship with the state, main targets, typical tactics, geographical scope, and desire for visibility. The

Table 3.2. Major types of armed nonstate groups

	Criminals	Mercenaries	Terrorists	Rebels/insurgents	Warlords
Basic interest	Economic	Economic	Political	Political	Economic/political
Primary goal	Domination of illicit flows to maximize profit	Reestablishing order in designated areas	Discrediting states and ideologies by inciting state repression in response to violence	Defense or liberation of population from external control so as to take over or replace the state	Defense or liberation of population from external control so as to acquire power
Organizational structure	Mixture of hierarchy and network, with move toward network	Hierarchical control by states that hire them	Horizontal networks of loosely connected subversive cells	Operational decentralization in revolutionary activities	Charismatic leadership, hierarchical control, and patronage systems
Relationship with state	Undermining state economic and judicial process, with little interest in state collapse	Serving state interests	Hostility toward the state-push for fundamental change in ideology or political system	Hostility toward the state-attempted acquisition of predominance of force	Pragmatic maintenance or acquisition of autonomy and of monopoly on force
Main targets	Unarmed civilians and competing groups	Disruptive nonstate forces	Unarmed civilians	Government security forces and competing groups	Government security forces and competing groups
Typical tactics	Corruption/violence	Violence	Violence	Corruption/violence	Violence
Geographical scope	Global presence	Global presence	Global presence	Local presence	Local presence
Desire for visibility	Low	Low	High	High	High

net effect of these differences is to show how counterproductive it is to conceptually lump the types together, as well as to show each type's distinct strengths and weaknesses.

The differences in basic interest and primary motivation among the five armed nonstate groups highlight their contrasting orientations with respect to security objectives. In terms of basic interest, criminals and mercenaries are more economically oriented, rebels/insurgents and terrorists are more politically oriented, and warlords exhibit a mixed pattern. In terms of primary motivation, criminals want to dominate illicit cross-national flows so as to maximize profit; mercenaries want to reestablish order in designated areas; rebels/insurgents want to defend or liberate a given population from external control so as to take over or replace the state; terrorists want to discredit the state by inciting repression in response to violence; and warlords want to defend or liberate a population and territory from external control so as to acquire power and control of an area.[50]

The differences in organizational style and relationship with the state among these armed nonstate groups provide meaningful indications of their level of formality and potential for cooperation. In organizational style, criminals display a mixture of hierarchy and network, with noticeable movement toward network structures; mercenaries exhibit hierarchical control by states that hire them; rebels/insurgents display operational decentralization in revolutionary activities; terrorists display horizontal networks of loosely connected subversive cells; and warlords display charismatic leadership, hierarchical control, and patronage systems.[51] As to relationship with the state, criminals undermine states' economic and judicial processes, with little interest in state collapse; mercenaries serve state interests (since the state is usually their employer); rebels/insurgents exhibit coercive hostility toward the state and attempt to attain predominance of force; terrorists exhibit coercive hostility toward the state while pushing for fundamental change in a state's ideology or political system; and warlords pursue pragmatic maintenance or acquisition of autonomy and attempt to attain predominance of force.[52]

The differences in main targets and typical tactics among armed nonstate groups show distinctions in restraint and enemy identification. In terms of main targets, rebels/insurgents and warlords focus on official government security forces and competing groups, mercenaries emphasize disruptive nonstate forces, and criminals and terrorists concentrate on unarmed civilians (criminals also focus on competing groups).[53] In the tactics typically chosen, criminals and warlords rely on a mix of corruption and violence, while mercenaries, rebels/insurgents, and terrorists rely more on violence and the threat of violence.

Finally, the differences among these groups in geographical scope and desire for visibility reveal key differences in ambition and desired global image. In terms of geographical scope of activity, criminals, mercenaries, and terrorists seek a global presence, while warlords and rebels/insurgents seek only local or regional control.[54] As to desire for visibility, criminals and mercenaries usually prefer to operate "under the radar," while warlords, rebels/insurgents, and terrorists prefer high visibility to attract new members, signal strength, or extract concessions.

These distinctions among the five types of armed nonstate groups are not immutable, for three reasons. First, one kind of armed nonstate group can easily morph into another, and the boundaries among them are blurring. For example, the Palestine Liberation Organization went from being labeled as a terrorist group to receiving official recognition as legitimate by the United Nations. Second, armed nonstate groups have responded to international police pressure by extending their cooperation with one another and engaging in "marriages of convenience," recognizing in the process common underground tactics, reliance on similar weaponry, and use of the same international financial, commercial, transportation, and communication infrastructure systems that provide both anonymity and multiple access points.[55] For example, in the Madrid terrorist bombings of March 11, 2004, the Moroccan drug traffickers merged into a local terrorist group, exemplifying the collusion among terrorists, insurgents, warlords, militias, and criminals that creates "much more formidable challengers to the state."[56] Indeed, "while the modus operandi of criminal groups, insurgents, and terrorists most often diverge, mounting evidence suggests the interaction among or between these entities is increasing."[57] Third, complicating responses to armed nonstate groups is the extent to which they "are cooperating and collaborating with each other in networks that span national borders and include fellow tribal groups, criminal groups, and corrupt political elements."[58] Security-policy makers often face "a cauldron of traditional and emerging threats that interact with each other and at times converge."[59] The guiding principle behind these groups' mutation and collusion appears to be not ideological affinity but rather pragmatic operational opportunism. With their complex web of external ties, these groups seem willing to work with anyone else—legitimate or illegitimate—who can help them to achieve their goals, and so they accept a much wider array of temporary allies than states do in dealing with global security challenges.

Predicting the interaction patterns among armed nonstate groups is considerably more difficult than predicting the interaction patterns among states. Because of their marriages of convenience, these groups "operate through a mixture of confrontation and cooperation even when on opposing sides."[60] Because of their fluidity, past modes of behavior may change without warning. For example, one might wonder how transnational criminals could ever turn against transnational terrorists when criminals make a lot of money by selling weapons to terrorists; yet because such criminal groups respond to economic incentives, they can (and have done so in the past) alter their alliances to conform to the most attractive offer on the table. Because their number and variety are increasing, creating even just a definitive taxonomy of armed nonstate groups is a real challenge.

MAJOR TYPES OF ARMED NONSTATE GROUP CONTROL ATTEMPTS

Out of the wide range of circumstances surrounding armed nonstate groups pursuing control of an area, this study focuses on the major patterns, summarized in Figure 3.3. Armed nonstate group security control attempts can be classified in two ways: by the differences among governance dilemmas serving as a stimulus for armed nonstate group action, and the differences among the armed nonstate group responses to these provocative stimuli. Together these two categorizations allow systematic comparison of control attempts' impact on stability, which is critical because of the substantial variation evident among them.

As with the major types of armed nonstate groups, the major types of armed nonstate group security control attempts are not fixed. Over time, there can be dramatic changes in the governance dilemmas within an area and in armed nonstate groups' responses to them in undertaking their control attempts. Both types of change can readily cause security vulnerabilities to transform, opportunities and limitations to shift, and control attempts to be reclassified and reinterpreted, significantly altering the resulting stability impact. For example, at different times, the Taliban in Afghanistan has experienced each of the four predicaments outlined in its attempts to gain security control within the country; and in response, international praise or condemnation has fluctuated

Figure 3.3. Major types of armed nonstate group control attempts

---

GOVERNANCE DILEMMAS ELICITING ARMED NONSTATE GROUP ACTION

Control attempts where there is no functioning central governing authority

Violation of the stability function of providing predictable order through authority

Difficulty of establishing law and order in an area unused to any effective governance

Control attempts where there is an ineffective central state government

Violation of the stability function of providing basic survival goods and services to the affected population

Vulnerability of affected groups may be invisible to society at large

Control attempts where multiple internal factions are coercively competing for power

Violation of the stability function of preventing internal disruption by ceasing conflict

Reluctance by outside powers and international organizations to enter such a bloody predicament

Control attempts where an unsanctioned outside force has seized power

Violation of the stability function of preventing external disruption by precluding unwanted foreign coercion

Possible need to resort to "fighting fire with fire" approach to maintain or restore order

---

ARMED NONSTATE GROUP RESPONSES TO GOVERNANCE DILEMMAS

Control attempts and armed nonstate groups' internal commitment

Extent to which armed nonstate groups possess coercive strength

Extent to which armed nonstate groups demonstrate willingness to use their capabilities

Control attempts and armed nonstate groups' external support

Extent to which armed nonstate groups attract mass public support

Extent to which armed nonstate groups receive outside funding and support from states or other nonstate groups

Control attempts and armed nonstate groups' predictable continuity

Extent to which armed nonstate groups have a status quo versus non–status quo orientation

Extent to which armed nonstate groups exhibit longevity and unity

Control attempts and armed nonstate groups' strategic adaptability

Extent to which armed nonstate groups indicate openness to power sharing

Extent to which armed nonstate groups harbor realistic expectations about their limitations accordingly. Nonetheless, overarching patterns of difference do emerge among armed nonstate group control attempts.

Differences among Governance Dilemmas Eliciting Armed Nonstate Group Action

Each type of governance dilemma that elicits armed nonstate group action associates with failure in attaining one of four essential stability functions: (1) having no functioning central governing authority within a given territory, so that lawlessness prevails, links with failure to meet the stability function of promoting predictable order through authority; (2) having a state government with authority over an area but the security needs of all or part of its citizenry remain unfulfilled links with failure to meet the stability function of providing for basic survival needs to the affected population; (3) having multiple factions coercively competing for power and control within a state links with failure to meet the stability function of preventing or restraining internal disruption by ceasing violent conflict or perpetuating peace; and (4) having an unsanctioned outside force seize power and severely oppress large numbers of people links with failure to meet the stability function of preventing or restraining external disruption by precluding unwanted coercive foreign intervention.

Only one of the four types of armed nonstate group control attempts—the second one, where a state government has authority over an area but the security needs of its citizenry are unfulfilled—involves a direct confrontation between an armed nonstate group and a central state government. This reinforces the point that the primary underlying dynamic is not private groups directly and forcibly wresting control from the state.

Instead, underlying these private security control attempts are tangible security deficiencies: "(1) illegitimacy, whereby citizens of a state do not see the leadership of a state as the rightful wielders of power; (2) incapacity or impotence, whereby the wielders of power do not have the means to address the problems facing their citizens; and (3) excessive force, whereby the use of coercive power is an oppressive response to problems."[61] When affected societies recognize these security governance deficiencies, they endeavor to rectify them in ways conducive to armed nonstate group involvement:

> Communities that have been cut off from an effective state authority—whether out of governmental indifference to marginal frontier territories, or because of protracted warfare, or because of vested local and external interests in perpetuating conditions of state failure—consistently seek to devise

arrangements to provide for themselves the core functions that the missing state is supposed to assume, especially basic security. These local efforts at governance vary widely in their effectiveness. Collectively, they reinforce the obvious but often overlooked observation that local communities are not passive in the face of state failure and insecurity, but instead adapt in a variety of ways to minimize risk and increase predictability in their dangerous environments.[62]

The first two governance dilemmas, where no functioning central governing authority exists within a given territory and where a state government has authority over an area but the security needs of its citizenry are unfulfilled, have received the most global attention: for example, the World Bank highlights that the number of states lacking effective sovereignty rose from eleven in 1996 to twenty-six in 2006.[63] Yet the other two governance dilemmas, where multiple internal factions are coercively competing for power and where an unsanctioned outside force has seized power and is engaging in severe oppression, seem just as volatile and dangerous from a security standpoint.

In the first governance dilemma, involving control attempts where there is no functioning central governing authority, an armed nonstate group may appear as the only way to implement an internal solution to the problem of widespread domestic disorder and possible complete chaos associated with a classic power vacuum. Sometimes unruly elements want to keep an area ungoverned so illicit activities can flourish unnoticed and unregulated. In many cases, no central state government can form with the requisite institutions, infrastructure, resources, and legitimacy to manage the lawless area, and few alternatives may be realistically available to ensure continuity in the existing community. It may be difficult for anyone to restore order within an area unused to any form of effective governance. The country of Somalia illustrates this security challenge.

In the second governance dilemma, involving control attempts where a state government controls an area but security needs remain unfulfilled, an armed nonstate group may appear as the only way to fulfill citizens' security needs in the face of a ruling power that is ignoring, unable to fulfill, or purposely violating its end of the social contract. A weak state that has been unable to regulate its citizens and its own agents often causes a "culture of impunity" to emerge, defying any attempt to impose law and order.[64] This predicament can develop especially when dealing with internal groups against which the state discriminates—often because of racial, religious, or ethnic differences—or with internal groups that are so impoverished and destitute that the state provides for minimal protection or basic survival needs.

If the neglected people have arms and military training greater than that of state-controlled armed forces, then armed nonstate group control attempts become even more likely. Indeed, "with failures in governance resulting in a loss of regime illegitimacy and undermining the notion of 'citizenry,' identity cleavages further serve to alienate the individual from the state and lure them toward nonstate actors."[65] This predicament can occur in both remote frontier zones and urban areas where dangers are so high that government police or soldiers do not enter them either to patrol or to apprehend disruptive forces. A key obstacle may be that the vulnerability of these marginal groups is invisible to the rest of the society, perpetuating the security gap and reducing the likelihood of effective remedies being implemented by the state. Because even in democratic societies such disadvantaged groups usually constitute only a minority of the state's citizenry, normal political channels are often insufficient to improve their security plight. Jamaica illustrates this security challenge, with posses filling in the void where the central state government does not provide security.

In the third governance dilemma, involving control attempts where multiple factions coercively compete for power, an armed nonstate group may appear as the only way to cope with seemingly endless internal violent conflict that fosters dysfunctional turmoil within an affected area. Often violent conflict among differing groups warring over territorial control creates a predicament that the central government cannot resolve, or in which it does not wish to risk intervention. These unruly forces competing for security control are often extremely dangerous—terrorizing political opponents and wreaking havoc, with innocent people being killed or injured and property being destroyed. Because both outside state powers and international organizations may be extremely reluctant to enter such a bloody predicament with any serious commitment to stay as long as is necessary until stability is restored, an armed nonstate group may see a golden opportunity to seize control. Any group wishing to establish order in such a conflict zone usually needs to outwit and outmuscle the warring groups. What is ultimately desirable may be the establishment of a new coercive hierarchy for promoting effective deterrence of would-be aggressive battling forces. Exemplifying this predicament are the long-standing security governance dilemmas associated with warring private factions in the Philippines;[66] and the Taliban's elimination of the dominant control by predatory warlords when it established control in Afghanistan, before the American intervention.[67]

In the fourth governance dilemma, involving control attempts where an unsanctioned outside force has seized power and is engaging in oppression, an armed nonstate group may appear to be the only way to eliminate the disruptive coercive external intervention. The pressing need in this instance is not to interfere with state government control but to reduce the control of the dangerous outside force that seized power. In this predicament, the armed nonstate group fighting the disruptive outside force may have to resort to a volatile "fighting fire with fire" response, in which vulnerable people use the same kind of private coercion to protect themselves as is being used to threaten them.[68] Two recent examples illustrate this pattern. On the high seas off the coast of Somalia, private security firms have been hired to interfere with the dominant control by pirates (some of whom come from outside the country) because the area needing protection is too large for the government navies of the world to patrol effectively;[69] and in Mexico City, private police and citizen security patrols "see themselves on the fault lines of 'war' against criminal forces who threaten to destroy the nation"[70] and who have assumed (with the involvement of some nonindigenous elements) control in areas of the city. In these kinds of predicaments, generating substantial popular support is crucial for the success of an armed nonstate group working against the illegitimate outside force that seized control of the area.

Differences among Armed Nonstate Group Responses to Governance Dilemmas

Four elements characterizing armed nonstate group responses to governance dilemmas stand out: (1) internal commitment, the extent to which these groups possess coercive strength and demonstrate willingness to use their capabilities; (2) external support, the extent to which they have mass public support and receive outside funding and support from states or other nonstate groups; (3) predictable continuity, the extent to which they have a status quo versus non–status quo tilt and exhibit longevity and unity; and (4) strategic adaptability, the extent to which they exhibit openness to a wide variety of responses, including power sharing, and harbor realistic expectations about their limitations. The first two elements address the capacity associated with these armed nonstate group security control attempts, while the second two elements address the orientation embedded in these control attempts.

Beginning with armed nonstate groups' internal commitment: the first requirement is coercive strength, the extent to which these groups are able to attain and maintain effective control over an area and put down violent disruptions. For example, some otherwise promising tribal warlords may not be able to clamp down on disruptive terrorist or criminal activities within designated areas. Coercive strength depends not only on armed nonstate groups' size and possession of military technology, but also on their training, discipline, and coordination in how to use such technology and on their ability to find innovative ways to supply their needs. Equally important is the second requirement, the extent to which armed nonstate group are willing and steadfast in their use of coercive strength when needed in their security control attempts. Although most armed nonstate groups appear to be more than willing to apply sufficient coercive force when opportunities present themselves, this pattern is not universal: some groups vacillate in their control attempts and security goals, inconsistently applying force and withdrawing it in an ambivalent way. If a private security provider lacks commitment to deal with existing turmoil, its control attempts could be disastrous even if it has significant coercive capabilities.

Regarding external support in a nonstate group's security control attempts, popularity with the mass public constitutes a real asset. As Chapter 4 discusses, in many countries citizens are becoming increasingly dissatisfied with protection from the central state government, and are thus they are open to other sources of stability. Because armed nonstate groups tend to operate locally without a huge bureaucratic infrastructure, the public may feel the group understands its needs better. When citizens approve of what armed nonstate groups are doing, the costs of their protection go down; in contrast, antagonism or distrust from the mass public can be deadly to a security control attempt. A second key element is outside funding and support from states or other nonstate groups, because armed nonstate groups with diverse sources of support from outside their area of operation seem more likely to launch successful security control attempts and to weather a greater variety of unforeseen challenges. Given the likelihood of severe fluctuations in incoming funds and fickle supporters, it is beneficial to have a wide range of states and outside groups from which to solicit extra help and cash and equipment. Such support need not come just from those who approve of a group's cause or who are disgruntled with an ongoing security predicament; instead, a group can successfully elicit outside help simply on the basis that it is opposing another group considered a lot worse by the funding or support source.

One important dimension of armed nonstate groups' predictable continuity is their orientation toward status quo versus non–status quo goals.

Numerous strong and capable armed nonstate groups willing to apply their strength lack any interest in promoting stability. For example, rebels or insurgents may be so invested in overthrowing the existing political regime that they have no motivation to become stability enhancers; and terrorists—with perhaps the most notable illustration being al-Qaeda—may be so obsessed with fostering a climate of fear of violent disruption that any form of stability would undercut their objectives. A key distinction exists between those armed nonstate groups whose disinterest arises from absence of desire to participate in security governance and those whose disinterest arises from antagonism toward the existing state regime. A second important dimension enhancing armed nonstate group control depends on whether these groups have unity and strong leadership, have been around for a while, and possess a coherent long-range plan for achieving their security goals. The result can be much greater domestic and global credibility. Armed nonstate groups exhibiting all kinds of internal splits can find their security control attempts doomed from the outset.

A central facet of armed nonstate groups' strategic adaptability involves openness to a wide variety of responses to governance dilemmas, including power sharing, which aid the success of security control attempts. The emphasis here is on the group's flexibility, as in whether it is willing to accept something less than monopolistic control of a particular area. Some groups have experience colluding with the state, and some do not; some are full of hatred and antagonism toward the state, and some are not; and some see themselves as in direct competition with the state for power, and others do not. For example, the Japanese Yakuza has a legacy of successful covert criminal collusion with central state government` officials. Armed nonstate groups' capacity to adapt can be remarkable, altering their mission, coercive tactics, and informal alliances depending on changes in the existing authority structures and in competing power challenges they face. A second facet of strategic adaptability is whether armed nonstate groups harbor realistic expectations about limitations, because control attempts are more likely to be successful if groups are prudent in evaluating the potential speed at which they can assume security control and the scope and limitations of their operations. Some groups possess unrealistic, overblown expectations—just as some states do—about their ability to achieve security and provide protection to an affected population. These unrealistic expectations may incorporate classic delusions of grandeur or inadequate recognition of a group's handicaps in light of persistent constraining systemic conditions. Successful responses to governance dilemmas depend on none of the parties potentially relevant to power sharing—the central state government, the armed nonstate groups, and the affected population—developing unrealistic expectations about the rapidity or benefits of such arrangements. In Afghanistan, for example, the American attempt to achieve stable governance lost some long-term support from the local citizenry because "the negative impact was amplified by the great hype that initially surrounded the process, raising great expectations among the Afghan population."[71] Anyone anticipating immediate dramatic positive transformation via private security control is bound to be disappointed.

CONCLUDING THOUGHTS

Contrary to their public image, armed nonstate groups and their security control attempts have substantial diversity among their goals, tactics, and rationales for existence. Most analysts lump the groups together into a single normative pot, categorizing them all as attempting to undermine state control, representing the most destructive examples of ruthless, violent group behavior, and constituting a bunch of irresponsible and reckless thugs requiring immediate eradication. Compared to other potential stability enhancers, armed nonstate groups have their strengths and weaknesses, but they are not always the worst of the lot. Each type of group operates out of its own self-interest, but this self-interest does not always diverge from what is best for the stability of the state and the society.

So on occasion armed nonstate groups may see incentives in promoting a predictable environment, in attracting public support, and in cooperating with the state. Frequently these groups exercise power in situations they did not create and where not many viable alternatives exist, including where there is an authority vacuum, an inept governance system, a clash of different internal contenders for power, and an undesired outside force coercively intervening. One cannot automatically discount any possible stabilizing contribution by these groups despite their long record of violence, because effective coercion sometimes is exactly what is needed to establish stability. Likewise, one cannot automatically discount any possible stabilizing cooperative relationships between these groups—despite their collusive relationships with each other—and central state governments, because armed nonstate groups are nothing if not pragmatic in how they select their marriages of convenience. Armed nonstate groups—which can often adapt to and take advantage of instability faster and better than states—may not only thrive but also sometimes constitute a logical response to a world full of too much fear, hatred, and anger and too little civil discourse to resolve pressing security differences.

The important distinctions identified among armed nonstate groups and control attempts serve equally to reinforce that not all are suitable for stability promotion. Some groups fulfill the most negative stereotypes of disruptive violent subnational and transnational forces, seeking actively to create as much turmoil as possible within countries, negatively affecting both societal functioning and political regime continuity. Other groups, more oriented toward the status quo, may inadvertently foster unexpected backfire effects. Still other groups stand on the sidelines and watch societies disintegrate without lifting a finger. Regardless, the preceding analysis strongly suggests the need to engage in careful discrimination among armed state groups and their security control attempts before formulating policy to manage them.

4 THE TRANSFORMATION IN GLOBAL SECURITY CONTROL

IT IS DANGEROUS to assume that the global security environment has been unchanging during the volatile decades since the end of the Cold War. Instead, the identity and tactics of those forces most capable of enhancing stability have been in a state of significant flux. This warrants a close examination of the changing state of global supply of and demand for security and the resulting global shift in security governance.

The context for this ongoing security transformation is global anarchy, where there is an absence of overarching authority, promoting lawlessness (in contrast to a hierarchical system in which there is deference to a higher authority).[1] In recent years, "an increasing number of state and nonstate actors have displayed an indifference to international norms and law as well as conventional forms of conflict resolution, and have demonstrated a preparedness to adopt offensive strategies that have the potential to challenge the traditional security architecture."[2] Anarchy may stem from rampant crime, disease, ethnic strife, government corruption, overpopulation, resource scarcity, tribalism, weak or dysfunctional institutions, and widespread poverty.[3] The combination of anarchy and high internal violence often can trigger external coercive intervention.[4] A common normative international relations assumption is that the presence of systemic anarchy impedes security, making the labels "ungoverned" or "anarchic" automatically suggest a system's inherent security undesirability. Moreover, in analyzing anarchy, a normative bias toward the state is evident: if an area is outside the control of a central state government but under some form of private authority, the area is often inappropriately labeled ungoverned rather than as alternatively governed. Definitional controversies surrounding global anarchy include (1) whether state security governance reduces anarchy more than nonstate governance does; (2) whether armed nonstate group security governance depends on, contributes to, or detracts from anarchy; and (3) whether a meaningful threshold exists for moving from global anarchy to global order within an increasingly multipolar world with multiple conflicting core values.

CHANGING GLOBAL SECURITY SUPPLY AND DEMAND

In today's international system, a security role reversal is in process, in which armed nonstate groups fulfill for citizens security functions that traditionally have been the domain of central state governments. This change, displayed in Figure 4.1, can best be analyzed in supply-demand terms: (1) the state supply of effective security is decreasing, (2) the public demand for security is increasing (linked to diversifying threats), and (3) the armed nonstate groups' potential to provide security is increasing. Given the international community's reluctance to intervene in a state's internal turmoil, national military downsizing, and the glut of highly skilled military personnel available, the supply of armed nonstate groups and the demand for them appear to be escalating in unison.[5] This supply-demand change is not so much a product of anyone's intentional planning but rather results from the convergence of several simultaneous trends.

The Global Decline in State Supply of Protection

Going back to the Treaty of Westphalia in 1648 (ending the Thirty Years War), when the international state system was first formalized, helps provide a context for understanding the modern erosion of state security authority. As the nation-state first was emerging, the "feudal anarchy" of localized jurisdictions yielded to the "ordered centralism" of a broader authority, "which ruled over a pacified area with the aid of a bureaucracy, a professional army, and the power to levy taxes":[6]

> Indeed, the very emergence of the modern nation-state is associated with the suppression of brigands, private armies, and other autonomous military formations by the central government. To protect the nation from foreign invasion and to preserve social stability, the nation-state has been endowed by law and practice with certain fundamental powers: to levy taxes, to conscript young men (and sometimes young women) into the armed services, and to regulate the production and distribution of firearms. When a state can no longer provide such protection, its authority withers and failure is likely."[7]

Figure 4.1. Changes in global supply and demand for protection

DECLINE IN STATE SUPPLY OF PROTECTION

Government military downsizing
Government forces unsuited for unconventional threats
Growing length and complexity of conflicts
Tentativeness in Western governments' use of force
Unwillingness/inability by states to allocate enough security resources
Human insecurity escalation due to state action

INCREASE IN PUBLIC DEMAND FOR PROTECTION

Rising sense of perceived threat
Spreading domestic insurgencies, civil wars, weak/failing states
Expanding subnational and transnational disruptive forces
Growing interdependence and globalization
Exploding mass migration
Escalating fears due to media scares and state corruption

INCREASE IN ARMED NONSTATE GROUPS' SUPPLY OF PROTECTION

Proliferation of armed nonstate groups
Entrance of the glut of ex-soldiers legitimized by security vacuums
Swelling private protection in both developed and developing states
Privatization of military, police, prison, and home protection
Facilitation of "fortress mentality" by private groups
Superiority of localized private over centralized state protection

Contributing to this need for larger and more complex administrative units were improvements in communication and transportation, representing early forms of globalization. The political authority of the state derived from an implicit social contract between the rulers and the ruled, in which citizens were loyal and obedient to the state in return for protection.[8] The capacity of the state to provide this protection in turn derived from its "monopoly of the legitimate use of physical force within a given territory,"[9] considered to be the "ultimate symbol"[10] of national sovereignty. The primary justifications for this exclusivity of government coercion appears to have been to maintain order and to protect human life, even though historically other motivations—such as keeping the regime in power—often took precedence.[11] Providing security was without doubt "the crucial historical variable in the rise of the state";[12] and indeed states may have arisen as a "security racket," "trading protection to merchants and others in return for revenues and other services, and in the process for providing a framework for the organization of production, exchange, and accumulation."[13] The relationships between the formation of the state, its ability to wage war, and its capacity to provide protection were mutually reinforcing:

> [I]n order to defend or establish national sovereignty, states engaged in armed warfare, with inter-state violence fueling both the domestic monopolization of the means of coercion and modern state formation. To successfully wage and win wars the state created new institutions (government bureaucracies), new revenue sources (taxes), and new avenues for securing legitimacy (citizenship rights) which then allowed it to extract funds and moral support from the citizenry to employ armed actors, in the process building stronger state-society connections.[14]

Through this arrangement, states attained a degree of legitimacy (in their citizens' eyes) and institutionalization to manage expected services.

Up until recent decades, the state appeared to be on a uninterrupted course of gradually expanding its global dominance in the security realm through four distinct eras: "(1) a stateless era (by far the longest), (2) an era of small-scale states encircled by vast and easily reached stateless peripheries; (3) a period in which such peripheries are shrunken and beleaguered by the expansion of state power, and finally, (4) an era in which virtually the entire globe is 'administered space' and the periphery is not much more than a folkloric remnant."[15] To many observers, raising the responsibility for providing the public good of security from the local level to the central state government level appeared to be a step in the right direction. From this perspective, it is easy to see how some analysts might conclude that nonstate authority has become a relic of the past.

However, there is no reason to assume that the Westphalian state system is optimal in all circumstances as a means of providing global stability. It is evident that "the state always was and continues to be a less than perfect mechanism to express, enable, or contain the diversity of the world,"[16] and there has been a long "global history of populations trying to avoid, or having been extruded by, the state."[17] At various times, other configurations of political control—including those involving armed nonstate groups—have functioned well for stability promotion, as "for at least three thousand years mercenarism has been a feature, often the major feature, of institutions of organized violence."[18] Looking at the broad sweep of legitimized violence from the origins of the nation-state to the present, observers remain skeptical about the utility of a government monopoly on the use of force being under all circumstances the smoothest, most effective, and sole acceptable path to the attainment of security:

> The contemporary organization of global violence is neither timeless nor natural. It is distinctly modern. In the six centuries leading up to 1900, global violence was democratized, marketized, and internationalized. Nonstate violence dominated the international system. Individuals and groups used their own means of violence in pursuit of their particular aims, whether honor and glory, wealth, or political power. People bought and sold military manpower like a commodity on the global market. The identity of suppliers or purchasers meant almost nothing.[19]

Global norms and public expectations about security governance have changed over time, and in the process the public-private balance has exhibited both continuous and discontinuous transformation.[20]

A state monopoly on instruments of violence, viewed from an economic perspective, does not appear to be a fixed component of maximizing expected utility, for the choice of public versus private control is ideally determined by economic efficiency:

> As from the late 19th century, efficiency and the public provision of security happened to coincide, historically, with the emerging nation-state. But today, efficiency and the exclusively public provision of security may not coincide anymore. I claim that in our time the increasing privatization of various degrees of security functions also is an efficiency response to a different, evolving constellation of constraints.[21]

Thus while government control of the armed forces was an efficient response when the state system first evolved, that may not always be the case anymore, either domestically or internationally.

Furthermore, a broad global historical examination of effective authority patterns reveals that "the modern nation-state is the exception rather than the rule," as frequently national governments "lack the capacity to implement and enforce central decisions and a monopoly on the use of force."[22] Indeed, "states are a recent innovation in governance,"[23] and they are by no means eternal:

> The state's attainment of a near monopoly of legitimate force is not permanent. Instead, it is temporary and reversible. The end of the Cold War, economic globalization, and the spread of cheap, light weapons are making the state's monopoly on legitimate violence increasingly tenuous, most dramatically in the Middle East, Central Asia, and Africa, but everywhere else, even in northwestern Europe itself.[24]

For a variety of reasons to be discussed later in this chapter, there has been a post–Cold War decline in state capacity and willingness to apply coercive force in order to protect citizens. States have not been attentive or quick to adapt to changing trends: "the geriatric, ossified state sits befuddled as it slowly discovers that the forces of globalization render its 'hard shell' into so much Swiss cheese."[25]

After 1989, Western military establishments significantly downsized, reducing their capacity to maintain security through the use of force, and then were unable to cope with the ensuing outpouring of unconventional threats. Even when the American military budget sharply rose after the 9/11 attacks, the traditional military training of government soldiers was not well suited to deal with these unorthodox dangers. Furthermore, the downsizing associated with the supposed post–Cold War "peace dividend" "released millions of people from armed service but left intact the infrastructure of violence," as demobilized soldiers from the proxy armies maintained by the superpowers "gravitated toward mercenary armies, militias, and gangs."[26] Thus the ratio of those armed personnel employed by national governments to those working for private outfits moved in a nonstate direction.

Western states have become more tentative in their use of force[27] irrespective of the constraints posed by downsizing. Again, this trend has hampered their ability to coercively provide protection. The inability of the United States to achieve a ground force victory in Vietnam "persuaded a generation and more of American and Western generals that the use of Western and particularly American ground forces in foreign conflicts is a mistake"; indeed, the "mounting human and financial costs" resulting from helping to manage "seemingly intractable civil wars" overseas has created a kind of "intervention fatigue" among Western states.[28] Moreover, "the unanticipated length and complexity of post-conflict operations in Iraq and Afghanistan" provided incentives to move away from reliance on uniformed government soldiers.[29] American political leaders have to some extent become "quite terrified of taking casualties" through foreign coercive interventions, and as a result private contractors have begun to look attractive: a while ago an American ambassador in Europe confessed "that his country could no longer emotionally, psychologically or politically accept body bags coming home in double figures."[30] When even the greatest military power in the world is unable to manage global turmoil, and conventional state military forces alone are unable to manage external threat,[31] the demand escalates for low-risk private means—potentially involving armed nonstate groups—to promote or maintain stability.

As a consequence, in today's world "state authority is not absolute, exclusive, or necessarily primary."[32] Indeed, "in the twenty-first century, it is becoming increasingly clear that the conventional modes of political steering by nation-states and international regulations are not effectively dealing with global challenges such as . . . new security threats."[33] Within this changing context, "the national monopoly of legitimate organized violence has been eroded from above by the transnationalization of military forces" and "eroded from below by the privatization of organized violence."[34] Many state governments cannot or will not provide adequate protection and provide for basic survival needs to their citizenry, and state security structures and standard operating procedures often appear to be ill suited to existing dangers. Specifically, "states are being overwhelmed by complexity, fragmentation, and demands that they are simply unable to meet; they are experiencing an unsettling diminution in their capacity to manage political, social, and economic problems that are increasingly interconnected, intractable, and volatile."[35] The current global security environment is not filled with stable well-functioning democracies, and some places—like the so-called "rogue states"—behave with little sense of obligation or responsibility to the broader global community.

The Global Rise in Public Demand for Protection

The mass public's demand for protection has appeared to increase, accompanied by expanding frequency and intensity of perceived insecurity. There are several precipitants of this trend, including growing (1) concerns about diversified stability-eroding global threats to Western interests; (2) uncertainties associated with interdependence and mass migration of peoples; and (3) mass public awareness of threat heightened by mass media scare tactics and mass public awareness of government security deficiencies heightened by exposure of corruption. Because security is both psychological and physical,[36] perceived insecurity by the mass public is at least as important as any assessment of "objective" security levels for gauging the success of state government protection. Although most people may be subject to more protective efforts than ever before, they often do not feel that what they receive is adequate. Particularly within the world's dense urban areas, numerous public opinion surveys indicate that people perceive that they are highly vulnerable to violence, with ineffective state protection, rising threats, unfulfilled security demands, and only themselves to rely on for personal safety.

The growing sense of threat came with the end of restraining bipolarity, which opened the door to different kinds of dangers, including increasing domestic insurgencies, internal civil wars, failing states, the spread of weapons of mass destruction, and violent acts perpetrated by subnational and transnational disruptive forces. These threats often have been covert, dispersed, decentralized, adaptable, and fluid, with threat sources difficult to identify, monitor, target, contain, and destroy. Past actions are not necessarily a sound guide to their future behavior. This pattern among armed nonstate groups reflects "the 'de-massification' of threats in the world," where "a single giant threat of war . . . is replaced by a multitude of 'niche threats'" in which "war will not be waged by armies but by groups we today call terrorists, guerrillas, bandits, and robbers."[37] Along with regular government armies, the participants in modern violent conflicts have included an assortment of "paramilitary units, local warlords, criminal gangs, police forces, mercenary groups," and other nonstate groups with coercive capabilities.[38] In the future, a "looming crisis of governance and widening security deficits" appears to be "inextricably linked to increasing global instability."[39] In facing these widening security challenges, states "often lack the patience" to persevere in the inevitably enduring and difficult contestations of power that ensue.[40]

The September 11, 2001, terrorist attacks on the United States, which destroyed the World Trade Center towers in New York and damaged the Pentagon in Washington, critically altered Western perception of threat. Terrorists armed only with box cutters destroyed four aircraft, killed almost three thousand people, and caused direct damage estimated at $18 billion, bringing the most powerful state in the world to a halt for a few days.[41] American citizens responded with heightened uncertainty and fear, along with a mix of shock, pride, anger, and resolve.[42] Since the attacks, many Americans (both in and out of government) have turned from wishful thinking to worst-case thinking about dire national security dangers.[43] On March 12, 2002, the American government initiated the Homeland Security Advisory System, a five-level color-coded public warning system designed to combine threat information with vulnerability assessments, to communicate to American public safety officials and the mass public the severity of incoming threat, and to guide American protective measures to reduce the likelihood or impact of a terrorist attack. Amplifying the sense of public uncertainty, however, was the reality that little systematic threat assessment undergirded this severity determination; no published criteria exist for the threat levels; and the Department of Homeland Security never explained the sources and quality of intelligence upon which threat levels were based.[44] Thus, in the wake of the 9/11 security trauma, confusion has often surrounded the required level of threat protection:

> Everyone understands instinctively that we can't do everything—100 percent security is impossible to achieve, especially in a nation like ours, which rightly places a premium on civil rights and civil liberties—and everyone agrees that for all we've already done, we need to do even more. But how much more? How much is enough? How little is too little? Exactly how secure are we? How much more secure do we need to be, or can we be? These are the key questions, yet no one inside or outside government seems to have the answer to them.[45]

After the United States undertook coercive military measures to respond to the 9/11 attacks, "the risk of further large-scale attacks on the U.S. mainland fell," but "no one knows by how much."[46] This persistent uncertainty about safety led much of the public to adopt a "better safe than sorry" security attitude, in which they assume that existing state protection is never sufficient.

As part of the rising uncertainties associated with increased interdependence and mass migration of peoples, the mass public is becoming more cognizant of how much that goes on in a given country is crucially affected by seemingly unpredictable internal and external forces. As self-sufficient and isolationist states are disappearing, people all over the world have realized that interconnectedness can create critical vulnerabilities from which they want protection. Interdependence creates the specter of unanticipated cutoff of natural resources or finished product flows from abroad, which can foster an uneasy sense of pending external disruption of one's cherished economic lifestyle. Mass immigration raises the specter of hordes of foreigners entering one's country legally or illegally, which can foster a sense of pending external disruption of one's cherished cultural values. Both trends make people feel that they (and their governments) have inadequate control over their own fates.

Mass public awareness of threat, heightened by mass media scare tactics and mass public awareness of government security deficiencies, heightened in turn by exposure of corruption, instant global communication of dangers and disruptions all over the world, has combined with rising expectations of protection to cause people to become increasingly dissatisfied with their security. This dissatisfaction seems especially focused on state-provided security, as the legitimacy of the state to manage existing fears may be "on the decline." For example, "instead of letting elected officials and their regulatory agents fight the problems of crime, growing numbers of citizens reject formal political channels and look for their own answers to the problems of insecurity in everyday life"; and "when citizens bypass state channels and turn to nonstate actors like private police for protection, the state itself loses a key function and some of its legitimacy."[47] Mass media promotion of fear, in both print and electronic media, highlighting acts of violence and terror, attracts a much larger audience than glorifying occurrences of peaceful cooperation and successful crisis management; as a result, the public can get an exaggerated view of the prevalence of dangers, from which they require protection. Mass awareness of government security deficiencies, in democratic advanced industrial societies—where the majority of the population is unused to constant insecurity and believes in a meaningful two-way social contract—allows more people learn about what is actually transpiring, making them more skeptical about the adequacy of their protection from peril. For example, increasing public awareness of "unprecedented levels of police corruption and impunity have contributed to rising public insecurity" and opened the door to armed nonstate forces entering the picture.[48]

The Global Rise in Armed Nonstate Groups' Potential to Supply Protection

As state capacity to ensure security has eroded, armed nonstate groups—whose independent power and influence has been growing significantly in international relations since the end of the Cold War[49]—have been ready to step in and fill the void. This pattern has become increasingly common globally:

> States continue to be the primary providers of security, but even in this realm nonstate actors are making inroads. Increasingly, we are being forced to think of security as a commodity that can be treated as either a public good or a

private good. Like the nobles of the medieval period in Europe who built castles as private investments in security, more and more people worldwide who can afford to do so are retreating into gated communities or hiring private security firms for protection.[50]

What results is "not so much collapse as reconfiguration," described by some observers as "the emergence of a new Middle Ages."[51] This transition can be called "security governance without government," in which an area may be dominated by relatively powerful armed nonstate groups that control access to natural resources, trade and businesses, and humanitarian aid; in such circumstances, these groups may "act as de facto key 'security providers' based mainly on violence, suppression and intimidation, but sometimes also on popular support"[52] and collusion with governments. In this regard, armed nonstate groups "often enjoy a legitimate social recognition to the extent that they step into a power vacuum left by a weak state and provide public goods that the state fails to provide."[53] This private form of security may on occasion "complement or outperform state efforts,"[54] where "the performance of traditional state functions in such communities may actually have improved as the official government has receded."[55]

Potentially violent groups have been around for millennia: "even Rome, at the height of its power, had to contend with roaming criminal bands that preyed on its citizens as well as with maritime pirates."[56] However, in the late twentieth and early twenty-first centuries, armed nonstate groups reemerged as a "major challenge to the Westphalian state," sometimes seeking to perpetuate and intensify state weakness.[57] This resurgence of armed nonstate groups has many roots, including stressful, desperation-inducing conditions affecting the mass population from which there appears to be no recourse: "from among the varied sources of human insecurity . . . resource scarcity, demographic pressures, socioeconomic deprivation, organized crime and corruption, and identity cleavages are most likely to make individuals susceptible to mobilization" by armed nonstate groups.[58] Indeed, "the contest between nation-states and VNSA [violent nonstate actors] takes place in an environment that is marked by an unprecedented degree of complexity and diversity: on one hand, the revolution in information technology enables a global recruiting campaign by religious extremists; while on the other, persistent socioeconomic deprivation and failures in governance expand the recruiting pool."[59] Within the current security setting, these various roots of armed nonstate group growth combine to accelerate their global power and influence. In addition, the post–Cold War cutback on uniformed officers left a glut of those possessing military expertise gained in previous eras looking to places other than governments for meaningful work.[60] Armed nonstate groups possess diverse motivations: they emerge because of either the pull of an attractive security void or an opportunity for adventure or the push of a desire to control one's own fate, fight for one's beliefs, or earn extra money.[61] Thus the rise of armed state groups is due to a lot more than the presence of failing or weak states.[62]

This sea change is occurring within developed and developing countries:

> Internally the state is being stressed by its inability to provide effective security for parts of it population. In contrast to the ever-increasing international and transnational aspects of economic and social activity, security is becoming much more local. As many nation-states fail to fulfill their basic social contracts, people turn to local solutions—often militias. In essence, the people are forced to turn to an earlier form of social organization—family, clan, tribe, region, and their associated militias—for protection. While particularly true in those states that were arbitrarily formed and encompass widely varying and even hostile groups, this is not just a third-world phenomenon. We have militias in the United States; we simply call them gated communities. In these communities, the home owners have decided that their government can no longer provide sufficient security and therefore have hired private militias to do the job.[63]

Despite differing circumstances, parallels exist when globally comparing the reliance for protection by the rich and the poor on armed nonstate groups:

> As the more prosperous players plug into a global economy . . . they retreat into secure enclaves protected by private security forces—a process former U.S. Secretary of Labor Robert Reich called the "secession of the successful." Marginalized communities have essentially done the same thing, using a different kind of private security force—the gang—to maintain order in the global cities' multiplying and expanding ghettos.[64]

In many cases, "armed groups have used violence strategically to undermine the authority, power, and legitimacy not only of weak states but even of the most powerful ones."[65]

Within developing countries, the dispossessed often find themselves with no alternative outside of an armed nonstate group's coercive security control. In many of these societies, effective authority traditionally has been on the local rather than national level, and so armed nonstate groups fit in nicely. To some inhabitants, the specter of failed and failing states has caused a fatalistic outlook that predictable protection will not be not forthcoming from the state, leading many people—including in seemingly stable places like South Africa—to utilize private security forces. Indeed, "some of the most violent cities of the developing world have become a mosaic of fortresses, creating a fragmented civil society in which families or streets or neighborhoods create their own forms of protection, often relying on armed force";[66] within this setting, "many individuals and groups, sensing the dangers of this chaotic environment for their own survival and recognizing the inability of states or international organizations to manage it, have retreated into a protective 'fortress' mentality—they have responded by finding private means of security, creating pockets of security within settings that would otherwise be entirely violent."[67] Enhancing the seemingly unending supply of potential members for armed nonstate groups within the global south is the demographic trend of "a continued or even intensifying 'youth bulge' in many developing countries."[68]

In advanced industrial societies, the proliferation of private security—replacing parts of the central government's military, police, prison, and property protection security infrastructure—highlights both its growing appeal and the public realization of states' failure to fulfill their most important function.[69] Many well-to-do citizens feel that they need to augment state efforts with privately provided home and auto security systems, gated communities, or armed vigilantes patrolling vulnerable neighborhoods. The awareness of privatization's efficiency in many economic sectors has helped increase societal acceptance of this private protection option. Even though the governments of these advanced industrial societies are usually well funded and well organized compared to those of developing countries, advanced industrial societies contain a lot more that citizens want to protect; so many of these citizens are not confident that state forces are sufficient to safeguard them from the unorthodox threats they face today, and they often find localized, highly visible private options to be more satisfying.

THE GLOBAL SHIFT IN SECURITY GOVERNANCE

The global decline in state supply of effective security, the global rise in public demand for security, and the global rise in armed nonstate groups' supply of security have together created pressures pointing toward a significant global shift in security governance from public to private hands. This kind of shift is not unprecedented, as during the nineteenth century in Western Europe, "there was also a plethora of political activity by nonstate actors who utilized migration channels and immigrant communities to mobilize transnationally and, at times, employed political violence that challenged state security interests."[70] Signaling this potential shift, "security and stability in the 21st century have little to do with traditional power politics, military conflict between states, and issues of grand strategy; instead, they revolve around governance, public safety, inequality, urbanization, violent nonstate actors, and the disruptive consequences of globalization."[71] Figure 4.2 compares the state-centric Westphalian system to one where armed nonstate groups help with stability.

There is little reason to assume that this impending shift in security governance is normatively inferior or superior across the board to the traditional state monopoly on security provision. Intense disagreement surrounds this

Figure 4.2. Nature of the global shift in security governance

---

Westphalian state system — rule exclusively by states

"Ordered centralism" entails rule over an area through a bureaucracy, a professional army, and the power to levy taxes.

State authority derives from the notion of a social contract between the rulers and the ruled.

State ability to provide this protection derives from its monopoly of the legitimate use of physical force.

States attain a degree of legitimacy in the eyes of their citizenry and institutionalization to process their demands.

Providing security has been the crucial element in the rise of the state and its acceptance in the eyes of its citizenry.

Post-Westphalian system — diverse sources of rule

Security governance without government emerges, where an area is dominated by powerful armed nonstate groups.

Armed nonstate groups are de facto security providers based on intimidation and sometimes on popular support.

Armed nonstate groups may enjoy legitimacy if they step into a power vacuum and provide for critical public needs.

People often turn for protection to more localized social organizations—family, clan, tribe, and armed nonstate groups.

Current security realities have many state governments functionally power sharing with many armed nonstate groups.

issue. It appears to be an open question whether or when this security governance shift would be most beneficial and detrimental to the people being protected and the international system as a whole.

On the plus side, some analysts now contend that "the devolution of state control over violence to nonstate actors . . . does not necessarily presage a descent into chaos,"[72] as they argue that sometimes the security governance shift can yield mutual benefits for both state and armed nonstate groups:

> Although at first glance the gangs seem to be at odds with the government, the local police frequently cooperate with the dons [the gang leaders] whose ruthlessly efficient rule can make the cops' jobs easier. The result is a tenuous quid pro quo: if the dons keep order, the police turn a blind eye to the drug trade. Besides, direct assaults on the gangs are often futile. Even when the police capture dons or their gunmen, convictions are next to impossible to obtain because potential witnesses remain silent out of loyalty or fear.[73]

Often these mutual payoffs are not recognized in advance but emerge slowly as the different public and private comparative advantages begin to emerge.

On the minus side, most analysts evaluate armed nonstate group involvement in security governance as universally undesirable: "by seeking to embed themselves irrevocably in a country's political system and win exclusive control over a segment of the population, mezzanine rulers [associated with armed nonstate groups] jeopardize domestic stability; when they resort to terrorism, piracy, insurgency, or other means to advance ideological, ethnic, or nationalist agendas, they pose a threat that goes well beyond the borders of the host state."[74] These skeptics assert that power sharing usually does not work smoothly within "an environment where traditional institutions of national sovereignty and the power of the nation-state still exist and must be reckoned with."[75] Because there is little explicit face-to-face discussion between states and armed nonstate groups, areas of friction often remain unresolved, and the security interests of the mass public can get lost in the cracks between these two very different protection sources.

Despite the importance of this potential shift in security governance, it has been largely ignored, downplayed, disparaged, or misunderstood because of an enduring bias for states and against armed nonstate groups. Often Western governments "tend to see such movements as temporary, destined to wither away."[76] In recent decades, both scholars and policy makers have poorly coped with fundamental discontinuity in the international system,[77] underestimating the role of private groups in governance[78] and overemphasizing the value of promoting and preserving the state system as the ultimate source of global stability.

From a theoretical standpoint, many scholarly analyses have treated the possible devolution in security authority from the state to armed nonstate groups as a backward step, reversing the progressive and potentially efficient upward movement of protection provision that they perceive to have taken place over the centuries. In contrast, only a few significant conceptual studies have analyzed this form of private protection provision: these rare efforts raise such notions as the "legitimate oligopolies of violence," where governance is "established at local level by various armed groups in order to secure a minimum of stability"; the "outsourcing of statehood," "where state institutions de facto hand over governance functions to nonstate actors"; and "transnational security governance," where "international and local actors, including armed groups such as militia, clan chiefs or (former) warlords, cooperate in an informal or formalised way so as to achieve a secure environment and to deliver services to the local population."[79]

From a policy standpoint, great powers have stubbornly persisted in promoting status quo preservation of the international state system—however arbitrarily determined in the past—and recently have lessened support for either new formal self-determination of peoples or the creation of new states for societies dissatisfied with existing security governance.[80] Similarly, intergovernmental organizations—still the global bodies possessing the most international legitimacy—systematically exclude armed nonstate groups from having any form of representation. Traditional diplomacy across national borders continues to operate as if these groups do not matter even when they exert tremendous influence over the course of events in key areas.

Partially because of this sustained inattention and negative predisposition, the global shift in security governance from state to nonstate control has not gone smoothly. States have openly resented armed nonstate groups' ascendancy and sought in vain to eliminate or constrain their operations. Central state governments' lack of receptivity to armed nonstate groups has caused these groups to be treated as threats: "while in the past, most threats to states came from other states, nonstate actors have increasingly posed major threats in the minds of policy-makers."[81]

In the process, armed nonstate groups have sometimes been induced to identify states as their opponents. International organizations have not had the frameworks in international law or diplomacy to incorporate armed nonstate groups, and therefore have mainly sided with states in largely futile attempts to return sovereign control to central state governments. This security governance transition has thus been fraught with hostility, misunderstanding, and resentment, with few if any successful efforts at public-private cooperation.

Causes of the Global Shift in Security Governance

The push toward a global shift in security governance—reflecting protection provided by armed nonstate groups in addition to states—has diverse causes, including those from a top-down international system perspective, a nation-state perspective, an armed nonstate group perspective, and a bottom-up mass public perspective. Together, global trends seem to be converging so as to enhance private as opposed to public power. Figure 4.3 highlights the major causes of this global transformation in the way people are protected. In those cases where state governments choose to outsource security provision to armed nonstate groups, causes may vary: states utilizing an armed nonstate group for security purposes may choose to do so either because it maximizes effectiveness or because it bears little public accountability for undesired consequences, deaths of citizens, or moral and legal dilemmas about the legitimacy of an action;[82] and government police forces in states relying on armed nonstate group provision of security may need the help in promoting order either because these police forces are overwhelmed by ongoing threats or because they are "ill-equipped, poorly trained, susceptible to corruption and apathy, and highly distrusted by civilian populations."[83]

Looking at this global shift in security governance from a top-down international system perspective, we see that accelerating globalization—involving the expansion of knowledge as well as markets across national boundaries[84]—has fundamentally weakened states in terms of diminishing central governments' abilities to be the sole determinant of what transpires within their boundaries, and has opened the door to alternative governance. Increased internal conflict and irregular warfare have occurred within multi-ethnic or resource-rich societies, ripping apart the fabric of these societies and any ongoing stability and allowing armed nonstate groups to take advantage of existing grievances in establishing their own control within contested areas.[85] Advances in communication and transportation technologies, along with the proliferation of arms and weapons technologies[86] (particularly small arms technologies), have empowered forces outside of government who desire to achieve some level of

Figure 4.3. Causes of the global shift in security governance

---

Top-down international system perspective

Globalization has weakened the international state system, opening the door to alternative governance structures.

Increased internal conflict is occurring within multi-ethnic or resource-rich societies.

Proliferating advanced communication, transportation, and weapons technologies empower nongovernment forces.

Growing population, migration, and inequality tensions have emerged between have and have-not societies.

Nation-state perspective

Many state governments cannot or will not provide adequate protection and survival goods/services to their citizenry.

State boundaries have become more porous, where goods, services, and people move more freely across them.

Ungoverned or contested spaces and failed or failing states have been appearing with greater frequency.

States incapable of exercising responsible sovereignty have a spillover effect of lawlessness into neighboring countries.

Armed nonstate group perspective

Group motivations are loyalty, a common enemy, "back to the wall" desperation, support for a cause, or economic greed.

Many groups do not undermine capable state structures, seek regime change, or even possess political aspirations.

Many groups work in a clandestine fashion for central state governments.

Groups understand how to take advantage of today's global security setting better than most states.

Bottom-up mass public perspective

Rising popularity of security privatization suggests that citizens often prefer private security to state security.

Mass public is cynical about government security capacity, particularly in managing unsanctioned violence.

For many of today's world citizens, identification with the state has become nominal.

People discontent with the status quo are highly receptive to alternative forms of governance.

coercive control: "technology diffusion gnaws away the monopoly of power states once enjoyed by providing smaller and smaller groups with sufficient tools to elude, or sometimes even to challenge, state authority."[87] Communications technology has allowed armed nonstate groups to benefit from the reality that satellite interconnectedness and the Internet have eroded government control over information and made it more difficult for any government to shut down lateral communications among its citizens.[88] As well, "relatively cheap and accessible military technologies, including improvised explosive devices and explosively formed projectiles, give unconventional forces [such as armed nonstate groups] an edge."[89] Growing tensions between the haves and have-nots—manifested through rapid population growth in many poor countries combined with native population decline in many advanced industrial societies, the large migration pressures from poor to rich countries, and the increased inequality and marginalization of key segments of the world's population[90]—have contributed to a pervasive sense of global frustration.

Considering this global shift in security governance from a nation-state perspective, many states violate the social contract by not granting citizens adequate security. National boundaries are increasingly porous, allowing goods, services, and people to move more freely across countries and to find ways to evade state authority.[91] Ungoverned or contested spaces and failed or failing states appear more frequently, as do state governments with authority but unable to fulfill citizens' needs or wants. Internal state governance problems permitting lawlessness create external contagion repercussions in neighboring countries when states "incapable of exercising 'responsible sovereignty' have a 'spillover effect' in the form of terrorism, weapons proliferation, and other dangers."[92] Within societies, preexisting identity cleavages,[93] particularly in societies whose national boundaries were arbitrarily determined, have also indirectly helped facilitate this shift in security governance.

Reflecting on this global shift in security governance from an armed nonstate group perspective, one may find that the popular "greed versus grievance" dichotomy[94] is inadequate to explain the complex motivations involved. Armed nonstate group motives include a sense of loyalty, a common enemy, a "back to the wall" survival instinct, a passion for a cause, and a desire for economic gain.[95] Contrary to widespread opinion, many of these groups do not seek to undermine capable state structures, to promote the collapse of the state, or even to further political aspirations: "it is important to emphasize that not all states and NSAGs [nonstate armed groups] are always engaged in zero-sum games, and not all NSAGs want to 'become' or 'take over' the state (or the full panoply of its functions)";[96] indeed, many armed nonstate groups "are motivated neither by anti-government ideals nor by regime change," and "are not struggling for political dominion, control of the state, or political inclusion so much as economic and subterritorial dominion as well as the coercive capacity to control key local nodes and transnational networks" facilitating their activities.[97] Moreover, many armed nonstate groups are "iceberg-like organizations, with below-the-waterline operational units that can be difficult to detect and disrupt"[98] and that can sometimes act clandestinely on behalf of states. These groups may use their arms and advanced technologies to insulate themselves from detection and apprehension by both state law enforcement authorities and whistle-blowing citizens:[99]

> Armed groups place a premium on the use of intelligence and security to protect themselves from states and rivals both inside their own and other armed groups. They usually specialize in local knowledge and conduct extensive surveillance and reconnaissance to find and exploit their enemies' weaknesses. They also use intelligence to penetrate and manipulate their adversaries.[100]

The goal of such groups is usually not complete state-like sovereignty or independence. Instead they often seek limited autonomy, including protection functions, that may or may not incorporate any transformation of the state governance apparatus. However, their willingness to assume governance roles has grown, and in many ways they now understand and know how to take advantage of today's global security setting better than most states do.[101]

Evaluating this global shift in security governance from a bottom-up mass public perspective, we see that the rising popularity of private security reflects citizens' preference for it over state-provided security, to the point where they find it natural that "private actors are increasingly engaged in authoritative decision-making that was previously the prerogative of sovereign states."[102] The reasons that the mass public may prefer armed nonstate groups to states include these groups' provision of vital social services, coercive incentives for compliance, and opposition to an enemy (including in some cases an unpopular regime).[103] In some instances, people think that state security is less likely to be attentive to their personal needs than private security providers, which focus more on human security—providing citizens with essential services needed for survival—rather than on regime preservation. People discontented with the status quo are usually receptive to alternative sources of protection because they see the state provision of security as either ineffective or wrong-headed. Many citizens have "become less connected to national states as a source of political allegiance or social and economic claim-making" and instead more tied to more local security alternatives offered by armed nonstate groups.[104] Deep public opinion divisions surround the choice of security providers, with some people concerned more about fairness and others concerned only about effectiveness: these views mix cynicism about government security capacity— particularly state capacity to restrain illegal violence[105]—with openness to private security alternatives. In democracies, these divisions often can induce security public policy paralysis. Because of these popular preferences, for many of today's world citizens "identification with nation or state has become nominal, even notional."[106]

Consequences of the Global Shift in Security Governance

Figure 4.4 summarizes the wide variety of consequences of the imminent global shift in security governance. This shift can create the opportunity for two opposing outcomes: severe friction over dominance between states and armed nonstate groups, or tacit collusion between states and armed nonstate groups. On one hand, some central state governments have escalated their attempts to restrain and negate the impact of these groups (for example, Russia with the Chechens), and some armed nonstate groups have escalated their disruptive antigovernment violence (for example, certain transnational terrorist groups). Moreover, in certain circumstances, the rise of armed nonstate groups has associated with the rise in subnational autonomy or separatist movements that end up completely disconnecting affected areas from the security control of an existing central state government. On the other hand, there has been a rise in private "statelets" that "coexist in a delicate, often symbiotic relationship with a larger state":[107] both the frequency and acceptability of some form of tacit collusion between armed nonstate groups and central state governments appears to increasing. Recently, even though armed nonstate groups are still generally opposed or ignored, states and international organizations have sometimes had to contend directly with armed nonstate groups, to the point where alliances have become necessary between states and these groups: for example, the United Nations directly dealt with Somali gangs on military, diplomatic, and economic levels; and the United States in its ongoing war in Afghanistan had "to align with warlords and militias on a regular basis."[108] On very rare occasions, armed nonstate groups "may even participate in their own form of

Figure 4.4. Consequences of the global shift in security governance

---

Severe friction or tacit collusion between states and armed nonstate groups

Some states have escalated a crackdown against these groups, and some groups have escalated antigovernment violence.

Subnational autonomy/separatist movements may disconnect affected areas from state security control.

Armed nonstate groups often forge a symbiotic relationship with central governments where tacit collusion is the norm.

States and international organizations may have to negotiate with these groups, which can have their own foreign policies.

Ambiguity in separating and harmonizing public and private authorities

Difficulty exists in distinguishing between public and private forces and between law enforcement and defense concerns.

Private police compete with public police for a monopoly over the means of violence and the legitimacy to use force.

Government military and armed nonstate groups mutually misperceive each other.

Distinctions blur between military and police activities and between internal and external security concerns.

Benefits of security governance shift

Armed nonstate groups have a comparative advantage over states in adaptability in providing security.

Armed nonstate groups facilitate the global free-market flow of goods and services, improving stability.

Armed nonstate groups deter worse outcomes for people in protected areas.

Armed nonstate groups focus on human security, enhancing the provision of basic survival needs to the people.

Costs of security governance shift

There is likely diminished accountability for actions taken and ambiguity about who is responsible for security.

There is likely reduced trust in government authority and eroding state sovereignty, signaling weakness.

A "might makes right" social order can emerge, retarding the development of civil society and democratic processes.

A "global playground" can reemerge, poorly understood and accepted compared to the traditional state system.

'foreign policy' by negotiating, baiting, or cooperating with the sovereign states in whose territory they operate."[109]

The global shift in security governance may also create more ambiguity in making distinctions, dividing control, and normalizing relationships between public and private authorities and between public and private forces. To the mass public, these two kinds of groups may look similar in rules, modes of operation, and even appearance, and in many situations the mass public might be uncertain who controls what. Friction can emerge between public and private sources of authority: for example, tensions have frequently escalated between private contractors and government army personnel.[110] Overall security can deteriorate "when 'private' police compete with 'public' police for a monopoly over the means of violence and the legitimacy to use force": for example, "in both Mexico City and Johannesburg, two highly violent cities, there have been instances of 'public' and 'private' police forces, not to mention communities themselves, engaging in conflict over who has the right to protect and arrest citizens."[111] Distorted expectations inflame existing difficulties: government security officials may see private forces as having inferior qualifications and experience, serving only to interfere with rather than to promote safety or to make law enforcement and stability more difficult; while armed nonstate forces may assume that the reason behind the demand for their services was the incompetence, inadequacy, or ineptitude of government military personnel.[112] Contestation of control between state officials and armed nonstate groups can contribute to a crisis of legitimacy, as "in contested governance, a group refuses to acknowledge the legitimacy of the government's rule and pledges loyalty to some other form of social organization, such as an insurgent movement, tribe or clan, or other identity group."[113] Frequent misunderstandings occur, such as "the perception by career militaries that their governments seek the support of armed contractors in order to sustain unpopular conflicts."[114] There is "a long tradition of [government] military personnel in many countries being more skeptical than others in government about whether nonmilitary people can do the things they do as well as they do."[115] Finally, "the use of contractors in war, particularly in areas once considered the exclusive domain of uniformed personnel, can have a corrosive effect on warrior ethos—that combination of discipline, selflessness, and cohesion that binds warriors in a collective covenant."[116]

Similarly, as a result of the projected governance shift, there can be confusion in distinguishing between narrow law-and-order and broader national-defense concerns. Traditional distinctions are blurring between military and police activities and between internal and external security.[117] Facets of the murky military/police divide include the emerging pattern of military forces becoming more involved in domestic security missions, such as border control; policing functions becoming more internationalized and militarized; the police and the criminal justice system relying more heavily on the military/war model for their rationale and policy dealing with crime, drugs, and terrorism; and criminality often being redefined as insurgency and crime control often being redefined as low-intensity conflict.[118] This subnational and transnational activity makes the bureaucratic dividing line between narrow law-and-order issues and broader national-defense concerns increasingly artificial and difficult to delineate, causing, in turn, some vital security threats to fall between the bureaucratic cracks.

For the ambiguities between public and private forces and between law-and-order and defense concerns, mutual finger-pointing constitutes a common explanation of violent disruptions jolting the status quo. Certainly, disagreements on the scope of legitimate authority can foster this finger-pointing. However, despite the security concerns generated by these two sets of ambiguities, one beneficial consequence is that the availability of multiple sources—public and private and police and military personnel—to enhance stability can sometimes promote useful competition, both among armed nonstate groups and between these groups and states, to see who can best provide protection. Some observers optimistically believe that this kind of competition "can motivate sovereigns to provide better governance."[119] Indeed, "local-level [private] governance in competition with central governance is not, by itself, problematic; competition in governance provides checks and balances in a healthy, federal political system."[120] This kind of competition can in the best circumstances promote a healthy redundancy in sources of protection for an affected population, allowing one to step into the void if the other is temporarily overburdened or incapacitated in providing effective security.

The global shift's primary security benefits include (1) promoting effective maintenance of order, employing more complex, fluid, speedier, and adaptive mechanisms than possessed by states,[121] which are then relieved by armed nonstate groups of security burdens that central governments cannot easily fulfill, reflecting a quid pro quo relationship involving complementary comparative advantages; (2) erecting fewer political barriers than states do that interfere with the global free-market flow of goods and services, thereby increasing the probability of international efficiency gains and cooperation[122] and of efficient diversity in stability enhancers; (3) deterring worse outcomes for people in protected areas, preventing more disruptive armed nonstate groups from entering and controlling the population and multiplication of illicit supply chains;[123] and (4) serving human security needs more successfully than states do, with greater effectiveness than central governments in protecting people and with combined public-private protection ensuring fewer security gaps for affected populations—under this system, "from the human security standpoint, the security of the individual is no longer defined exclusively within the realm of states and as a consequence of national security."[124] Armed nonstate groups may provide a low-risk way to maintain order temporarily in an area in the face of a governance vacuum, and through this service may forestall both the squandering of scarce government defense resources and the often futile pouring of outside aid into dysfunctional state governments.

The global shift's primary security costs include (1) reducing accountability for actions under national or international law,[125] along with ambiguity about who is responsible for provision of protection; (2) diminishing trust in and deference to government authority,[126] along with eroding state sovereignty and signaling state weakness domestically and internationally; (3) spreading a "might makes right"[127] social order and a "police state" mentality, including the societal intensification of militarization, arms races, and diversion of scarce resources to arms procurement,[128] retarding civil society development and short-circuiting democratic processes; and (4) stimulating the reemergence of a "global playground,"[129] representing a possibly cyclical[130] reversion to an older mode of global "rules of the game" that is much less well understood and accepted than the now largely broken-down traditional sovereign state system.

For example, "the lack of accountability and the acceptance of criminal behavior create a climate of intimidation that cows domestic opposition" and reinforces armed nonstate group control.[131] Armed nonstate groups' accessibility and adaptability can inadvertently make central government "national leaders look irresponsive, flat-footed, and corrupt—as indeed they may be"—reducing still further the perceived legitimacy of the state.[132] Together these security costs may not only promote state instability but also degrade human security: especially when multiple competing armed nonstate groups are present within a country, "as the fighting between these [paramilitary] bands intensifies, more and more people are likely to be caught in the crossfire or to be victimized in one way or another."[133]

CONCLUDING THOUGHTS

Regardless of the magnitude of costs and benefits surrounding the global shift in security governance, a significant shift in security authority is on the verge of occurring in many parts of the world. This transition is happening gradually and in many instances "under the radar" in ways that are not splashy and do not make the headlines. It is occurring in most cases not because (1) the people consciously chose—after carefully considering all the options—to go in this direction; (2) an armed nonstate group forced itself into a situation where it was not wanted or where there was already stable authority; or (3) the government explicitly sought out an armed nonstate group to help to provide stability. Instead, the global shift in security authority may simply be the natural product of existing security governance deficiencies needing desperately to be overcome, combined with the availability of private sources of stability who are ready, willing, and able to fill the void. Thus the nature of this bottom-up shift has been evolutionary and organic, creeping into parts of the world not under the spotlight in ways that have largely eluded systematic scrutiny.

Following the most basic principles of free-market economics, supply and demand imbalances should eventually reach a stable equilibrium if allowed to adjust in an unfettered way. According to that logic, a stable equilibrium might eventually be attained that incorporates mixed public-private security provision, given the global decline in state supply of effective security, the global rise in public demand for security, and the global rise in armed nonstate groups' supply of security. This would seem most likely to occur if effective public protection is not universally available, if private protection is a perfect substitute for public protection, if the mass public perceives that the benefits of private protection exceed the costs, and if the private protection is nonexclusionary within the area safeguarded. To date, any natural movement toward such a stable equilibrium has been systematically blocked, principally by efforts to artificially prop up a single structure—central state governments—as the sole means of providing security and stability in today's world. Other constraints on the forces of change in this direction, including intergovernmental organizations, have also stood in the way of authority shifting from public to private hands. Those parties involved in trying to prevent the shift from occurring, and who thus are keeping a stable global security governance equilibrium from happening, appear to be largely motivated by fears that allowing such a transition would lead to too many dire consequences involving too much unpredictable chaos and violence.

The manner in which this shift might occur could no doubt be substantially improved. If both participants and observers developed an attentiveness to and understanding of the gaps in global protection, then there should be ways to make the transition more harmonious, without the adversarial attitudes and actions currently characterizing the process. If government officials and the mass public realized that there are historical precedents for successful transitions of this kind, as well as for partial state reliance on local private groups for stability provision, and that there are both advantages and disadvantages to any system of security governance, then fears that this change somehow signals a sharp degradation in world order might diminish. If more observers recognized the huge variation among armed nonstate groups and the compatibility of some of their greatest strengths with existing global gaps in providing security to needy areas, then more hope might surround the anticipated consequences of this potential shift for the world's population.

Shifts in global security governance will occur in the future regardless of whether anyone is psychologically, politically, economically, and culturally prepared for them. However, disruptions to stability could be minimized if there were more acceptance and preparation for the changes that seem inescapably to lie ahead. National governments, armed nonstate groups, humanitarian organizations, and intergovernmental organizations all need to adapt to the reality that different kinds of security authority may serve different kinds of situations, and that cookie-cutter advocacy for a single standardized source of world order cannot function successfully in a world with so many different kinds and levels of security challenges and protection needed by the people.

5 CASE STUDIES OF ARMED NONSTATE GROUP CONTROL ATTEMPTS

TO INVESTIGATE THE IMPACT of armed nonstate groups on stability, this study examines a wide range of empirical evidence. The twelve cases selected for examination are the Chechens in Russia, Executive Outcomes in Sierra Leone, the Revolutionary Armed Forces of Colombia (FARC) in Colombia, the gangs in Somalia, Hezbollah in Lebanon, the Irish Republican Army in the United Kingdom, the Islamic Army of Aden in Yemen, the Lord's Resistance Army in Uganda, the Mara Salvatrucha in the United States, the posses in Jamaica, the Taliban in Afghanistan, and the Yakuza in Japan. In each case, private perpetrators attempt to assume security control, and in certain circumstances outperform often bloated, sluggish, and unwieldy state bureaucracies both in sizing up disorderly situations and in attempting to restore order. Nonetheless, a huge variance exists regarding the normative desirability of these security control attempts; indeed, in some cases, armed nonstate groups appear to have helped foster existing instability. Each case analysis includes the case's general background, an explanation of the elements in the case profile, and a discussion of the designated armed nonstate group's impact on local and regional stability.

Together these cases represent the four major types of security control attempts—successful and unsuccessful and constructive and destructive—by the five major types of armed nonstate groups across the world since the end of the Cold War. As discussed in the introductory chapter, most case evidence is by necessity subjective and secondhand, for no systematic, objective global database exists that catalogues such efforts, and so the cases attempt wherever possible to rely on multiple independent sources for key conclusions reached or controversies identified. Thus, although conclusions are inescapably tentative, the evidence presented seems sufficient to provide understanding of the patterns of armed nonstate group impacts on stability in a manner conducive to guiding security policy.

Tables 5.1 through 5.4 summarize the comparative profiles of the twelve cases of armed nonstate groups' control attempts. Table 5.1 describes the background characteristics of each case: the type of armed nonstate group perpetrator (including whether the group's membership is affected by a youth bulge); the country in which the armed nonstate perpetrator undertakes its security control attempt (including whether the control attempt largely takes place in urban or rural parts of the country); the period during which the control attempt occurs; the identity of the armed nonstate group perpetrator; the degree of unity within the armed nonstate group perpetrator; and the poverty level in the society affected by the armed nonstate group.

Table 5.2 describes the security control attempt by the designated armed nonstate group involved in each case: the group's security goals involved in its control attempts; the presence or absence of territorial ambitions by the armed nonstate group; the orientation of the group toward maintaining the political status quo or promoting change; the nature of any outside help and funding to the group; and the level of popular support for the group in the affected area.

Table 5.3 describes the authority facing the designated armed nonstate group in each case: the characteristics of the central state government's power at the time of the armed nonstate security control attempt; the nature of traditional authority in the affected area; the effectiveness of the state in providing security to the affected population; the bias of the state in providing security in terms of any discrimination it displays toward particular groups; and any public-private links between the state and the armed nonstate group perpetrator.

Table 5.4 describes the security context of the armed nonstate group security control attempt in each case: the identity of any menacing state or nonstate outsiders who threaten to disrupt the affected population; the nature of any ongoing conflict relevant to the armed nonstate group security control attempt; the level of violence and militarization within the affected society; the regional effects of the control attempt; and the overall impact of the armed nonstate group action on stability (assessing all four essential stability functions). Together these tables highlight patterns of similarity and difference among the twelve cases, and the attributes that they present form the basis for isolating the conditions under which armed nonstate group control attempts are most and least likely to enhance stability.

Table 5.1. Case profiles—background characteristics

Group name	Group type	Country site	Challenge dates	Identity	Unity	Area poverty
Chechens	Rebels (youth bulge)	Russia (rural area)	1991–present	Mountain tribesmen Radical Muslim beliefs	High	High
Executive Outcomes	Mercenaries	Sierra Leone (rural area)	1995–1996	Ex-apartheid South Africans Desire for profit	High	High
FARC (Revolutionary Armed Forces of Colombia)	Rebels/criminals/terrorists	Colombia (rural area)	1996–present	Guerrilla antistate ideology	High	High
Gangs (Somali)	Warlords	Somalia (urban area)	1991–present	Local tribal clans	Low (clan friction)	High
Hezbollah	Warlords/terrorists	Lebanon (urban area)	2006	Radical Muslim beliefs Opposed to Jewish state	High	Medium
Irish Republican Army	Rebels/terrorists	Great Britain (urban area)	1969–2005	Catholic beliefs Opposed to Protestant state	Low (violence split)	Low
Islamic Army of Aden (al-Qaeda affiliate)	Terrorists/warlords (youth bulge)	Yemen (rural area)	1998–2006	Radical Muslim beliefs	High	High
Lord's Resistance Army	Warlords/terrorists	Uganda (rural area)	1987–2006	Christian cult beliefs Opposed to oppressive state	Low (goal split)	High
Mara Salvatrucha (MS-13)	Warlords/criminals	United States (urban area)	1980–present	El Salvadoran migrants Desire for illicit profit	High	Medium
Posses (Jamaican)	Criminals (youth bulge)	Jamaica (urban area)	1983–present	Desire for profit in the drug industry	High	High
Taliban	Rebels/terrorists (youth bulge)	Afghanistan (rural area)	1996–2001	Radical Muslim beliefs Opposed to warlords	High	High
Yakuza	Criminals	Japan (urban area)	1995	Desire for profit in the construction industry	Low (age split)	Low

Table 5.2. Case profiles—control attempts by armed nonstate groups

Group name	Security goals	Territorial ambitions	Orientation	Help/funding	Popular support
Chechens	Achieve subnational political autonomy	Yes—rule within native Chechen land	Change	Islamic movement/illicit activity funding	Medium
Executive Outcomes	End internal antistate rebellion	No—restoration of state control of territory instead	Status quo	Government funding/mineral company support	Low
FARC (Revolutionary Armed Forces of Colombia)	Alter the existing regime/control drugs	No	Change	Drug trade/kidnapping and extortion funding	Differs by area
Gangs (Somali)	Achieve coercive tribal clan rule	Mixed	Status quo	Islamic movement/illicit trade and looting	Low
Hezbollah	Provide basic needs for war relief	No—gain Lebanese and Palestinian loyalty instead	Mix	Islamic movement/global network funding	High
Irish Republican Army	Unite Northern Ireland with Ireland	Yes—expulsion of Britain from native Irish land	Change	American and Libyan backing	Medium
Islamic Army of Aden (al-Qaeda affiliate)	Provide terrorists a safe haven	No	Mix	Islamic movement funding	Medium
Lord's Resistance Army	Achieve subnational political autonomy	Yes—eliminate oppression in northern Uganda	Change	Sudan funding/looting	Low
Mara Salvatrucha (MS-13)	Achieve firm turf control	Yes—expansion into profitable areas	Mix	Illicit activity funding/neighborhood taxes	Medium
Posses (Jamaican)	Achieve firm turf control	Yes—expansion into profitable areas	Mix	Drug trade funding/neighborhood taxes	Medium
Taliban	Achieve subnational political autonomy	Yes—expansion of control emanating from Kandahar	Mix	Opium profits funding	Medium
Yakuza	Provide for basic needs for disaster relief	No—expansion of control of industry	Status quo	Illicit activity funding/neighborhood taxes	Medium

Table 5.3. Case profiles—existing authorities facing armed nonstate groups

Group name	Government power	Traditional authority	State effectiveness	State bias	Public–private links
Chechens	Strong state	Local tribal rule	Medium	High Discriminatory	None—antagonism
Executive Outcomes	Failing state	National state government rule	Low	Medium	Private group hired by the state
FARC (Revolutionary Armed Forces of Colombia)	Weak state	National state government rule	Low	Medium	Bribery to corrupt officials, infiltration
Gangs (Somali)	No central government	Local tribal rule	Nonexistent	Nonexistent	None
Hezbollah	Weak state	National state government rule	Low	Medium	Private group has government seats
Irish Republican Army	Strong state	National state government rule	High	High Discriminatory	State bargains with private group
Islamic Army of Aden (al-Qaeda affiliate)	Failing state	Local tribal rule	Low	Medium	Mixed and changing
Lord's Resistance Army	Weak state	National state government rule	Low	High Discriminatory	None—antagonism
Mara Salvatrucha (MS-13)	Strong state	National state government rule	High	Low	None—antagonism
Posses (Jamaican)	Weak state	National state government rule	Medium	Medium	None—antagonism State accepts group
Taliban	Weak state	Local tribal rule	Low	Medium	Bribery to corrupt officials, infiltration
Yakuza	Strong state	National state government rule	High	Low	Private group colludes with state officials

Table 5.4. Case profiles—security context of armed nonstate group activities

Group name	Menacing outsiders	Ongoing conflict	Violence/ militarization	Regional effects	Stability impact
Chechens	Russian central government	Separatist struggle War in the North Caucasus	High	Separatist contagion	Mixed
Executive Outcomes	Revolutionary United Front	Rebels against regime Civil war	High	Increased exploitation of natural resources	Positive temporarily Long-run turmoil
FARC (Revolutionary Armed Forces of Colombia)	Paramilitary groups	Rebels against regime Civil war	High	Spread of instability and illicit drugs	Positive in rural areas Negative in urban areas
Gangs (Somali)	Rival clans	Civil war	High	Spread of criminal activity	Mixed
Hezbollah	State of Israel	Hezbollah-Israel war	Medium	Persistence of international conflict	Positive locally
Irish Republican Army	British government Ulster Volunteer Force	Rebellion Civil war	Medium	None	Mixed
Islamic Army of Aden (al-Qaeda affiliate)	Western powers and beliefs	Rebellion Civil war	Medium	Spread of terrorist activity	Negative
Lord's Resistance Army	Ugandan central government	Antiregime war	High	Spread of violence regionally	First mixed, then negative Child/female abuse
Mara Salvatrucha (MS-13)	Rival street gangs	Gang warfare	High	Spread of gang activity	Positive locally Negative in Central America
Posses (Jamaican)	Rival gangs	Battles with police	High	Spread of gang activity	Positive locally Negative in Caribbean
Taliban	Warlords	War on terrorism Civil war	High	Spread of anti-Western terror	Mixed Female abuse
Yakuza	None	None	Low	None	Positive Speedy disaster relief

CHECHENS IN RUSSIA

This case revolves around an armed nonstate group attempting to gain autonomy in a territory discriminated against by the central state government. After the Soviet Union collapsed in 1991, Chechnya formally declared its independence, saying it had never joined Russia voluntarily.[1] As a result, on December 11, 1994, the Russian military embarked on what it thought would be "a speedy and unproblematic military conquest to wrest Grozny away from Chechen secessionists," but the reality turned out to be a bloody and protracted battle in which the Russians were humiliated.[2] This conflict was extremely costly: "along with the civil war in Tajikistan, this first Chechen War of 1994–1996 was the most severe since World War II on the territory of what was once the Soviet Union, with casualties and fatalities approaching 100,000, refugees and homeless numbering in the hundreds of thousands, and the capital city of Grozny—as well as countless small towns and villages—virtually destroyed."[3] Indeed, "some observers have argued that Russia's efforts to suppress the separatist movement in its Chechnya region have been the most violent in Europe in recent years in terms of ongoing military and civilian casualties."[4] By the war's end in 1996, Chechnya gained nominal autonomy by proving remarkably resistant to Russia's troops.[5]

However, the ensuing cease-fire lasted only until 1999, when the Second Chechen War began, with the Chechen army entering into Dagestan, a region that also wished to be independent from Russia. In August and September 1999, a wave of terrorist bombings struck three Russian cities, including Moscow. Russian leaders accused Islamic terrorists from Chechnya of organizing the attacks, precipitating a new Russian military offensive to establish federal control of Chechnya. In late September, Russian warplanes began a campaign of air strikes against targets in Chechnya. In October, Russian ground forces entered Chechnya with the goal of capturing Grozny, and by early December they surrounded the city. Despite heavy bombing and artillery fire, rebels entrenched in fortified buildings managed to maintain control of Grozny for many weeks, waging fierce street-by-street battles against advancing Russian troops. Nonetheless, Russia was significantly more successful during the Second Chechen War, and when the fighting ended in early February 2000, Grozny was reduced to ruins. Fighting continued afterward in the mountainous regions of southern Chechnya, traditionally the stronghold of the Chechen rebels. In May 2000, Russian president Vladimir Putin, who repeatedly used the Chechen problem as an excuse for centralizing the federal government, declared that Chechnya would be ruled federally. In a globally publicized incident in October 2002, a band of forty-one Chechen guerrillas seized a theater in Moscow, taking about eight hundred civilians hostage and rigging the theater with explosives, with the demand for complete withdrawal of Russian troops from Chechnya. After pumping an opiate-based gas into the building, Russian special forces stormed the theater, killing all the rebels along with 129 hostages. In March 2003, the results of an official referendum in Chechnya on a proposed new constitution affirming Chechnya's status as a republic within the Russian Federation showed overwhelming majority support for the new constitution, which allowed Chechnya an unspecified level of autonomy and an elected government subordinated to federal law. Chechen rebels boycotted the vote, claiming that it was a political farce, and vowed to continue their secessionist struggle. The conflict persisted in 2006 and 2007, "but with a significantly lower number of battle-related deaths than in 2004 and 2005"; and "low-level violence continued into 2008"[6] and afterward.

So while in April 2009 Russia announced the end of the Second Chechen War, setting the stage for withdrawing thousands of federal troops from Chechnya, during the summer of 2009 there was an "upsurge in violence" in the North Caucasus.[7] Sporadic violence continued, as for example in March 2010, when Russian officials accused Chechen separatists in the deadly bombings that rocked two subway stations in central Moscow.[8] Thus, although high levels of conflict in Chechnya "appeared to ebb markedly" after 2005 with the killing, capture, or surrender of leading Chechen insurgents, "Russian security forces and pro-Moscow Chechen forces still contend with residual insurgency."[9]

The causes of the Chechen insurgency are multifaceted, involving political leaders, sectional interests within Russia, and regional groups within Chechnya "instrumentalising conflict for political and economic ends."[10] First, Chechnya's drive for autonomy from Russia "occurred under extremely unfavorable economic circumstances":[11] Chechnya suffers from lack of job opportunities, education, and economic stability, and it is a region that has been largely excluded from state benefits.[12] Indeed, "the standard of living in the southwestern republic is poor compared with the rest of Russia," with high unemployment and infant mortality.[13] Second, Russian government discrimination against Chechnya is a primary cause of unrest, as the regime made only minimal efforts to integrate Chechnya, leaving the region dependent on deliveries from Russia and without many internal job opportunities. During the Chechen wars, Russia failed to provide Chechens with significant economic incentives to stimulate development, and instead treated Chechens as criminals.[14] Third, Russian efforts to manage the Chechnya problem "reportedly are undermined by rampant corruption."[15] President Dmitry Medvedev identified these corrupt practices (along with unemployment) as "the chief sources of instability": "government employees on the take—from high-level republican officials to traffic cops—nourish organized crime and spark violent reprisals."[16] Fourth, "the Chechen population of about one million is mostly made up of Sunni Muslims, who maintain a distinctly different cultural and linguistic identity from Russian Orthodox Christians."[17] Ethnic Muslims concentrated in the North Caucasus are multiplying fast, even as Russia's total population shrinks."[18] Chechen society is traditional, composed largely of Islamic mountain tribesmen with tight clan loyalties and family ties, fiercely resisting both Russian domination (for two hundred years) and globalization pressures.[19] The Chechen rebel forces have been composed of "a conglomeration of individuals seeking to avenge relatives, mercenaries, Chechens brutalized by the war and determined to fight on, and fanatical Islamists."[20] Fifth, radical Islam "has reemerged as a powerful source of identity in the North Caucasus over the last 20 years," promoting among some elements of society armed rebels joining antigovernment militant groups.[21]

In terms of funding and support, outside assistance to the Chechens was reportedly extensive during the 1994–1996 war, "coming from radical Islamic extremists who found common cause with their Chechen counterparts." Later, "with the restart of the war in 1999, the existence of linkages between the Chechen resistance and transnational radical Islamic organizations expanded, fuelled by religious ideology."[22] The Second Chechen War was characterized by the Russian government as a "counterterrorist operation"[23] against fundamentalist Islamic militants linked to al-Qaeda and other international terrorist organizations. The Chechen movement has also funded itself by engaging in criminal activities such as counterfeiting money, extracting oil, and trading in drugs.[24]

The overall impact of the Chechen insurgency on stability has been mixed. From a Russian state security standpoint, Chechen violence has posed a "longstanding threat to the country's stability."[25] However, because the Russian government often treats Chechens as second-class citizens and excludes the region from economic development programs, from a human security standpoint the rebels have been the only source of protection and basic survival needs for many Chechens. Russia has brutally executed Chechens during many repression campaigns, and "as Putin's popularity ratings skyrocketed at home,

Russian military actions led to thousands of Chechen casualties among civilians and the creation of tens of thousands of new refugees."[26] The Russian government has attempted "to secure order by adding intelligence agents and beefing up the presence of federal border guards, along with redeploying police from elsewhere in Russia—but to little avail."[27] In the long run, "Russia undoubtedly would have fared better in Chechnya were it not for the corruption, cronyism, indifference, and administrative incompetence that pervade the Russian army, security forces, and political system."[28] Continuing skirmishes have impeded law and order.

Part of the difficulty in attaining a stable security solution in Chechnya has been the unrealistic expectations repeatedly voiced by Russian government leaders. President Boris Yeltsin had "envisioned that 'a small and victorious' war in Chechnya could help him win the 1996 presidential elections";[29] and in late May 2008, Prime Minister Vladimir Putin optimistically asserted that "Chechnya was becoming more peaceful."[30] However, the situation continued to remain volatile: in October 2009, President Dmitry Medvedev told Russia's Security Council that "the North Caucasus remains the country's foremost internal political problem," and in 2010 "Russian Interior Ministry officials announced that 'terrorist crime' in the North Caucasus was up by 60 percent in 2009 compared to 2008."[31]

Differences of opinion exist regarding the future of Chechnya's security and stability. Some observers fear that the prospects look bleak for greater security in Chechnya even with an independent government, as "Chechen society is riven apart by sectarian conflict and a growth in the power of militarised Islamic extremists, which would be enormously destabilising were an independent government to be restored without significant economic support from Russia and the international community."[32] Others report positive security developments within Chechnya, such as "the trickling down of federal money," "improved law and order," and a lessening of "everyday crime, such as burglaries and street robberies."[33]

The Chechen turmoil has fostered considerable regional instability over the years. Ingushetia's economy "suffered greatly during the Chechnya conflict, mainly from the influx of displaced persons which in effect doubled the population during intense periods of fighting in 1995 and 2000."[34] In August 1999, hundreds of Islamic guerrillas crossed into Dagestan from Chechnya and occupied several villages, proclaiming a separate Islamic territory; although Russian air and artillery attacks returned the villages to federal control, incursions into Dagestan by Chechen guerrillas seeking to create an Islamic state became increasingly common. The Chechen wars have contributed to "the accelerated social and economic decline of the region";[35] created hundreds of thousands of Chechen refugees in neighboring areas; strained to the breaking point the capacity of local governments; and fostered "destabilizing consequences throughout the Caucasus and southern Russia."[36] Recently, there has been even more regional violence: "a wave of assassinations, bombings, and suicide terrorist attacks spread well beyond the old war zone into the neighboring republics of Dagestan, Ingushetia, and Kabardino-Balkaria."[37] Thus, future regional stability prospects appear dim.

EXECUTIVE OUTCOMES IN SIERRA LEONE

This is the only case in this study where an armed nonstate group hired by the state acted as a coercive third party in an existing violent conflict between rebels/insurgents and the central state government. Sierra Leone is one of many African countries where armed nonstate groups have played a major security governance role (among other recipients of foreign assistance from armed nonstate groups are Angola, Liberia, and the Democratic Republic of the Congo).[38] In 1995, the government of Sierra Leone was facing a strong rebel movement led by the Revolutionary United Front. The civil war in Sierra Leone had spilled over in early 1991 from conflict in Liberia and "was conducted with almost inconceivable barbarity, mostly against unarmed civilians"; Sierra Leone government forces "had effectively ceased to exist as an organised force" (and, to make matters worse, the soldiers and rebels were virtually indistinguishable from one another):[39]

> The Republic of Sierra Leone Military Forces (RSLMF) evinced many of the limitations which have encouraged the growth of private militaries. It hardly qualified as an army, despite its size of perhaps 14,000 soldiers, two-thirds of whom had been hastily recruited, and lacked basic military professionalism. The military displayed no lack of corruption. The term "sobels" ("soldiers by day, rebels by night") described soldiers who also engaged in banditry or rebel activities, and RSLMF units sometimes fought each other.[40]

Over the course of the four-year war, 1.5 million of the people in Sierra Leone became refugees and more than 15,000 were killed.

Facing a desperate situation in which the insurgents had cut off the government's last major source of domestic revenue earlier that year, in which "much of the country, including the valuable diamond and rutile mines, was in the hands of the Revolutionary United Front," in March 1995 President Valentine Strasser's "besieged" government requested that Executive Outcomes (EO) come into Sierra Leone to assist in quelling the rebel movement, at a cost of $35 million.[41] Executive Outcomes was a South Africa-based private military company that provided direct combat support. Within months, EO had cleared rebels from the capital, removed rebel troops from the principal diamond mining areas, trained local self-defense units to replace the government army, and even attracted other foreign investors in the mining industry.[42] Executive Outcomes used expert intelligence and training of local African recruits to achieve this goal.[43] This impact is less surprising when one takes into account the widespread reports of an "unofficial alliance" between EO and the British-based Branch Energy Company, owned by the Canadian mining company Diamond Works:[44] although no formal official ties exist, "the mineral companies provide the introduction for EO which then provides the security environment that allows for the profitable extraction of the minerals that might otherwise be impossible to access; this close association puts the mineral companies at an advantage when negotiating contracts, as they can link their operations to the provision of security."[45] Shortly thereafter, EO was dissolved and ceased operations on December 31, 1998, accompanied by a statement that "EO no longer saw itself as having a role to play in conflict resolution in Africa."[46]

The government of Sierra Leone appeared to have a sound justification for hiring mercenaries from within the African continent to restore order in its country: "there were a variety of reasons for the employment of colonial troops but chief among them was that they were generally much cheaper than their European counterparts, often available in greater numbers, and better suited to tropical environments; as a bonus they often turned out to be excellent soldiers."[47] Moreover, the end of the Cold War made great-power assistance unlikely:

> Africa has suffered from very serious international marginalization following on from the end of the Cold War. During that conflict Africa became a battleground for the superpowers who conducted their rivalry via proxies such as Cuba and South Africa. The consequences of this rivalry still haunt Africa today, particularly in Angola. Nevertheless, during this period Africa was, to a significant degree, a centre of attention for the superpowers and many African leaders were able to exploit this to the political and pecuniary advantage of both

themselves and their countries. However, in the immediate aftermath of the collapse of the Eastern Bloc in 1989 Africa, as one writer has described it, "lost its political worth" and the states of Sub-Saharan Africa became "so much irrelevant international clutter." This political marginalization has been accompanied by growing economic isolation, with the continent accounting for less than two percent of international trade.[48]

So the Sierra Leone government, unable to cope with the armed challenge to its authority, had few options as to where to turn for help.

The particular choice of Executive Outcomes was controversial. Executive Outcomes began in 1989 as an incorporated South African company; its founders, Eeben Barlow and Lafras Luitingh, were "former members of South Africa's apartheid-era special forces"; and "most of EO's front line operatives have been recruited from former members of South Africa's special forces units that operated in the apartheid era."[49] Executive Outcomes was basically "a private army with access to some two thousand ex–South African Defence Force (SADF) combat veterans"—"most of EO's soldiers have come from South Africa's former 32 Battalion, the Reconnaissance Commandos, the Parachute Brigade, and the paramilitary 'Koevoet' or 'Crowbar,'" four groups which were "South Africa's spearhead for military destabilisation throughout southern Africa during the 1980s."[50] Although more recently most private military companies have helped provide training, logistics, military intelligence and analysis, and arms supply, EO engaged in direct combat operations. The result was that "many commentators, especially African ones, cannot help but ascribe evil motives to anything done by what have been described as 'apartheid's attack dogs.'"[51]

There is little doubt that the use of mercenaries had a positive short-run stability impact in Sierra Leone—from December 1995 to October 1996, "EO launched a series of offensives that secured the Freetown area, reoccupied the diamond and rutile mines, and eliminated the RUF bases," and "they established sufficient security for elections to be held in March 1996 that led to a civilian regime and forced the RUF to sign up to a peace accord in November 1996."[52] For many observers, this private military intervention was a model of success in restoring an established government's ability to impose law and order and in ending violent conflict:

> Executive Outcomes' role in Sierra Leone prompted a major rethink within the international community of the value and uses of PMCs [private military companies]. It had created stability in the West African state when the legitimate

government force could not and, moreover, established the conditions for democratic elections when the regional and international community could not or would not. It had prevented the continuation of barbaric acts against the civilian population by facing the opposition forces and training and educating government forces. It also worked closely with international emergency relief organisations.[53]

Indeed, "EO's operations in Sub-Saharan Africa demonstrated that a small disciplined force can have a great impact in situations where governments face challenges from warlords and other insurgents who may possess modern weapons and fervor, but who otherwise lack training, discipline and organization."[54] Although constituting "a heavy burden on an economy such as Sierra Leone's," the security provided "was essential for its future well being and in reality was not available elsewhere."[55] Moreover, "EO did not mount any major civic action programmes but its ability to defeat rebel groups militarily, and its correct behaviour towards the general population created popularity with civilians."[56] Executive Outcomes promoted state security by protecting the regime from the rebel insurgency, and promoted human security by protecting the civilian population from barbaric rebel violence. However, EO did not provide for—and was not called upon to provide for—basic survival needs for the people of Sierra Leone.

Despite fostering short-term stability, this private intervention by an armed nonstate group did not succeed in restoring long-term stability to the country. In contrast, this involvement may have been at least partially responsible for some long-range problems. Sierra Leone became subject to extensive influence from and dependence on profit-seeking foreign mercenaries;[57] and, specifically regarding EO, "serious problems, including its linkages with Western commercial interests, its often less-than-permanent victories, and its possible militarisation of Africa, may lessen its contribution to state security."[58] Moreover, although in 1996 Sierra Leone's democratic elections went well, with the new government continuing to rely on EO for security; when such dependence ended in February 1997, this new regime was overthrown by a coup the following May.[59] Executive Outcomes was by no means alone in not being able to address long-term stability in Sierra Leone:

A criticism leveled at private security companies in general, and EO in particular, is that they have failed to deliver lasting solutions to the problems of Angola and Sierra Leone. In their defence, it must be stated that they never claimed that that was what they were trying to do. They offered particular solutions to specific problems. As for long-term solutions, it is not just private security companies that have failed, so have the United Nations and regional organisations.[60]

Nonetheless, "the international community was frustrated by the lack of transparency, which only bred suspicion"; and "perhaps most important for the people of Sierra Leone, the stability that Executive Outcomes provided did not last after the company left, pointing to a lack of depth in the PMC's operation."[61] Turmoil has continued on and off since that time, with civil war continuing well into the twenty-first century.

From the beginning, fears emerged about regional effects, specifically the broader implications of EO's actions for sub-Saharan Africa that included a "worry that Executive Outcomes' training and combat skills may only increase the militarisation and destabilization of a desperately poor continent."[62] The success of EO's intervention in Sierra Leone may have increased natural resource mining in the region, as "mineral exploitation companies may well have benefited from the activities of these mercenaries and even encouraged them," given that "international companies want access to Africa's natural resources and desperate governments need to raise revenue from their exploitation."[63] Although EO has since disbanded, in the future state governments facing security challenges could turn to mercenaries rather than attempt peaceful negotiations to resolve the conflicts.[64] However, this pattern is not yet common, as regional and global observers varied in their reactions to the EO intervention; and the role of mercenaries in Africa to deal with ongoing conflict did not mushroom as a result of this case.

THE FARC IN COLOMBIA

This case revolves around a rebel group trying to wrest political and economic authority from the central state government. The peasant-based left-wing guerrilla group called the FARC formed out of the Communist Party in 1966. Colombians have since witnessed decades of civil war and protracted guerrilla fighting, with the FARC and the state government "locked in a violent contest focused on determining who exercises political power, redressing historically rooted socioeconomic grievances of marginalized classes, and competing ideas on the type of political and economic system Colombia should have."[65] Explanations of Colombia's civil war and political violence include poverty, inequality, unjust government oppression, and state infrastructure weakness.[66] The civil war between the guerrillas and the state had been somewhat contained before 1992, but after 1996 both the scope of the conflict and the number of armed combatants sharply escalated.[67] The pattern of growth was dramatic: "the FARC progressively expanded its fronts from 27 in 1984, to 60 in 1992, to 80 in 2000, involving approximately 15,000 to 18,000 members."[68] The Colombian government responded to the FARC "by steadily increasing military expenditure and courting increased U.S. military and cournternarcotics assistance."[69] In working to negotiate an end to the guerrilla insurgency, the Colombian government created in 1998 of a safe haven for the FARC—where no government troops could enter—in southeastern Colombia. Peace negotiations between the government and the FARC followed between 1999 and 2001, and during 2000 the two sides agreed on an ambitious agenda including agrarian reform, historically the FARC's most fundamental concern; but the two sides made little progress on substantive issues, and by the end of 2001 negotiations had collapsed.

The disruption from the conflict has affected southern rural areas in particular, whose poor populations (as well as students and urban intellectuals) called for a Cuban-style revolution (a popular bottom-up guerilla uprising). The FARC has argued that political leaders have done nothing to help the rural population fight poverty and achieve development, and that these officials assassinated labor leaders who were opposed to the regime. The FARC rebellion is based mainly on class division rather than ethnic, national, or religious differences: the FARC's demands include land reform, rural development, greater opportunities for political participation, and ultimately a radical restructuring of Colombia's liberal capitalist order. The FARC has recruited men and women mainly from rural areas where unemployment is extremely high and where many people feel abandoned by the government. In those areas, the FARC often has appeared to be the only viable choice for young people, giving them employment, basic survival needs and financial security, and meaning in life. The FARC has been able to provide some of its members with decent standards of living as a result of drug production and trade, higher living standards than many rural Colombians could afford even with increased government aid; as a result, the Colombian government "may find itself hard pressed to convince the remaining guerrillas to give up their lucrative, if clandestine, lifestyle for the uncertainties of reinsertion into civil society."[70]

The FARC has three principal sources of income: kidnapping and extortion, cattle rustling, and the production, processing, and trafficking of illicit drugs.[71] The FARC has especially "embraced the drug industry as an important source of income," and estimates of the FARC's drug-related income vary from $269 million to $530 million.[72] Indeed, the FARC "is notorious for its increasing involvement in the international narcotics trade,"[73] and has in the past derived much of its funds from Colombia's major drug cartels.[74] Many analysts call the Colombian government a "narcodemocracy," with drug traffickers having purchased the compliance of key personnel in every major government institution.[75] Colombia's past emergence as Latin America's preeminent drug supplier—particularly for cocaine—was due to its geopolitical position, its vast central forests that hide secret processing laboratories and airstrips facilitating the traffic, the strong entrepreneurial skills of the Colombian people, and the willingness of the Colombian community in the United States to function as a distributor network.[76] American and European citizens' insatiable "appetite for narcotics Colombia produces has been central in undermining Colombia's law and order, economy, and democratic institutions."[77] In Colombia "drug-related income has led to an intensification and militarization of the intra-state conflict."[78] Today many drug operations have moved to other countries in the region (including Mexico), where "the drugs still flow" despite massive American investment in the global "war on drugs."[79]

In terms of stability, the FARC has had a negative impact in urban areas. The modern era of "narco-guerilleros-paramilitary warfare" (fighting among cartels, insurgent armies, and paramilitary groups) has led to hundreds of thousands of displaced persons and massive numbers of kidnappings and deaths. As a result, "the amount of human suffering inflicted on civilians during the Colombian internal conflict has been enormous," with atrocities committed against innocent civilians, fighters from rival groups, and cartel members.[80] In this context, Colombia "has one of the highest homicide rates, and the highest kidnapping rate, in the world."[81] At least partly because of the FARC's activities, citizens throughout much of Colombia have not enjoyed the level of security they have the right to expect, and "those few who had the courage to stand openly and call for governmental action became the targets of assassination."[82] The disruption of central government security seems particularly acute because the semblance of democracy is riddled with corruption and controlled mostly by oligarchic interests. Indeed, "the ambiguous relationship between the paramilitaries and the [government] armed forces was revealed in the peace negotiations of 1998–1999, when the FARC demanded—and the government consented to—the removal of several high-ranking army officials suspected of having close ties to the paramilitaries."[83] Although it has been weakened, the FARC continues to pose a "serious threat to stability in parts of Colombia: for example, in February 2009, the FARC tortured and murdered 17 indigenous Awa tribe members; and in March 2009 a FARC mortar attack killed 4 Colombian soldiers."[84]

However, the FARC has generated positive effects on stability for the rural population, especially in the southern parts of the country. In these rural areas, while not exactly eradicating violent conflict or promoting rules and order, the group has addressed employment, basic needs (food and shelter), purpose in life, and investment. The FARC's positive stability impact in areas largely neglected by the Colombian government has occurred because "in these areas, guerrilla groups are not viewed as foreign or predatory actors, but as the main regulators of economic activity and, in some circumstances, as the foremost contributor to political security."[85] There has been a consistent demand for effective governance, be it from an international recognized central government authority or from unconventional armed nonstate groups; so "given the historical weakness of the Colombian state, then, it should not be surprising that one of the means of survival chosen by marginalised citizens has been to create and support guerrilla goals."[86] Citizens in rural areas have been skeptical about the Colombian government, underconfident about its institutions, and reluctant to participate in governance processes:

> It is assumed by Colombian policymakers that the end of the war should result in the consolidation of state control over all national territory. Yet the legitimacy of the state is questioned not only by the guerrillas, but also by large sectors of the population—particularly in rural areas—who have been subject to forced displacement, human rights violations, and loss of property at the hands of state security forces. Many people are sympathetic to the view that the distribution of political and economic power in Colombia is highly inequitable. For these reasons, a military victory over Colombia's illegal armed groups may remove the immediate threat posed to state sovereignty and national security, but alone is incapable of restoring state legitimacy, let alone addressing the underlying structural causes of conflict.[87]

Lack of faith in the "tattered and dysfunctional"[88] Colombian central government is reinforced by the expressed need for self-defense by local elites in the face of "continued failures on the part of the national state to provide security and protection to those elites."[89] Ultimately these concerns about the central government translate into public receptivity in rural areas to armed nonstate groups.

On a broader regional level, the FARC's activities in Colombia have some ominous security effects. Drug trafficking undermines not only Colombian state security, but also state security in other poor states enmeshed in the expanding drug web. Indeed, since 1999 there has been "unprecedented internationalization of the conflict, both in terms of spillover effects to neighboring countries and in terms of direct international involvement."[90] In this regard, The Heritage Foundation has argued that "the threat to U.S. and hemispheric security posed by Colombia's narco-democracy cannot be overestimated."[91] A "drug-insurgency nexus" has emerged, one where some analysts claim that leftist guerrillas work hand in hand with drug dealers to help undermine the United States government through the influx of illicit narcotics, thereby weakening the Colombian government and accelerating the pace of revolutionary change there.[92] States neighboring Colombia have been extremely concerned about the export of disorder from that country affecting their own governments' political stability.

GANGS IN SOMALIA

This case revolves around armed nonstate groups trying to assume authority in the complete absence of a central state government. There is a long and bloody history of fighting and violence within Somalia,[93] which "has gone without any functioning central government since January 1991."[94] Since civil war broke out in 1991, attempts to resolve the conflict—along with attempts at state building—have so far been unsuccessful: "in the early 1990s Somalia's situation deteriorated when it became a testing ground for new international institutions—in the form of a multi-lateral peacekeeping operation—for managing the problems in the new world."[95] Because "most inhabitants are ethnic Somalis, it is the clan rather than ethnicity that most influences identity."[96] However, deep inter-clan grievances persist,[97] with warfare regularly occurring among clan factions run by warlords: "able to arm their militias with the vast amount of weaponry, these new chieftains were interested only in power and the spoils of war."[98]

There is no long-standing tradition of centralized government in Somalia. Armed nonstate actors seem to be the only forces with a realistic potential for providing any form of security in the country, as by now outside states and the international community have largely given up attempts to restore order.

The Somali people appear to possess an especially cynical mentality about their state and statehood: "for many Somalis, the state is an instrument of accumulation and domination, enriching and empowering those who control it and exploiting and harassing the rest of the population."[99] So from this perspective, receiving protection or provision of basic survival needs from a central state government would not seem much better than receiving them from local clans.

In terms of funding, "much of the social infrastructure (i.e., health and education) that exists in Somalia is funded by Islamic charities and, to a lesser extent, by Western NGOs."[100] Moreover, "Somalia is an excellent location for short-term transshipment and transit operations," allowing "easy and undetected smuggling of people and material": "local partners in such short-term operations are easily contracted for the right price," and "al-Qaeda and other groups have used Somalia in the past and will likely continue to do so" in the future.[101] Local robbery and looting is rampant, and Somali warlords find that exporting the narcotic *qat* "offered a particularly lucrative source of income."[102] Furthermore, the urban gangs have on occasion colluded with and profited from the now infamous maritime pirates—after the April 2009 seizure of an American ship captain—who engage in illicit commerce and interfere with legitimate trade running off the coast.[103]

As to the overall impact of the Somali gangs on stability, the picture looks bleak. Because of past Somali government control problems, many people in Somalia are opposed to any reinstitutionalization of central government rule:

> [There are] ... many local actors who do not engage in illegal activities but who oppose state revival out of well-founded fear, especially fear that a revived central government will become a predatory, repressive force as was the case under Barre's regime in the 1970s and 1980s. For business people who have benefited from state collapse, the return of a central government may carry too many risks—of high taxes, corruption, expropriation, and nationalization. Among clans and other social groups is the fear that the central government will again come under the control of a narrow coalition of clans that will use the state as an instrument of domination at their expense. Some civic groups and the media fear unwarranted restrictions on their activities by a revived state.[104]

In recent years, Somalia has been at or near the top of the Failed States Index, which ranks the most unstable countries in the world; for example, in 2010 "Somalia saw yet another year plagued by lawlessness and chaos, with pirates plying the coast while radical Islamist militias tightened their grip on the streets of Mogadishu."[105] There is no end in sight for the anarchy in this area.

When viewed in terms of the first essential stability function of promoting law and order, Somalia has shown itself as the epitome of lawlessness, having "disintegrated to a level of violence and chaos that was hard to imagine," where "death, disorder, and destruction went utterly unchecked."[106] Unjust discrimination occurs within this system, as "larger more powerful clans have used the tools of domination against weaker groups."[107] Not surprisingly, "the Somali public consistently cites personal security as its most pressing need."[108] However, as the sole security source in much of the country, Somali gangs contribute at least some level of local authority:

> The fact that efforts at state-building and national reconciliation have failed so consistently for more than a decade has made it easy for observers to conclude that politics and governance in Somalia is mired in anarchy. But a closer look reveals an impressive if fragile level of local governance. Collectively, these developments do not add up to anything resembling a conventional state. But the mosaic of local politics and informal social pacts which has evolved does provide Somali citizens with some level of "governance," if not "government." In some cases, these informal and sub-national polities deliver more effective public order than in most neighbouring states in the Horn of Africa.[109]

In the absence of formal government providing security, one witnesses "the rise of local, informal polities that have, in fits and starts, increasingly provided many Somali communities with variable levels of governance, public security, and even social services"; in a sense, this is somewhat akin to "what today is called 'good governance'—effectively providing core functions of public security or other services demanded by local communities, and earning legitimacy as a result."[110] Particularly in rural areas, "Somalia has repeatedly shown that informal systems of governance can ensure the rule of law and in some instances surprisingly high levels of personal security":[111]

> The pastoral zones have never come under the effective control of the state, so the collapse of the state has not been as traumatic for nomadic populations as outsiders often presume. There, protection and access to resources in a political world that loosely approximates the anarchy of the international system have long been secured through a combination of blood payment groups (*diya*), customary law (*xeer*), negotiation (*shir*), and the threat of force—mirroring in

intriguing ways the practices of collective security, international regimes, diplomacy, and recourse war, which are the principal tools of statecraft that modern states use to manage their own anarchic environments.[112]

A beacon of hope exists in Somaliland, a semiautonomous region in northwest Somalia, where what is most critical is a cultural tradition of civil discourse rather than violence—"a very strong commitment by civil society to peace and rule of law, which serves as a strong deterrent to would-be criminals, warlords, and politicians tempted to exploit clan tensions from violating the basic rules of the game."[113] Armed nonstate groups are not alone in establishing order, for in parts of Somalia "where authority is weaker and contested, a complex mix of community organizations, private companies, Islamic foundations, and local and international aid agencies have stepped in to fill the vacuum left by government. . . ."[114] Ironically, however, when considering just state security, "the very success of local adaptation to state collapse could also impede state building by reducing local incentives to support a revived state."[115]

Somalia has also failed in the second essential stability function of providing for basic survival needs to an affected population, to the point where fighting among the Somali warlords has led to a "quintessential humanitarian disaster." Many civilian deaths have occurred from famine and lack of basic survival needs, such as food that was bottlenecked by these warlords[116] (including the July 2011 blocking of global food aid to deal with severe famine). Moreover, "today, Somalis feel the indignities of statelessness in restrictions against international travel, in their secondary status in many countries of asylum, marginalization in economic transactions, and a lack of international protection and security."[117] However, some local warlord-run polities have managed to provide some basic social services, operate piped water systems, and regulate marketplace interactions.[118] Any stability success from "the political fragmentation of Somalia is intricately linked to the force of kinship-based patronage networks that developed in Somalia as state power and legitimacy eroded."[119] In many ways, formal state structure in Somalia appears to be no longer necessary for participation in the global economy and exercise of political power, as Somali warlords "do not rely on state institutions, but can survive and profit from economies that are non-territorial, linked to international trade and financial networks facilitated by modern communications equipment."[120]

As well, the absence of effective state government in Somalia has prevented attainment of the third essential stability function of restraining internal violent disruption. Instead, it has opened the door to endless warfare: "war and feuds occur constantly" due primarily to cultural traditions, "desert living conditions, lack of resources, and continual droughts."[121] Nonetheless, since "attempts to revive a central state structure have actually exacerbated armed conflicts,"[122] the predicament might have been even worse were it not for some armed nonstate group actions. Over time, fewer private constituencies in Somalia may be benefiting from armed conflict, as warlords found their capacity to foment conflict reduced because of shrinking financial support and war-weary clans, and "those interests in favour of peace—or at least suspension of armed conflict—have grown appreciably."[123] From 1995 to 2006, the duration and scope of armed conflict in Somalia dropped noticeably.[124] However, since 2006, al-Shabaab—a hard-line militia group composed of domestic and foreign youth, which controls much of southern Somalia—has waged an insurgency against Somalia's transitional federal government: designated by the United States as a terrorist group and claiming the support of al-Qaeda, al-Shabaab (unpopular with the most Somalis) blocked the arrival of desperately needed international food aid after the onset of the worst drought in sixty years and the ensuing famine, until late summer 2011.[125]

The turmoil in Somalia has also impeded the country from attaining the fourth essential stability function, precluding unwanted foreign coercive intervention, by attracting some of the worst elements of humanity, including al-Qaeda terrorist operatives. Since the early 1990s, Somali warlords have received "advisory instruction" from al-Qaeda when dealing the American military intervention, and al-Qaeda appears to have "found a ready-made recruiting ground in failed states such as Somalia, in which daily life was characterized by excessive political and economic stagnation, rampant corruption, and brutal repression."[126] Al-Qaeda's intent was to use Somalia as a staging ground for international attacks.[127] However, while "in theory, the protracted collapse of formal law-enforcement capacity should provide an attractive safe haven for a wide range of criminal elements—terrorists, smugglers (of drugs, guns, people and other contraband), money-launderers, pirates, and criminals on the run; in fact, Somalia has proven to be relatively inhospitable terrain. . . ."[128] So al-Qaeda leaders may have "greatly underestimated the costs of operating in Somalia" and "overestimated the value to Somalis of their version of jihad."[129]

The outlook for regional stability is extremely dim. In recent years, "Somalia's protracted anarchy posed a direct security threat mainly to the neighbouring states of Kenya and Ethiopia."[130] Maritime piracy has been thriving off the coast of East Africa, with attacks growing from 41 in 2007 to 122 in 2008.[131] Thanks to weak regulation in Somalia, the entire range of global shipping commerce through the Horn of Africa is in peril, and the result has been to cause some businesses to avoid the area completely.

HEZBOLLAH IN LEBANON

This case revolves around an armed nonstate group stepping in to provide the order and basic security not supplied by the central state government to a war-ravaged area during a violent conflict between Israel and Lebanon in 2006. Hezbollah ("party of God") emerged as an organization in 1982 in response to the Israeli invasion of Lebanon.[132] A Shi'a Muslim organization strong in southern Lebanon, Hezbollah was heavily influenced in its establishment by the Islamic revolution in Iran in 1979, especially since it was backed by Iran. Social and political marginalization of the Shi'a in Lebanon led to mobilization calling for the implementation of Islamic law: "Hezbollah's founding document calls for Islamic rule in Lebanon, an end to Western imperialism, and the destruction of the state of Israel."[133] In October 1983, this Hezbollah "literally exploded into the world's consciousness with devastating suicide attacks on the U.S. embassy and marine barracks in Beirut, causing over 250 American casualties; as a result, Washington concluded that there was little peace to keep in Lebanon and withdrew its forces in 1984."[134] Since that time, Hezbollah has carried out over 179 terrorist attacks, killing more than 800 people and injuring more than 1,500.[135]

Hezbollah is unusual among armed nonstate groups in that it actively participates in legislative governance by holding seats in the Lebanese parliament. Having previously labeled the electoral system as corrupt, Hezbollah decided to enter the political arena in 1992. Its political platform is diverse, covering not only religion but also economic exploitation, political inequalities, and security. The group has been "popular among Lebanon's Shi'ite plurality and is respected by many non-Shi'ite Lebanese."[136] As of 2009, Hezbollah "holds 28 seats in the Lebanese parliament and enjoys the status of a political organization that negotiates directly with governments, both its own and foreign"; and Hezbollah's strategic communications capabilities now "include a sophisticated television, radio, print, and web media apparatus."[137] Hezbollah's ability to project multiple faces aids the group in successfully functioning within the current global security setting:

> By mixing religion, ideology, social welfare, politics, and occasional violence, Hezbollah has gained legitimacy with local communities and developed

sophisticated institutional practices, which give it strength and resilience. The movement is at once a religious organization, an aid organization, a political party, and a paramilitary force. This makes it hard for governments to know how to categorize and confront it. The U.S. government, for example, considers Hezbollah a terrorist organization and has banned its television programs, financial arms, and charity activities from operating in the United States. The British government proscribes only Hezbollah's military wing, including its External Security Organization, but allows the group's political, social, and welfare elements to proceed unhindered. The disparities between countries' domestic counterterrorism legislation helps Hezbollah because it inhibits a consistent, unified Western response to its activities.[138]

Hezbollah "has expanded from an underground militia to a political party with a highly efficient apparatus, an extensive welfare network and a small semi-professional resistance organization":[139] it "operates as a political party, but at the same time it is a terrorist organization, a highly trained militia, and a clandestine criminal organization with illegal enterprises in Lebanon and abroad."[140]

During the 1990s, Hezbollah made a concerted effort to expel Israel from Lebanon, responding to Israel's establishment of a "security zone" in southern Lebanon in 1985. In this effort, Hezbollah utilized guerrilla warfare rather than terrorist tactics, since "the vast majority of Hezbollah's actions were focused on Israeli military personnel on Lebanese soil" rather than on innocent civilians.[141] Hezbollah has also given money, weapons, and personnel to the Palestinian freedom movement in Israel.[142] This armed nonstate group has thus played a unique and pivotal role in the relationship between two neighboring states, using one (Lebanon) as a safe haven from which to attack and undermine the interests of the other (Israel).

On July 12, 2006, Hezbollah captured two Israeli soldiers with the hope of negotiating a prisoner exchange, and in response Israel declared war on Lebanon, launching massive air strikes, an air and naval blockade, and a ground invasion from the south. Hostilities ceased on August 14, and Israel lifted its naval blockade on September 8. The 2006 war had a devastating impact, not so much on the Lebanese government but rather on the people and their personal property:

> The 33 day war that followed Hezbollah's capture of two Israeli soldiers in July 2006 was widely considered to be more destructive than previous Israeli invasions or occupations of Lebanon. Approximately 1,200 Lebanese were killed,

one million were displaced and direct war damage was estimated at US $4 billion, with an additional $6 billion in indirect costs. Israel's response went far beyond an operation to rescue its two soldiers, though it was goaded by Hezbollah rocket attacks deep into Israeli territory that killed 43 civilians. Roads, bridges and public utilities were targeted, and thousands of housing units were destroyed or damaged, particularly in the Shia-dominated areas of Beirut Southern Suburbs (BSS) and southern Lebanon. Most civilians returned home within hours of the cessation of hostilities in mid-August 2006 (thus averting the humanitarian problems associated with long-term displacement), but returnees faced hazards from enormous quantities of unexploded ordinance [sic].[143]

Not coincidentally, the damage was most severe in parts of Lebanon where Hezbollah's support was the greatest. Over time, Hezbollah has proved to be "the single most effective adversary Israel has ever faced": "its fighters and leaders have demonstrated exceptional dedication and an ability to learn from mistakes and innovate quickly"; and Palestinians cite "Hezbollah's combination of skilled operations, willing sacrifice, and emphasis on long-term struggle as a guide to their own efforts."[144] Hezbollah is now well organized under a charismatic leader, has strong finances, effectively supplies education, welfare, and emergency aid to its supporters, and has a military branch capable of deploying advanced weapons systems.[145] The group's leaders have "seamlessly fit together political and military roles that resulted in the large-scale support that the party enjoys today."[146]

Hezbollah relies on diverse international sources for funding and support, and thus is not immediately vulnerable to having its income bottlenecked:

> Both Hezbollah's terrorist actions and its guerrilla warfare are facilitated by the group's extensive international network. Hezbollah operatives have been found in France, Spain, Cyprus, Singapore, the "triborder" region of South America, and the Philippines, as well as in more familiar operational theatres in Europe and the Middle East. The movement draws on these cells to raise money, prepare the logistical infrastructure for attacks, disseminate propaganda, and otherwise ensure that the organization remains robust and ready to strike.[147]

Interestingly, among Hezbollah's foreign resources are Colombian drug traffickers,[148] who reinforce the global reach of Hezbollah's funding network.

Long before the 2006 war with Israel, Hezbollah had a positive stability-enhancing reputation in Lebanon. Over the years since the group's formation, "in marked contrast to the Lebanese government, it offers relatively efficient public services and runs effective schools and hospitals":[149] Hezbollah's welfare services are "an important source of popularity because of their extensiveness, their efficiency and their reputation for integrity," for whenever the state failed to provide for basic survival needs, "Hizbollah steps in—whether it is a Christian village in the Bekaa valley cut off by an avalanche, or impoverished Shi'a in Beirut lacking water, electricity, and sewerage services."[150]

In the wake of the 2006 war, Hezbollah fostered a positive impact on the stability of the affected population in Lebanon through substantial reconstructive efforts, including "substantial economic resources" and "elaborate welfare and education programmes" in Lebanon during and after the 2006 war with Israel.[151] Jihad al-Bina, the reconstruction wing of Hezbollah founded in 1988, undertook this reconstructive activity, benefiting from possessing both an extensive organization structure and an ability to tap into the resources of the Shi'a community.[152] Distributing more than $100 million within seventy-two hours of the cessation of hostilities, Hezbollah appeared to be the "most effective" of all the on-the-ground humanitarian assistance organizations, as, for example, "it directed bulldozers to tear down damaged buildings" and "its volunteers staffed registration centres to assess the needs of returnees."[153] Although Hezbollah's own actions triggered the 2006 Israeli-Lebanese war, the group did an effective job providing for basic survival needs to the affected population, including food and shelter. The group has since established a massive system of hospitals, schools, and relief centers for the Lebanese people.[154] Hezbollah's accomplishments have been so remarkable that "Hezbollah was able to provide a higher quality of social service to some communities in the midst of a civil war than they had previously received from the Lebanese state"; and the organization is "Lebanon's largest nonstate provider of healthcare and social services and operates schools of such high quality that even non-Muslims send their children to them."[155] Indeed, despite the group's many unsavory activities, today Hezbollah can be considered the "poster child" for how an armed nonstate group can enhance stability.

The net effect of Hezbollah's success in delivering significant aid to displaced, destitute, and homeless people was to mute Lebanese citizens who might have otherwise criticized Hezbollah for triggering a conflict that devastated much of southern Lebanon[156] and to cause Lebanese people benefiting from Hezbollah-sponsored aid to approve of the organization. Indeed, after the war "the mood in Beirut's southern suburb on September 22, 2006 was one of unrestrained jubilation; Hizbullah's 'divine, historic, and strategic victory against Israel' was being celebrated by a gathering of more than a million people. . . ."[157] As a result of Hezbollah's massive postwar reconstruction effort,[158] it "won the loyalty of many Lebanese":[159] its broad-based Lebanese support encompassed 96 percent of Shiites, 87 percent of Sunnis, 80 percent of Christians, and 80 percent of Druze.[160] Given the diversity of groups residing in Lebanon, this level of domestic popular support for an armed nonstate group is impressive.

The Lebanese government, in contrast, did little more in the aftermath of the 2006 war than to pay some financial compensation to those who had lost their homes.[161] As a result, "the inevitable comparisons being drawn between Hezbollah effectiveness and Lebanese government ineptitude raise questions about the future of the . . . government and its ability to withstand domestic criticism over its leadership during the current crisis."[162] Moreover, as usual, "European states and Western-backed financial institutions focused their attention on providing aid primarily in the form of programmes for better governance."[163] Indeed, many states providing assistance in the war-torn area tended "to be slow paced, wedded to bureaucratic procedures and prone to attaching conditions to financial assistance."[164] The contrast between state and nonstate humanitarian assistance getting quickly and effectively to the war-ravaged area could not have been starker. However, in response to Hezbollah's reconstructive assistance, "Western political and media sources voiced concern that Hezbollah's apparent reconstruction efficiency was due to Iranian funding,"[165] as both Iran and Syria had close ties to Hezbollah.[166]

Despite its positive impact on internal stability, Hezbollah has had devastating effects on stability in the region. Aside from the effects of the 2006 war with Israel, "since the outbreak of the al-Aqsa intifada in October 2000, Hezbollah has provided guerrilla training, bomb-building expertise, propaganda, and tactical tips to Hamas, Palestinian Islamic Jihad, and other anti-Israeli groups."[167] This outreach allows Hezbollah to disrupt the peace process at little cost to itself, and "exporting its model of conflict while limiting actual attacks allows the movement to continue its fight without alienating its Lebanese constituents (many of whom fear an Israeli backlash) or its backers in Tehran and Damascus (who fear U.S. retaliation)."[168] Consistent with its extremist goals, Hezbollah seems willing to undertake a wide range of subversive activities in the Middle East to disrupt the status quo.

IRISH REPUBLICAN ARMY IN THE UNITED KINGDOM

This case revolves around an armed nonstate group attempting to unify a nationality by wresting designated territory from outside control by a central state government. The activity in the United Kingdom of the Irish Republican Army (IRA), identified both as a terrorist group and a rebel/insurgent group, is one of the three instances in this study of armed nonstate groups attempting to gain security control in Western advanced industrialized societies. The formation in the early twentieth century of the IRA, an Irish Catholic republican revolutionary military organization, was fueled by a desire for freedom and a response to British occupation of Ireland, specifically reacting "to the formation of the Ulster Volunteer Force (UVF), a militia loyal to the Ulster Unionist Party and opposed to the granting of home rule to Ireland by the Westminster Parliament."[169] The IRA's mission was to end British rule in Northern Ireland and establish an independent united Irish republic, and for that purpose the IRA used violent terrorist tactics against Britain to try to force withdrawal of British military forces from Northern Ireland. Members of the IRA viewed this conflict as an "anti-colonial and anti-imperial" struggle.[170]

For centuries, "Ireland had been divided between a Protestant majority which almost uninterruptedly identified with Britain and a Catholic minority looking to a united and politically autonomous Ireland."[171] The revolutionary uprising of the Irish Catholics was largely fueled and sustained by the working class, who felt it was disadvantaged compared to its Protestant counterpart.[172] Over the years there has indeed been significant anti-Catholic discrimination in Northern Ireland."[173] Operating mostly within a territory with just over a million and a half people, and for most of that time within a support base of a minority of the cultural Catholic population of approximately 650,000, the IRA's organizational endurance was impressive,"[174] especially considering Britain's concerted opposition.

In 1969, the more extremist Provisional Irish Republican Army split off from the rest of the IRA (which was more restrained) and began an all-out war against the British army, killing hundreds of people in the early 1970s. This group not only defended Catholic enclaves, but also bombed military and commercial targets, with the underlying goal of increasing the cost of British governance of Northern Ireland. In response, the British army staged hundreds of raids against the IRA, and arrested and interned many suspected participants and supporters without trial.

The IRA has used ruthless methods to destroy its enemies, often at the expense of innocent civilians. Their prime tactics included "gun battles, crossfire, snipers' bullets, and ambushes; explosions . . . antipersonnel devices, and [some deaths] in riots or affrays."[175] In the period between 1969 and 1994, the

IRA was responsible for approximately 1,750 deaths, making Northern Ireland most violent region in the European Community.[176] Because IRA violence inflicted substantial casualties on the civilian population, some of their potential supporters were alienated from the cause. While a majority of Northern Irish Catholics supported a nationalist agenda, not all were willing to employ violent means to achieve the goal of a unified Ireland; part of the challenge facing the IRA has been "the division of opinion in Ireland among nationalists, as well as between nationalism and unionism."[177]

The IRA's sources of money and weapons include unusual as well as the usual suspects. First and foremost, key links were established with the sizable Irish Catholic population in the United States. However, since "the IRA throughout its history has engaged in alliances with a range of forces ideologically incompatible with one another . . . in accordance with their perceived practical needs," the IRA obtained backing from Libya at the same time it did from the United States[178] (the large quantity of small arms received from Libya was reportedly in retaliation for Britain's participation in the 1986 Libya bombing). Aside from this outside funding, money has been raised in Ireland "from protection, bank and post office robberies, republican clubs, local collections, [and] kidnappings."[179]

In 1995, parties opposing the conflict decided to address the situation through negotiations regarding "proposals for changes in the Government of Ireland Act, which set up the Irish Constitution's claims to the area, and cross-border institutions."[180] But it was only in 1998 that the parties reached a settlement, known as the Belfast Agreement or the Good Friday Accords. The agreement incorporated both political and military aspects addressing the grievances of both sides: (1) ending the armed conflict through a cease-fire, (2) decommissioning weapons, (3) demilitarization, police reform, and prisoner release, (4) recognition of Northern Ireland as part of Britain by the Republic of Ireland, and (5) balancing political power so as to give Catholics a greater voice.[181] The motives for IRA use of violence and IRA laying down arms were equally political:

> [T]he IRA's argument was not always subtle or nuanced, but the questions to which it related (legitimacy, government, independence, sovereignty, territory, force, and order) were all crucial to the state and to politics. Violence, and the belief in the necessity and primary efficacy of force, were what centrally defined IRA politics; once it came to be thought, at the end of the 1990s, that more

conventional politics in fact offered superior rewards, then the IRA began to cease to exist.[182]

The 1998 Belfast Agreement increased power sharing in Northern Ireland and made sure that any Irish unification would occur through public referendum.[183] The IRA was relatively successful in moving toward its goals up through the Good Friday Accords, though initially without decommissioning its arms. The peace process culminated in July 2005, with the IRA renouncing its use of violence and its armed campaign against British rule in Northern Ireland, choosing instead to pursue only peaceful means to achieve its political ends.

In terms of the stability impact, the IRA produced mixed results. At the same time it was protecting the Catholic population and forestalling external interference in Northern Ireland, the group was promoting violent conflict, erosion of civil society, and disruption of law and order. At times, the IRA acted as an agent of social control and security, driven by the need to preserve cross-class unity in the national struggle.[184] The Northern Irish Catholics argued that the British government was treating them badly by withholding opportunities such as adequate education, employment, and public housing, and the IRA saw itself as fighting for equal treatment of Catholics. In support of this claim, "the IRA in urban areas of Northern Ireland ran welfare assistance as well as a violent punishment system during the height of its power,"[185] thus helping to promote human security by providing for basic survival needs to much of the affected population, even if not advancing law and order or peace in the area.

The IRA viewed their violent initiative as being "primarily in response to defensive need, to urgent danger"—protecting against disruptive external intervention from Britain—and "an overriding need for a defence force to protect vulnerable Catholic communities from sectarian attack."[186] In reality, "the impulse toward communal self-defence made sense" because "there was a need for Catholic self-protection in the late 1960s (and beyond)," as in Northern Ireland "Catholic communities did (and do) come under attack, and the state was not providing anything like adequate protection."[187] Unfortunately, often the IRA's "defensive record has, in practice, been a poor one," where "IRA violence made more rather than less likely the prospect of Catholics suffering violence."[188] Moreover, "the post-1960s violence in Northern Ireland—for which the IRA was significantly, but not solely, responsible—greatly deepened the political and personal divisions and lack of trust between the two communities there."[189] Nonetheless, "IRA violence certainly prevented the imposition of a solution from which they were excluded, and it gave republicans greater leverage in the negotiation of the final deal arrived at in 1998—one which included republicans in government, prisoner releases, significant reform to the state and the hope of its ultimate dissolution."[190]

As to regional effects on stability, even though some IRA shootings and bombings occurred outside of the United Kingdom in other parts of Western Europe, the group's violent efforts had little impact on the rest of Europe. Owing to Great Britain's geographical separation from the European continent and the idiosyncratic issues at stake in the conflict between the IRA and England, this localized armed nonstate group activity did not spark any insurgency or violence among other groups within the region. Unlike cases where religion creates international repercussions—such as the involvement of the global Islamic movement in helping certain armed nonstate groups—no global pan-Catholic turmoil occurred in the IRA case.

ISLAMIC ARMY OF ADEN IN YEMEN

This case revolves around an armed nonstate group linked to international terrorism trying to control a central state government. The Islamic Army of Aden (IAA), also known as the Aden-Abyan Islamic Army (AAIA), is the Yemeni affiliate of al-Qaeda that has claimed responsibility for kidnappings and bombings against Western targets in Yemen and abroad.[191] Operating primarily out of the southern Yemeni provinces, this Sunni Muslim extremist group made its first formal public statements in mid-1998, when the group announced its intentions to overthrow of the Yemeni government, "to establish a state based on strict adherence to Sharia law and to expel all Western influence from Yemen and the greater Middle East."[192] This group later endorsed al-Qaeda leader Osama bin Laden after the American retaliatory strikes on his terrorist training camps in Afghanistan.[193]

The IAA "first drew world-wide attention to itself in December 1998 when it claimed responsibility for kidnapping sixteen westerners, mostly Britons, on an adventure holiday in Yemen."[194] The IAA made the headlines again in October 2000, when it attacked an American army destroyer, the USS *Cole*, killing seventeen U.S. sailors and injuring thirty-nine others.[195] This successful attack followed a January 2000 attempt to bomb another American warship, failing when the raft carrying explosives sank immediately after launch.[196] The IAA has also claimed responsibility for a suicide boat attack against the French oil tanker *Limberg* in 2002.[197] The group's anti-Western tilt continued with bomb attacks on American and British interests in Yemen, threats to Western doctors and tourists in the country, and open support for the attacks against the American embassies in Africa.[198] The organization itself "is probably a loose guerrilla network of a few dozen men."[199] During the Afghan-Soviet war of 1979–1989, many Yemenites joined the Afghans, learning how to fight and the jihadi ideology.[200] Because Islamic militants have been suffering setbacks in Afghanistan and Pakistan, many fighters are fleeing to Yemen to reassemble the movement.[201] Recently the IAA's influence has been waning, with its members last arrested in 2006.[202]

The Islamic IAA's primary source of funding and support appears to be al-Qaeda, although in addition "the IAA has traditionally conducted criminal activities as a means of raising money."[203] Before he was killed, "authorities suspect the IAA receives financial and material support from al-Qaida leader Osama bin Laden in exchange for public support of al-Qaida's agenda."[204] Al-Qaeda has been present in Yemen since the late 1980s, exploiting the central state government's lack of control by setting up training camps, recruiting from the tribes, harboring terrorists, and establishing illicit business fronts. While some tribes collaborate with the radicals based on ideology, others utilize the al-Qaeda connection merely for funding.[205] In the late 1990s, the IAA emerged as a structured affiliate of al-Qaeda,[206] and it announced in October 2003 that it was formally "joining" al-Qaeda.[207] Al-Qaeda's presence in Yemen is multifaceted—"rather than one affiliate, it was reported that several affiliates were working there on behalf of al-Qaeda."[208] Indeed, "the Yemeni government has a history of making tactical accommodations" with al-Qaeda.[209] In recent years, al-Qaeda's presence in Yemen has escalated.

The government of Yemen has not had a consistent policy in dealing with extremist violent groups like the IAA. It has apparently "progressed from passively tolerating these groups to actively opposing them": for example, "in 2005, the Yemeni government implemented a program to reconvert or persuade arrestees to renounce the ideology of these groups."[210] However, in fall 2003, President Ali Abdullah Saleh announced that he would release and grant amnesty to dozens of militants with links to al-Qaeda as long as they "pledged to respect the rights of non-Muslim foreigners living in Yemen or visiting it"; this prompted more than fifty IAA members to turn themselves in to authorities.[211] Yemeni government officials had earlier "quietly tried to incorporate the IAA and its founder Abu al-Hassan into the political system, but on Nov. 8, 1998, al-Hassan called on the president, the Consultative Council, and the parliament to resign and face criminal charges under Islamic law."[212]

Central government control is absent in many parts of Yemen, especially the rural areas—the regime itself admits a lack of control of sixteen of the country's nineteen provinces.[213] Yemen has been a tribal culture for millennia, and the central government is struggling to enforce national allegiance and respect for the law.[214] If the deterioration of the central state government's authority and legitimacy continues, its future is in jeopardy: "Yemen may slowly devolve into semi-autonomous regions and cities," and "for the central government, the civil war in Saada and the secessionist movement in the South represent threats to the very survival of the state."[215]

The frustrated and dissatisfied Yemeni people were receptive to the IAA, as "the neo-Islamist current is hardly the only dissident element in Yemeni politics," for "many people are protesting deteriorating economic conditions and the arbitrary powers of security forces."[216] The Yemeni people appear not appear to see the need for a strong central government: in the Yemeni countryside, "trying to introduce central government control may well increase, rather than decrease, popular support for insurgent and terrorist groups, perhaps even turning latent insurgencies into active ones."[217] This antigovernment sentiment permitted the long-term persistence of the IAA: "although the Yemeni government has sought to crush the group and has claimed that it is no longer capable of carrying out its operations, Western intelligence services believe it is still planning operations to advance its political and religious agenda."[218]

The IAA appears to have made matters worse on stability. The context for evaluating this stability impact is a dismal one: Yemen is the poorest country in the Arab world, with oil and water quickly being depleted, jihadism rising, corruption (particularly in the army) becoming endemic, the southern areas seceding, and warfare impending.[219] Moreover, "a rapidly expanding and increasingly poorer population places unbearable pressure on the government's ability to provide basic services."[220] On the 2010 Failed States Index—designed to indicate a country's overall instability—Yemen ignominiously climbed to the fifteenth spot, as "long-ignored Yemen leapt into the news when a would-be suicide bomber who had trained there tried to blow up a commercial flight bound for Detroit."[221] Within this setting, the Islamic Army of Aden has had ample opportunity to promote instability. Thanks in part to this group's activities, "war, terrorism, a deepening secessionist movement, and interconnected economic and demographic trends have the potential to overwhelm the Yemeni government, jeopardizing domestic stability and security across the region."[222] Although the tribal culture has opened the door to effective armed nonstate group rule, militarization of the population—due to participation in the Afghan-Soviet war and wide availability of weaponry—has expanded the negative stability impact:[223] the Yemeni Interior Ministry "estimates that the country's approximately 19 million people own some 50 million personal weapons."[224] Overall, the IAA has accomplished little in Yemen in terms of providing for basic survival needs to the population, promoting rules and order in the society, ending internal violent conflict, or deterring unwanted disruptive external coercive intervention. In the end, "while western intelligence agencies and think-tanks vaguely and gloomily forecast that a power vacuum and chaos in Yemen would open the door to a jihadist takeover and an important victory for al-Qaeda that might destabilise Saudi Arabia and so threaten the rest of the world, Yemenis able to afford the luxury of thinking about anything but their immediate daily needs felt themselves to be participating in a real and current, not imagined and future, drama: the disintegration of their country."[225] As of mid-2012, security in Yemen has deteriorated, and the choice of Yemen as a primary target by the United States for its violent anti-terrorist drone strikes has placed protection of the mass population in the country even more in jeopardy.

The IAA appears to have negative effects on regional stability. As a result of its links to al-Qaeda and the absence of effective central state government control, Yemen has become a safe haven for terrorists from all over the world, with it now being considered as one of the principal sites of the most extreme forms of anti-Western terrorism, and consequently a potential source of regional and global instability. Although no unimpeachable evidence of IAA-instigated disruptions have occurred so far within neighboring Oman, Saudi Arabia, Qatar, or the United Arab Emirates, the potential for significant contagious violence certainly exists.

LORD'S RESISTANCE ARMY IN UGANDA

This case revolves around a bizarre armed nonstate group with mystical beliefs trying to assert control over a part of a country discriminated against by the central state government. The Lord's Resistance Army (LRA) is a militant group formed in 1987 and engaged in an armed rebellion in northern Uganda against the Ugandan government in what is now one of Africa's longest-running conflicts. The northern part of Uganda, an area that "does not hold known strategic reserves of any key resources,"[226] is inhabited mainly by the Acholi people. This group has a lengthy history of antagonism toward central government authorities due largely to being both politically and economically marginalized by the government and militarized as army soldiers (dominating the ranks) during colonial times.[227] Many of the Acholi have engaged in armed resistance against a Ugandan central government that appeared to them to favor those living in southern Uganda, the focal point of agricultural development. Over time, the Acholi people have had "serious and legitimate complaints" against the central government of Uganda, including reports of atrocities by government soldiers against the Acholi population that strengthened distrust and hostility toward the central government.[228] The Acholi region "is the laggard of the nation in terms of any basic human development indicator—the proportion of households below the poverty line in the north when compared to the rest of Uganda is not only low, but actually increased from 1997 to 2000, in contrast to other regions."[229] The human security impact of this violent conflict has been staggering: "at its height, the conflict caused the displacement of over 1.8 million people, about 90 percent of the population of Acholi, forcing them to live in squalid, overcrowded camps."[230]

Despite its relatively small size—with an estimated five thousand to ten thousand members[231] at its peak—the LRA has "carried out its own external and internal policy" and has "made itself autonomous from the state."[232] The LRA originally emerged out of the Holy Spirit Movement, started in 1985–1986 by Alice Auma (Lakwena), who convinced many Acholi people that the Holy Spirit possessed her and whose beliefs combined "elements of missionary Christianity interacting with indigenous cosmology."[233] In 1987, Joseph Kony, who claimed to be a cousin of Lakwena and who wanted to attract her supporters, founded his own movement, which eventually was named the Lord's Resistance Army. In 1988, after Lakwena's forces were decisively defeated in battle, Kony recruited the remnants of her Holy Spirit Movement for his own purposes. At first, Kony he seemed to be "the bearer of an apocalyptic vision, a mouthpiece of a widely accepted view that the Acholi people [were] on the verge of genocide";[234] but as time passed, "the realities of this conflict appear to be far away from any of the Lord's moral dictates,"[235] and "the Holy Spirit tactics were replaced with guerrilla tactics."[236] Kony fought a war against the Ugandan government involving surprise attacks on villages using quasi-independent armed groups operating in northern Uganda and southern Sudan, and the central Ugandan government increasingly suffered from a war of attrition.[237]

Some analysts see the LRA conflict "as an extension of postindependence civil war strife," with inequality being "the main source of social conflict in Uganda, generating the structural violence from which all subsequent political, military, and civilian violence would erupt."[238]

The specific goals of the LRA, which "blends the intensity of religious ideology with brutal guerrilla tactics,"[239] have been much debated and are somewhat wrapped in mystery. Although some large-scale attacks by the LRA have been clearly designed to underscore the central government's inability to protect the country's citizenry, "the rebels' vision of an alternative society is poorly articulated, to put it mildly, just as rampant atrocities undermine the credibility of the LRA as a popular political protest."[240] To many observers, "the movement lacked any real political agenda and its activities were reportedly oriented around revenge for the humiliation of defeat by the NRA and in retaliation for southern aggression against the northern population."[241] However, the clearest expression is by James Alfred Obita, former Secretary For External Affairs And Mobilisation, and Leader of Delegation of the Lord's Resistance Army, who stated that the LRA's objectives are to remove dictatorship and stop the oppression of the people; to fight for the immediate restoration of competitive multiparty democracy in Uganda; to see an end to gross violation of human rights and dignity of Ugandans; to ensure the restoration of peace and security in Uganda; to ensure unity, sovereignty and economic prosperity beneficial to all Ugandans; and to bring to an end to the repressive policy of deliberate marginalization of groups of people who may not agree with the LRA ideology.[242] Nonetheless, for some observers, the stated LRA ideology appears to have little to do with the group's actual behavior.[243] Moreover, different strands have existed, with different types of participants looking for different payoffs: for the simple foot soldiers, the LRA's killings and pillages seemed simply a way to obtain goods that would otherwise be out of reach; while for the leaders, the actions also gave them material goods but more importantly power and superior status.[244]

Although LRA-initiated violence in Uganda has diminished since 2006 and the group's size has dwindled to fewer than five hundred, resolution of the conflict has proven to be elusive.[245] The LRA persists in part because it "abducts recruits from the population to sustain what has, in the past, proved a 'marketable' insurgency"; and the target population has generated "the leadership's only source of political capital."[246] Furthermore, rumors abound that the war continues because it has fostered corruption as a source of lucrative income for high-ranking government and military officials.[247]

From 1990 until 1999, the LRA was funded by the Sudanese government, and some analysts believe that the conflict is a function of the geopolitical rivalry between Uganda and Sudan, with the LRA having been the equivalent of "hired guns" used by the Sudanese government to destabilize Uganda.[248] The alliance between the LRA and the Sudanese government yielded "significant military benefit" to the LRA, with this armed nonstate group having "created rear bases in friendly Sudan that housed large numbers of LRA fighters, their wives, and other personnel."[249] In addition, "the LRA's primary source of supplies is through looting"—"trucks carrying valuable goods are regularly looted, especially for anything that can easily be sold in the trading centers, such as bicycle tires or farm tools."[250] Thus a combination of different internal and external funding allowed the LRA to continue its operations.

The stability impact initially seemed positive then later turned negative. Given little government investment in the region and the perceived neglect of the Acholi people, the LRA has provided its participants with basic needs and a meaning to life (a life endorsed by God). Especially in the LRA's early days, the northerners seemed to view the organization favorably and be looking toward the group for protection of themselves and their property from and retaliation of the National Resistance Army (NRA): "the LRA attracted popular support in the late 1980s when it was viewed by the population as a credible counterforce to the NRA government."[251] The preexisting militarization of Ugandan— and especially Acholi—society contributed to the popularity of this violent group.[252] Despite its faults, the LRA has offered "an alternative to the abuses of the central government" for "a narrow constituency of the politically and socially dispossessed" in Uganda.[253] In terms of military success, "the LRA's tactics make it extremely good at asymmetric warfare and thereby allow it to survive in long-term war against the much more (conventionally) powerful Ugandan state."[254] Although violent, the LRA was most effective during this initial period in providing for basic survival needs to the discriminated-against population in northern Uganda.

However, this rosy picture of the LRA stability impact quickly dissipated. In March 1991, a failed government attempt to eradicate the LRA caused Kony to retaliate with large-scale mutilation of suspected sympathizers. As a result, by the early 1990s, "the LRA faced a reduction in popular support (and we may infer a commensurate reduction in voluntary recruitment)" because of "the overall demise of many of the northern armed groups at the time—which suggests a general loss of faith in armed struggle—and popular grievance at the LRA's targeting of the civilian population."[255] Indeed, "whatever popular support it [the Lord's Resistance Army] initially enjoyed among the Acholi people of Northern Uganda has been largely forfeited by its use of terror tactics."[256] There is little doubt that now "the LRA is in total breach of human rights":[257] the international community condemns the LRA for its employment of child soldiers, with the Western media especially condemning "the brutality of the LRA and its practice of kidnapping children."[258] Nearly 80 percent of the LRA combatants are abducted children, as it is estimated that the LRA war has created close to twenty thousand child soldiers;[259] and women are equally mistreated, as the LRA holds many as sex slaves for the soldiers and as forced laborers. Overall, "the mutilation and summary execution of non-combatants, the abduction of children and adults for use as foot soldiers, sex slaves and porters, the rounding up of civilians in camps—1,200,000 at the end of 2003—have measured the cadence of this conflict with the regularity of a metronome."[260]

The LRA has promoted regional instability, recently moving many of its forces into southern Sudan, the Democratic Republic of the Congo, and the Central African Republic.[261] The result has been spreading violence: for example, in March 2002, after a massive Ugandan government offensive against the LRA in southern Sudan, the LRA responded by attacking refugee camps in northern Uganda and southern Sudan, killing hundreds of innocent people. The United States now classifies the LRA as a terrorist organization, and in 2005 the International Criminal Court charged the LRA's leadership with war crimes and crimes against humanity. Because of the role that Ugandan-Sudanese animosity played in funding the LRA, this regional spread of violence is unsurprising. In the end, it is hard to imagine that a group as brutal and ruthless toward its own people as the LRA is could meaningfully enhance stability and security in the region.

MARA SALVATRUCHA IN THE UNITED STATES

This case revolves around an armed nonstate group that emerged from a street gang composed of illegal immigrants with a high demand for personal security within a lawless gang-infested area largely ignored by the central state government. This case, along with that of the IRA and the Yakuza, illustrates the ways in which armed nonstate groups operate within advanced industrial societies. The origins of the Mara Salvatrucha can be traced back to massive El

Salvadorian emigration to the United States in the 1980s resulting from the civil war there.[262] In the context of the wars and insurgencies in El Salvador, Guatemala, and Nicaragua, "thousands of people, including young men, fled North, a great many arriving as illegal aliens in Los Angeles, California; a certain percentage of these young men had been involved in the conflict, either on the side of the governments or the insurgents, and were familiar with guns and armed combat."[263] Fleeing civil unrest, nearly one million El Salvadorans—representing one-fifth of El Salvador's population—relocated to the United States, with a majority going to the district of west downtown Los Angeles.[264]

Because of poverty, racism, and prejudice, many African American and Mexican American street gangs had already formed in Los Angeles, and the massive wave of El Salvadorans did not assimilate easily into the established gang culture in West Los Angeles. Facing violence from these gangs, as well as a difficult work situation, the El Salvadorans banded together into *maras* (small gang units) of *salvatruchas* (street-hardened El Salvadorans).[265] As a result of the hostile gang presence in the area, the El Salvadoran newcomers established what would become one of the most dangerous gangs in the United States: the Mara Salvatrucha, also known as MS-13. The gang is estimated to have thirty thousand to fifty thousand members worldwide, with eight thousand to ten thousand residing in the United States.[266]

The structure of the Mara Salvatrucha is "elaborate, flexible, and redundant with a leadership cadre and another to back it up," able to "function as networks, with extensive transnational linkages" for functions such as recruiting, logistics, attacks, intelligence, and propaganda.[267] This group has developed its own distinctive set of cultural norms that set it apart from other gangs:

> They increasingly arm their members, including with heavier weapons such as M16s, AK-47s, and grenades. Their members are reported to be increasingly sophisticated in using these arms. They use unique tattoos, have their own symbols and graffiti, and their own language both written and through hand signals. Each mara has its own internal rules which are very elaborate. Even in view of these unique, and at times bizarre or grotesque characteristics, probably the most defining characteristic of the maras, is the use of violence. Indeed, their unique vocabularies emphasize precisely the criminal activities and violence. From initiation, to ascension into leadership positions, to discipline, everything is based on violence.[268]

The Mara Salvatrucha is now widely considered to be the fastest-growing and most violent of all the street gangs in the United States.[269]

The American government did not remain passive in the face of this ominous development, but its stern action toward this armed nonstate group ended up backfiring. What "with the peace processes ending the war in El Salvador in 1992, and spreading throughout the region by the mid-1990s, the U.S. Government deported the *maras* on release from prison back to their countries of origin."[270] Specifically, the Federal Bureau of Investigation and the Immigration Customs Enforcement officials "deported hundreds of gang members since most hard-core gang members were undocumented aliens":[271] "between 1998 and 2005, the USA deported almost 46,000 convicts to Central America, in addition to 160,000 illegal immigrants caught without the requisite permit; three countries—El Salvador, Guatemala and Honduras—received over 90% of the deportations from the USA."[272] Many of those arrested were deported back to El Salvador, where the local governments were even less equipped to handle gang violence. Indeed, Mara Salvatrucha was established in San Salvador in 1992 "by the *clicas* (cliques, cells, or groups) deported from the United States" that replaced "earlier, less violent, and less sophisticated gangs."[273] Afterward, "to the surprise of federal law enforcement," deported members reorganized themselves abroad and then "returned to the United States together with new recruits to spread through the United States in different locations."[274] Recently there has been a surge of reemigration of gang members from Central America to the United States.[275] This armed nonstate group spread within the United States from Los Angeles to New York and Washington, D.C., with each city unit operating relatively independently but with cross-city coordination increasing of late.[276]

The Mara Salvatrucha's two principal sources of income are the drug trade and extortion,[277] as the protection racket is very much a part of its profitable operations. The Mara Salvatrucha is now complicit in committing a wide variety of crimes, including random killings and assassinations for hire, hijackings, theft, rape, and assaults on law enforcement officials. On the international level, the group engages in drug smuggling, gun running, and human trafficking.[278] Unlike local petty street gangs, Mara Salvatrucha's global infrastructure has facilitated a much larger and more dangerous scale of operations.

In terms of the stability impact, the Mara Salvatrucha initially had positive stability implications for the affected El Salvadoran community, providing

El Salvadoran immigrants living in a hostile environment in Los Angeles with protection of their person and belongings. The American government and urban police officials have often deliberately avoided inner city conflict areas because of the costs, risks, and lack of positive security payoffs, and this decision has meant that many inhabitants of these areas were either completely vulnerable to gang violence and extortion or completely relying on gangs for security. The Mara Salvatrucha gangs in West Los Angeles offered "street protection, refuge from home, and alternative family, and financial security"; as well as "stability, identity, status, and protection."[279] For the El Salvadoran migrants, the Mara Salvatrucha provided for basic survival needs, an internal system of rules and order, and insulation from the disruptive presence of nearby rival gangs, even though there was no relief from the intrusion of violent conflicts. This security emerged in an area largely devoid of any form of effective government protection. Even the richest advanced industrial society in the world contains areas where the central state government and public police knowingly cede authority to an armed nonstate group. However, from a United States government internal security perspective, the Mara Salvatrucha has posed a major threat to law enforcement authorities: American law enforcement has become concerned "that MS-13's evolution from decentralized cliques to a more formal command-and-control structure could hasten the shift from its focus on marginally profitable small-scale crime—such as neighborhood drug dealing and armed robbery—to high-profit criminal enterprises such as overseeing major drug-smuggling or arms-trafficking networks; shifts of this nature traditionally lead to a rise in high-profile violence such as assassinations, kidnappings and large-scale gang warfare as competing gangs battle for control of the businesses."[280]

The return of Mara Salvatrucha members to Central America has hurt regional stability.

> The U.S. deportations are damaging Central American stability—as understaffed, under-funded and ultimately ineffective security and intelligence services attempt to battle the gangs. For example, simultaneous prison riots broke out across Guatemala on Aug. 15, pitting MS-13 members against their rival 18th Street gang. During the fighting, police lost control of several prisons as MS-13 members—some of whom were armed with assault rifles and grenades—attacked their 18th Street enemies. Security forces later regained control of the prison, but not until after 35 people had died. The level of coordination and the

type of weapons used by the prisoners illustrate MS-13's disturbing capability in Central America. In El Salvador, meanwhile, the government has instituted la mano dura (the strong-hand) policy to deal with the gangs, but has been unable to render MS-13 inert.[281]

As a result of state organizational and financial inabilities to address the gang problems, Mara Salvatrucha gangs are now flourishing not only in El Salvador, but also in Guatemala, Honduras, Panama, Costa Rica, and Mexico. In the long run, the security effects were devastating in Central America:

> The instability process tends to move from personal violence to increased col-
> lective violence and social disorder to kidnappings, bank robberies, violent
> property takeovers, murders/assassinations, personal and institutional cor-
> ruption, criminal anarchy, and the beginnings of internal and external refugee
> flows. In turn, the momentum of this coercive process tends to evolve into more
> widespread social violence, serious degradation of the economy, and further
> governmental inability to provide personal and national security and to guar-
> antee the rule of law.[282]

For example, "of the 138 murders committed in El Salvador in January 2005, 79 or 48.9 percent were committed by the maras"; and "in 2003, 60 percent of the criminal activities in El Salvador were due to the maras."[283] Members of Mara Salvatrucha are now truly "transnational in that they move readily throughout the region, including into and out of the United States and Canada"—"if they are pursued in one country, El Salvador for example, they move to neighboring Guatemala or Honduras to escape capture."[284] Unfortunately, common characteristics in the affected Central American countries make them vulnerable to violent street gang activity: "the political institutions are new, democratic legitimacy is problematic, the countries are poor, social problems huge, the military are supposed to be out of domestic roles and missions, and the police are inadequate; and, the rule of law, with all of the bases in law, enforcement, and the judicial system, remains tentative."[285] Indeed, "the maras are already acting as surrogate or alternate governments in some areas, including in El Salvador and Guatemala," for "the governments have all but given up in some areas of the capitals, and the maras extract taxes on individuals and businesses: if people don't pay up, they are killed," as "the governments are unable to do anything about it due to a lack of police personnel and resources."[286] Furthermore, recently concerns have emerged about possible links between MS-13 and Islamist militants, particularly al-Qaeda.[287] In sum, "insofar as the maras threaten democratic values, respect for human rights, and territorial security and sovereignty, they are a threat to U.S. national security."[288]

POSSES IN JAMAICA

This case revolves around a drug-funded criminal group with political connections trying to assert control in urban areas outside of the central government's effective security reach. The Jamaican government's inability to extend promised social services and fulfill its part of the social contract has left a power vacuum that is being filled by posses (gangs). Their initial foray into drugs and gunrunning began in the early 1980s. The Jamaican posses have some affiliation with Jamaican political parties, including the Jamaica Labour Party (JLP)and the People's National Party (the Jamaica Labour Party posses control mainly the west and south sides of Kingston, Jamaica; and the People's National Party posses mostly operate in the eastern and central sides of the city). As with most gangs in Central America, the Jamaican posses are the by-product of poverty, unemployment, lack of social mobility, deportation of Jamaican criminals from the United States, and political problems in the country.[289] Indeed, the main motivation behind the posses is business and economic gain,[290] as "a lack of opportunity and unemployment is key to young people's involvement in gangs."[291] The organization of the Jamaican posses is hierarchical, with powerful leadership, middle managers, and workers at the bottom: at least 85 different posses exist, with anywhere between 2,500 to 20,000 members.[292] Partly as a result of the posses' nefarious activities, Jamaicans often rate gangs and gun violence as the most serious forms of violence in the country: "between 1999 and 2001, there were more than 2760 murders in Jamaica, and homicide rates in the vicinity of 40 murders per 100,000 inhabitants have placed Jamaica near the top of the list of countries with the highest rates in the world."[293]

Because the Jamaican government realizes that it is powerless against the posses, a delicate relationship has developed between the posses and the state, necessitating some level of mutual sensitivity. Because the government is unable to provide essential services, many citizens perceive the posses as legitimate.[294] The role of the Jamaican posses has changed over time: "in the past, gangs were at the beck and call of politicians"; then "gangs analysed what politicians did to get control"; now "gangs set up a mechanism that allows them to be independent and no longer totally dependent on the power structure."[295] A Jamaican gang leader states, "We have our own justice, the state does not provide justice; that is one of the things that gives rise to gangs—inadequate justice."[296]

In Jamaica, the local gangs make significantly more money than the government and are better equipped militarily. This disparity is noteworthy given the economic decline and demographic explosion of the country as a whole:

> [W]hile the decades from 1950 to 1970 were a period of progressive economic growth based on colonial exports, such as sugar and bananas, and diversification into manufacturing industry, bauxite extraction and tourism, the following three decades have been characterised by economic decline, stagnation under structural adjustment (introduced in the 1980s), and increasing dependence on tourism (much as the economy was dependent on tropical exports before 1950). To compound matters further, the period 1990–2000 has seen debt payments more than double so that they account for almost half the GDP, while the doubling of the population in Kingston between 1960 and 1991 has spurred the development of the city's colonial slums into an impenetrable and violent ghetto.[297]

Indeed, "today it is estimated that any given gang-cartel combination earns more money in a year from its illicit activities than any Caribbean country generates in legitimate revenues."[298] Illicit drug revenues are crucial here, as "Kingston has emerged as a node in the international drug network linking Colombia to the UK and the USA"—"Jamaican posses rapidly became street-level dealers for Latin American drug runners"; and "Kingston now stands at the centre of a US$3–3.6 billion dollar crack-cocaine trafficking network, the value of which was estimated as equivalent to 40–50 percent of Jamaica's Gross Domestic Product in 2001."[299] Jamaican criminal drug traffickers may have "switched to cocaine because of the relative ease with which it can be shipped, in comparison to marijuana, and because of the large profits to be made."[300] Beyond cocaine, the posses also have been trafficking other illicit drugs such as heroin, PCP, and methamphetamine, as well as engaging in falsifying documents and monetary transactions.[301] Finally, "recruitment to the downtown Kingston gangs is constantly fuelled by the deprivation of the ghetto, expressed particularly in low-class status and unemployment, and the stigma attached to anyone who lives there."[302]

Despite their disruptive activity, the Jamaican posses have provided considerable local security. These posses provide a wide variety of protective services to Jamaica's marginalized population. The posses exemplify a reasonably effective form of nonstate provision of social services, such as education, public health, and employment, with an eerie similarity to traditional state governance:

> The local gang maintains its own system of law and order, complete with a hold-
> ing cell fashioned from an old chicken coop and a street-corner court. It "taxes"
> local business in return for protecting them, punishing those who refuse to pay
> with attacks on property and people. It provides a rudimentary welfare safety
> net by helping locals with school fees, lunch money, and employment—a func-
> tion that the . . . government used to perform. But over the last couple of de-
> cades, keen to reduce spending, it has scaled back many of its operations, leaving
> a vacuum. As one kind of authority has withdrawn, another has advanced.[303]

The posses are ruthlessly violent toward anyone they feel has disrespected them; and because they are deeply engaged in illicit drug activity, they participate in gun battles with the police, shootings of rival gang members, and killings of their own members who steal illicit drug profits. Yet they also can act as social workers in their respective neighborhoods.[304] Specifically, "the central gang members, who tend to be only a few young men, are in charge of nearly every aspect of the communities and areas they control—essentially becoming a local government; they rule through intimidation and violence, as well as provide protection and welfare services, such as distributing food and materials for education, and allocating jobs to impoverished areas neglected by the state."[305] Thus, despite the persistence of violence, the posses provide for basic survival needs to the area population, and even implement a form of local justice to establish rules and order in an area where state control is receding.

Since the state does not consistently fulfill its end of the social contract— "areas of Kingston are out of the control of state authority"[306]—the posses seem to be the only potential sources of stability in many areas. In fact, "the proliferation of small gangs and inter-gang disputes, protection of drug turf, and revenge killings have marginalised political actors in the violent events of downtown Kingston" to the point that "the balance of power in the communities has shifted to gang leaders away from the elected political representatives, and many dons who command 'respect' are regarded as neighbourhood protectors, despite their reliance on violence."[307] Indeed, "politicians have been replaced as the primary source of economic and lethal resources by 'drug dons,' known euphemistically as 'community leaders.'"[308] More specifically, "the dons provide services that the state cannot—patronage, favors, conflict resolution, and a sort of neighborhood court of appeals, not to mention employment in the narcotics business."[309] However, recently the situation in Jamaica has deteriorated to the point where many Jamaicans now complain that their country "suffers from severe anarchy and violence."[310]

Traditionally, the police have been complicit in the posses' provision of protection:

> Jamaica's police have a long history of giving protection to ghetto gunmen, originally at the behest of the politicians. With the politicians out of the picture, the police have been increasingly drawn into a one-to-one relation with the gunmen. The tradeoff is one involving the offer of protection by the police from the law, and payment for that protection (or the offer of a share in drug profits) by the gunmen.[311]

In contrast, "in recent years the Jamaican police have developed a zero-tolerance to gang activities, including drug trafficking, and many dons have died in assassinations carried out by specialist police squads, such as the Anti-Crime Investigative Detachment and the more recently formed Crime Management Unit."[312] Thus, it has become more difficult for the posses to thrive.

Nevertheless, Jamaican posses have promoted regional political instability. They "project power to overseas outposts, largely in the United States, Canada, and the United Kingdom (where they are known as 'yardies')"; in turn, "posses in the United States ship guns, ammunition, illegal aliens, drugs, and money to and from their counterpart gangs back home."[313] The result is ominous from a security perspective: "turf wars fought in U.S. cities are played out along the same lines as in Jamaica, and assassinations are ordered in the United States for targets in Jamaica and vice versa."[314] In the process, Jamaican posses have collaborated with other criminal groups, including Los Angeles-based gangs and Nigerian thugs.[315]

TALIBAN IN AFGHANISTAN

This case revolves around a tribal Muslim militant group trying to establish control within a country with a weak central state government. The Taliban originated near Kandahar as a small group who followed the teachings of a mullah who later offered sanctuary and support to Osama bin Laden and al-Qaeda.[316] The group governed most of Afghanistan and its capital city of Kabul between September 1996 and October 2001.

The Taliban was initially a mixture of mujahideen who fought against the Soviet invasion of the 1980s, and a group of Pashtun tribesmen who spent time in Pakistani religious schools, or *madrassas*, and received assistance from Pakistan's Inter-Services Intelligence agency. The leaders practiced Wahhabism, an orthodox form of Sunni Islam similar to that practiced in Saudi Arabia; these leaders' interpretation of Islamic law has been criticized by Muslim leaders as unorthodox. With the help of government defections, the Taliban emerged as a force in Afghan politics in 1994 in the midst of a civil war between forces in northern and southern Afghanistan: "the Taliban graduated from being one of the many armed groups to a dominant political force when they seized a large stockpile of arms in 1994 and took Kandahar by October—suddenly, Afghanistan had a new military force with which to be reckoned."[317] Indeed, "discontented with the rule of the mujahideen, the Taliban, a traditionalist Islamic player, initiated an internal jihad campaign starting in 1994, with the aim of achieving some form of order and implementing Sharia, Islamic law, in the country."[318] The Taliban gained an initial territorial foothold in the southern city of Kandahar, and over the next two years expanded their influence through a mixture of force and negotiation. On September 28, 1996, the Taliban captured Kabul, the Afghan capital, and took control of the national government. Its goals were "liberating Afghanistan from the corrupt leadership of warlords and establishing a pure Islamic society."[319] Once in control, the Taliban solidified its ties to Osama bin Laden.[320]

The Taliban has relied heavily on the opium trade for financial resources,[321] as at its peak it controlled 96 percent of Afghanistan's poppy fields,[322] and the drug trade allegedly has provided $100 million a year to this armed nonstate group.[323] An irony is embedded here, for the Taliban claims to operate under Islamic law, yet that law forbids drug trafficking.[324] The Taliban taxes poppy farmers, drug laboratories, and storage facilities using a sophisticated illicit network, and to augment its income it extorts supplies from shopkeepers and from trucking, construction, and telecommunication firms.[325] Notably, "Pakistan has also given strong diplomatic support to the Taliban, in accordance with its recognition of the Taliban regime in 1997, backing its position in the international arena; besides official Pakistani support, the Taliban was supported financially and militarily by Pakistan's intelligence service and developed ties with influential lobbies and private commercial groups, which traded goods and smuggled contraband, including an extensive trade in narcotics, between the two countries."[326] Today, despite having been removed from controlling power in Afghanistan by the United States, "remnants of the Taliban are being aided by al-Qaeda operatives, powerful warlords, and drug-trafficking organizations";[327]

and these remnants "have terrorist capabilities, deploy insurgent technologies, such as improvised explosive devices, draw a steady income from the narcotics trade, and enjoy support from a network of madrasahs."[328] Recently, the Taliban introduced a new code of conduct to try to reduce extortion and exploitation of the local population, but these new regulations have received only spotty enforcement.[329]

The West has long associated Taliban rule with the spread of transnational terrorism. In retrospect it is ironic that the United States supported the Taliban from 1994 to 1996 because the American government viewed the Taliban as anti-Iranian and potentially pro-Western.[330] However, the United States quickly changed its policy as it began to realize that from the time the Soviets withdrew from Afghanistan in 1989, "a chaotic, Taliban-dominated Afghanistan and adjoining areas of Pakistan became hospitable venues for the continued training, recruitment, indoctrination, and team-building of violent jihadist groups whose resentments would be focused elsewhere."[331] In August 1998, "as the Taliban was about to take over the entire country, U.S. missiles destroyed camps near Kabul run by Osama bin Laden, who was accused of being responsible for the 1998 bombings of the American embassies in Kenya and Tanzania."[332] Although Pakistan's position changed somewhat after the 9/11 terrorist attacks on the United States, and "although the Pakistani government is formally an American ally in its war on terrorism, the border areas between Afghanistan and Pakistan, particularly North Waziristan, have become a safe haven for the Taliban and al-Qaeda forces to regroup and train," and "the Taliban is now operating from Pakistan and is one of the main sources of violence in Afghanistan."[333]

After the 9/11 attacks on the United States, President George W. Bush demanded that the Taliban turn over Osama bin Laden and the al-Qaeda leadership; when the Taliban refused, the United States and its allies began military operations against the Taliban on October 7, 2001. The invasion's goals were to remove the Taliban from power and prevent Afghanistan from being used as a terrorist base. The Taliban "was defeated after nine weeks, and then, along with al-Qaeda forces, turned instead to waging continuous guerrilla warfare against the coalition troops in Afghanistan."[334] Before its formal ouster by United States–led forces in December 2001, the Taliban controlled some 90 percent of Afghanistan's territory, although it was never officially recognized by the United Nations.[335] After the Taliban was defeated, chaotic warlord politics reemerged,[336] with the Taliban insurgents fighting the American-backed government regime in Kabul. In 2005, "the armed conflict between remnants of the ousted Taliban regime and the Afghan government escalated further"; in 2007, "the intensity of the Taliban insurgency reached new heights"; and from 2008 onward, "violence remained at a high level."[337] Currently the group continues its struggle in Afghanistan and northwest Pakistan.

The stability impact of the Taliban is mixed, with one analyst concluding that the Taliban in Afghanistan is "as destabilizing as it is stabilizing."[338] Prior to the Taliban's rise to power in 1994, the $2.5-billion-a-year opium trade "was critically hampered by predatory warlords"; in contrast, "the emergence of the Taliban presented the traffickers with a regulatory force that could assure the transaction costs were significantly lowered and business was carried out in a more predictable fashion."[339] Angry at the excesses of the predatory warlords, the Taliban "willingly provided protection to the illicit smuggling enterprise"— "not only did the reduction in transaction costs satisfy the needs of the traffickers, but it also greatly pleased the general population, who also found it much easier to move their products to markets"[340] There is little doubt that the Taliban, governed by its extremist ideology, perpetuated widespread violence and engaged in severe human rights violations, particularly toward women, who were often publicly abused and were often sold into sex slavery through human trafficking networks. At the same time, the Taliban in its heyday provided basic survival protection to much of the population, kept disruptive warlords at bay, and through application of Islamic law instilled a crude justice system to enforce rules and order.

Many citizens in Afghanistan saw some benefit, especially initially, from Taliban rule:

> Public reaction to the Taliban's rule was not wholly negative. While the rigid social standards fostered resentment, the Taliban cracked down on the corruption that had run rampant through the government for years. The new leaders also brought stability to Afghanistan, greatly reducing the infighting between warlords that had devastated the civilian population. Seven years after their ouster, the Taliban continues to provide a semblance of stability in regions where coalition and government officials have been unable to restore order and provide basic service.[341]

Weary from the seemingly unending violence and corruption associated with warring warlords, many Afghans were at first positively disposed toward the Taliban. So American opposition to the Taliban and association of the group with al-Qaeda's terrorism has not always been embraced by the mass public (although segments of the population have been sympathetic). As a result of the American ending of Taliban rule, "for now, the prospects of peace and stability in a reconstructed Afghanistan do not seem very promising, certainly not in the near future."[342] Sporadic fighting continues, and—regardless how long U.S. troops remain in Afghanistan—"the military actions used decisively to defeat the Iraqi army and overthrow Taliban forces in Afghanistan have spurred persistent insurgencies in both countries, resulting in very unstable and dangerous environments."[343]

Afghanistan is a tribal region, and to a certain extent the Taliban united tribes under the umbrella of religion. Although this does not reflect Western notions of stability, one could argue that strict religious laws contributed to the stability of the country (to the extent that it was ever a reasonably united state). Tribes, not the central government, have historically been the sources of stability in Afghanistan:

> [T]he concept of autonomy in Afghanistan has strong roots in its social and political history. For centuries, ethnic and communal groups lived in their own territory, independent from one another. Traditional society was fragmented and segmented . . . only when there was an external threat did these autonomous groups come together and form a united front to fight the invading forces. Throughout Afghanistan's modern history there were many attempts by the central government to take away autonomy from the local ethnic groups. These attempts created a wide range of armed resistance by the local community against the central government, which kept the notion of autonomy strong among ethnic and communal groups.[344]

In particular, "the ethnic fragmentation of Afghan society impeded the establishment of central governments to employ effective and permanent control over the numerous peoples making up Afghan society."[345] When there is no tradition of central government, people may not trust state regimes and instead prefer nonstate actors as sources of stability. When there is no emotional or practical allegiance to a government, it seems unlikely that the population will challenge the dominance of armed nonstate groups. When times get rough, there is a demand for security and—in the absence of public patriotism—people do not question from where the supply comes.

The chaotic security context for Taliban rule in Afghanistan helps explain the stability and security benefits from this rule perceived by some:

Neighbors of two girls kidnapped and raped by Kandahar warlords asked the Taliban's help in freeing the teenagers. The Taliban attacked a military camp, freed the girls, and executed the commander. Later, another squad of Taliban freed a young boy over whom two warlords were fighting for the right to sodomize. A Robin Hood myth grew up around Mullah Umar resulting in victimized Afghans increasingly appealing to the Taliban for help against local oppressors.[346]

In the aftermath of the war with the Soviet Union, warlords and criminals effectively ruled Afghanistan, and "this chaotic social and political environment gave rise to a vacuum of leadership and gave momentum to the appearance of a political force that promised to stop the infighting and further destruction of the country."[347] The mere appearance of a united, stability-enhancing group in Afghanistan led many Afghans to believe in a more secure future for their country.

As the United States sought to end Taliban rule in Afghanistan, initially neither of the "United States' two main security interests in Afghanistan that justify waging a war" focused directly on restoring stability within the country: "one, that terrorists who wish to strike the United States and its allies not use Afghanistan as their base; and two, that insurgent groups not use Afghanistan's territory to destabilize its neighbours, especially Pakistan."[348] However, in 2005, following the American government's recognition that "failed and failing states are breeding grounds for terrorists and insurgents,"[349] the American mission statement changed, and the objective for the war in Afghanistan transformed into "stability operations," elevated "as a core mission comparable to combat operations."[350] Unfortunately, while "a key part of the U.S. stabilization effort is to build the capacity of the Afghan government," that "objective that appears to be making only slow progress, particularly in the southern provinces."[351] Stabilization efforts have met with some modest success but have been unsatisfactory in terms of how quickly these gains have been achieved, and how vast the resource expenditures have been to achieve such modest gains. Stability operations often seemed doomed to fail from the outset, because the underlying original instability causes were not rectified and any temporary stability gains were not self-sustaining after eventual American withdrawal. Moreover, "vague mission, vague roles, and insufficient resources created significant civil-military tensions,"[352] leading to doubts about the military's ability military to create strong enough bonds with villagers to make a meaningful impact.

Efforts to promote stability in Afghanistan also have been impeded by "the lack of coordination among the different agencies and organisations involved" and have "hindered any systematic planning for the activation of local development strategies"; especially puzzling was that these efforts "often did not prevent ex-combatants from being re-absorbed by new or old systems of patronage run by warlords and local commanders."[353] The American killing of Osama bin Laden on May 4, 2011, did little to change the pattern of instability, although there is some evidence that the Obama administration has secretly entered into direct talks with senior Afghan Taliban leaders to explore peace possibilities.[354]

In terms of broader regional security implications, "the long-standing violent conflict in Afghanistan has had spillover effects in neighboring countries in Asia and implications for international stability."[355] Specifically, "the Taliban conquest of Kabul and the continuing civil war endangered the stability of the Central Asian republics, which were particularly threatened by the potential rise of antiregime Islamic movements; these threats led Tajikistan to allow Russian deployment along its border with Afghanistan, to prevent any possible Taliban incursions and to rein in the smuggling of opium and heroin into Tajikistan."[356] The Taliban's harboring of terrorist elements also posed a threat to regional instability, allowing a base of disruptive operations that could easily affect neighboring countries as well as the world at large.

YAKUZA IN JAPAN

This case revolves around a criminal group providing basic survival needs to natural disaster victims in response to the sluggishness of the central state government. On January 17, 1995, the port city of Kobe, Japan, experienced a 7.2 magnitude earthquake.[357] It had the equivalent impact of more than 340 kilotons of TNT, killed more than 5,500 people, left more than 300,000 homeless, and destroyed more than 199,999 houses, with total damage estimated at $95 billion.[358] The response of the Japanese government to this natural disaster was both slow and ineffective. The government was reluctant to swallow its pride and ask for help from its Self-Defense Forces, causing four hours to pass between when the quake hit and when officials finally requested aid, and internal military assistance took a full two days to arrive in force.[359] Bureaucratic red tape blocked Japanese relief efforts, as the government bureaucracy appeared to be "more concerned with the preservation of its own control, of the national 'face,' than with emergency relief . . . when the crisis struck, the central government was paralyzed, and the city, prefectural, and national police, fire brigades, water authorities, highway authorities, and Self-Defense Forces were shown to be unreliable."[360] Although Japanese s rarely rail against their government, in this case there was widespread criticism of the ineptitude of the official authorities, and even the prime minister admitted that the government response had been "confused."[361]

Into this void stepped a transnational criminal organization—the Japanese Yakuza. There are upward of 86,000 members operating under this Japanese criminal umbrella.[362] This venerable criminal nexus dates back to 1612, though it was not until the nineteenth century that many of the currently prominent factions emerged. With the unification of Japan at the beginning of the seventeenth century, some of the samurai warrior class formed gangs and "committed frequent outrages against ordinary townspeople."[363] Today, "membership is not illegal although the police regulate their activities."[364] The Yakuza have evolved over the years, and there is now somewhat of a generational divide: while the older generations have been known for their obedience to hierarchy and to Yakuza law, many younger recruits are considered to be "punks" and reckless, so much so that now "older members are dismayed with the decline of moral values and increasing gun use among the up and coming generation of Yakuza."[365]

Relations between the Japanese police and the Yakuza are symbiotic, with reciprocity an ingrained part of the system, allowing each to survive in its own sphere. For example, occasionally the Yakuza will allow the raiding police to confiscate some of its weapons or illicit goods so the police appear to be accomplishing their given task,[366] and sometimes police may ignore Yakuza activities or accept bribes to drop charges.[367] This relationship exists not just for profit, but also because "there is a great deal of personal rapport between the Yakuza and the police; local cops know local gangsters by name, and there is an easy familiarity between them."[368] In addition, many Japanese law enforcement officers have right-wing political views, making them sympathetic to the Yakuza members who "are ultra-nationalistic and conservative on matters of foreign policy" and "vigorously anti-communist."[369] The Yakuza seems alone among transnational criminal organizations in possessing such a high level of home state legitimacy. The government can move forward and pass new laws limiting or putting pressure on the Yakuza, but it is impossible to cut them off because the Yakuza have been such a tradition and because the two entities have become fused together. If the two were cut from one another, the state government would be in trouble because so many corrupt politicians would still seek the material comforts they had received from the Yakuza; and the Yakuza would find themselves at a loss without state access and would fight not only against the government but also against other factions to gain the upper hand. The result would be a destabilizing, endless war in which the economy would suffer, with both sides fighting for power and continuing to attempt to manipulate key Japanese companies over which they had influence.

The Yakuza are similarly embedded in Japanese society. From magazines to movies to video games, the Yakuza play a prominent role in Japanese pop culture and have woven themselves into the fabric of the society, so much so that even well-established rules seem to bend for them. They make themselves untouchable by setting up, manipulating, or taking over companies with close connections to the government. Armed with "the unique advantage of relative acceptance within Japanese culture,"[370] "what differentiates the Yakuza from other organized crime groups is the societal acceptance of its members": "membership is respected and these 'businessmen' carry business cards and conduct operations out of offices alongside legitimate businesses." The Yakuza even hire out on occasion to protect against other criminal groups.[371]

In terms of funding, during the 1960s and 1970s, the Yakuza began to delve into the illicit drug trade, and more recently the group has engaged in arms and contraband smuggling. By 1989 the Yakuza received one-third of its income from the sale of drugs, one-third from gambling, protection payments, and intervention in civil disputes, and one-third from indeterminate sources.[372] More recently, aside from drug running and the sex trade, Yakuza criminal operations began skimming a percentage of laborers' wages; smuggling weapons; engaging in loan-shark activities; running underground protection, security, and legal services; coercively acquiring valuable real estate; facilitating local prostitution; forcing kickbacks in the construction industry; pirating products in the entertainment industry; and indulging in gambling and extortion (with annual profits from protection rackets alone estimated at nearly $1 billion).[373] In 2007, Yakuza overall black market business earnings alone were estimated at over $10 billion.[374]

Yet the Japanese Yakuza positively affected stability in the wake of the Kobe earthquake. Their efficient provision of much-needed assistance to the citizens after the earthquake[375] illustrates the capacity of an armed nonstate group to respond with greater speed than a state during crises. Although there was no ongoing violent external conflict needing resolution, no violent internal conflict, and no danger of unwanted disruptive coercive foreign intervention, and no need to institute a functioning law-and-order system because the central government had one in place, the Japanese Yakuza was successful in providing for basic survival needs to a panicked population at a time of grave emergency. The Yakuza's image incorporated a Robin Hood quality after the Kobe earthquake—"the Yamaguchi-gumi Yakuza clan quickly mobilized providing ·on the scene assistance to Kobe's earthquake victims long before the national government resolved to act."[376]

> In the absence of prompt and effective response by governmental authorities, non-governmental organizations such as the infamous *yakuza*—relying on their nationwide network and clear lines of authority—were able to transport relief supplies (water, food, toiletries, diapers, etc.) to the Kobe area and distribute them to local residents with considerable aplomb and efficiency.[377]

The Yakuza gained respect by handing out free food and water to those made homeless by the earthquake:[378] the Yakuza claimed that they distributed approximately 8,000 meals per day,[379] and that they "eventually gave away nearly 1 billion yen worth of goods and 20,000 free boxed lunches."[380] However, this generous aid may not have been motivated by pure altruism:

> "Right after the earthquake, the yakuza came here and set up a stand to serve noodles for free, and I was kind of impressed," said one woman who was made homeless in the quake. "But then afterward, they asked for a written testimonial saying how great they were, so they could take it to city hall and get more construction business."[381]

Nonetheless, this Yakuza action highlighted government ineffectiveness in a security crisis. At a time of such emergency, rapid speed and tight organization were at a premium, and this criminal group outdid the state in this regard.

The case of the Yakuza suggests that, because of the inelastic demand for security in areas with high living standards, in well-run democratic advanced industrial societies citizens may be willing to take advantage of aid from criminal organizations, or any armed nonstate group for that matter, in emergency situations when no government assistance is immediately in sight. To most people, the idea of preserving a moral high ground with regard to criminals, warlords, rebels, and terrorists may be appealing only for so long as they have ready access to basics such as food, water, and protection. During a crisis such as an earthquake that disrupts the ability of the mass public to get survival

needs, it is not uncommon for central state governments to be unable to mobilize and respond as quickly as needed, and so it is not surprising that more
decentralized and flexible armed nonstate groups might have an advantage in
providing assistance. Even though Japan has a long history of earthquakes, and
the Japanese government had felt beforehand that it was prepared for such a
disaster because of the careful way construction had been done, the scope and
devastation wrought by the Kobe earthquake was so large that it was beyond
the government's capacity to handle in a timely fashion. Although in contrast
the Yakuza had done no preparation for disaster relief, the criminal group was
in a better position to provide immediate assistance. Given that long before the
earthquake the Yakuza already had a high level of acceptance among government officials and the public, the group—seizing on an opportunity to further
its objectives—was in a prime position to step in and help. Interestingly, to
keep from undermining government authority, "there is an unwritten agreement amongst the police and the Yakuza groups that is acceptable for them to
perform volunteer activities during a crisis but not to seek publicity for it."[382]

No regional stability effects are evident in this case, because the disaster
affected only Japan—an insulated island state. Neither the natural disaster disruption nor the criminal relief affected other countries. Despite some positive
appreciation for its efforts in this case, the Yakuza did not inspire other transnational criminal organizations—or other types of armed nonstate groups—
in other societies to attempt to play a role in natural disaster relief in subsequent years.

The March 11, 2011, Sendai earthquake (with its associated severe nuclear
reactor problems) showed the persistence of the patterns evidenced in this
case. In the 2011 Sendai disaster, the Yakuza provided the same kind of stability-
enhancing response as it did in Kobe in 1995. It was reported in 2011 that "in
regions where official rescue/aid teams have not established a foothold, Yakuza
are setting up mobile aid tents to give out supplies and provide shelter for the
disaster victims":[383] specifically, "Yakuza groups have been sending trucks from
the Tokyo and Kobe regions to deliver food, water, blankets and toiletries to
evacuation centres in northeast Japan, the area devastated by the March 11
earthquake and tsunami which have left at least 27,000 dead and missing."[384]
In addition, the Yakuza reportedly helped direct traffic in the Tohoku region,
opened their offices as shelters, and sent supplies to the reactor site.[385] The
Yakuza moved more than 100 tons of supplies to the Tohoku region and even

went into radiated areas "without any protection or potassium iodide"; as a Yakuza member said, "There are no yakuza or katagi (ordinary citizens) or gaijin (foreigners) in Japan right now. We are all Japanese. We all need to help each other."[386] One again, as with the Kobe earthquake, this positive and stabilizing action by the Yakuza received hardly any publicity, and as a result the image of the criminal organization remained unchanged from the past.

6 ANALYSIS OF CASE STUDY PATTERNS

THE CASE STUDY FINDINGS illuminate overarching patterns about the success and failure of armed nonstate groups and armed nonstate group control attempts, as well as the conditions when armed nonstate groups promote and retard stability, and the additional lessons learned. Although tentative, given their reliance on twelve case studies, these patterns appear to be robust. Because recent history reveals that proper differentiation has not occurred in this regard, the results of this investigation seem salient in helping to refine security policy.

The first step in this analysis—examining the relative success among the major types of armed nonstate groups and armed nonstate group control attempts—enhances comparative understanding of the differences involved. Some winners and some losers emerge from the findings, as summarized in Figure 6.1, which highlights the marked disparities between armed nonstate groups and confirming the need for discrimination among them.

RELATIVE SUCCESS OF ARMED NONSTATE GROUPS

The five major types of armed nonstate groups, whose differences were described in Chapter 3, are not all equally effective in enhancing stability. From a conceptual standpoint, at first glance considerable controversy appears to surround the identification of which groups are best and worst for stability promotion. On one hand, armed nonstate groups that respond to economic incentives and are reasonably accepting of the status quo—criminals and mercenaries—seem to be the most promising. The logic here is that, if an armed nonstate group is status quo oriented and responds to a state's positive and negative incentives, then it is much more susceptible to outside state influence

Figure 6.1. Stability promotion winners and losers

Among armed nonstate groups

The winners are criminals and mercenaries, as the outcome usually enhances stability at least temporarily and locally.

The losers are rebels/insurgents and warlords, for most of these groups generate, at best, mixed, stability outcomes.

Among stability functions

The winner is fulfilment of basic survival needs to the population, as armed nonstate groups usually supply them.

The loser is absence of internal violent conflict, as local violence usually continues with armed nonstate groups.

Among armed nonstate group control attempts in terms of governance dilemmas that elicit armed nonstate group action

The winner is where there is an ineffective central state government, which invites armed nonstate group involvement.

The loser is where multiple factions are coercively competing for power, which fosters turmoil.

Among armed nonstate group control attempts in terms of armed nonstate group responses to governance dilemmas

The winner is where control attempts exhibit high internal commitment, external support, and strategic adaptability.

The loser is where control attempts exhibit low internal commitment, external support, and strategic adaptability.

---

in its quest for control of particular areas, and it is much more likely through a top-down process to see stability as serving its own self-interest. On the other hand, armed nonstate groups able to combine using fear and terror tactics with attracting respect and sympathy from the affected population in their ideological fervor to pursue non–status quo goals—terrorists and rebels/insurgents—seem to be the most promising (warlords, which have mixed attributes in this regard, fall in neither camp). The logic of this claim is that, if an armed nonstate group has coherent ideals for reshaping the world in a non–status quo direction, then through generating fear and respect from the mass public it is much more likely in a bottom-up way to be able to create a stable security environment.

Patterns Linked to Armed Nonstate Groups

In reflecting on this conceptual controversy, it appears that the benefits of top-down malleability and reluctance to radically overturn existing norms (fitting in with the existing system, appealing more to satisfied elites who simply want order restored) would outweigh the benefits of ideological coherence for stimulating bottom-up extreme change (appealing to frustrated masses who want revolutionary transformation). Even though (as Chapter 3 points out) the primary advantage of private compared to public stability enhancers lies in the ability of private groups to focus on bottom-up human security needs, the top-down sensitivity of certain armed nonstate groups to state norms and preferences seems more important in this context. Although criminals and mercenaries can be vulnerable to criticism "for acting with excessive expediency and for accepting unfair status quos or corrupt leaders in the interests of pursuing other goals," "thereby sacrificing longer term improvements in governance,"[1] they do seem to have a general advantage over rebels/insurgents and terrorists in creating stability. Private militias are simply more predictable than ideological rebels.

From an empirical standpoint, the case study findings roughly confirm this expectation. The winners here are criminals and mercenaries, as when these groups initiate security control attempts the outcome usually enhances stability at least temporarily and locally. In contrast, the losers are terrorists, rebels/insurgents, and warlords, for most cases studied these groups generated, at best, mixed stability outcomes. Those groups with narrower interests incorporating more pragmatism and flexibility (such as Executive Outcomes) seem likelier to enhance stability, while those with broader ideological goals (such as the IRA and LRA) incorporating societal transformation in predetermined ways seem likelier to be disruptive and instability-promoting.

Broader Power-Sharing Implications

The relative success of armed nonstate groups requires broad historical reflection beyond this study's twelve cases when considering the potential for power sharing between states and nonstate groups. In examining patterns across time, mercenaries have for centuries been hired by states to do their bidding, and criminal organizations have long established collusive relationships with state governments. Because these two groups are motivated by money rather than ideology, states have found that they can control these groups to their advantage. In contrast, because terrorists and rebels/insurgents are inherently antagonistic toward the existing state regime, successful power-sharing arrangements with the state have not been historically evident.

Mercenaries perhaps have been the most common type of armed nonstate group used for enhancing stability. Mercenaries differ from the other armed groups in that their basic mission is usually to help restore order in a chaotic society, so "within the post-Cold War environment, those experiencing a variety of different forms of disruptive turmoil have begun to turn more to private security providers as a crucial component of the solutions to these problems."[2] In past decades, many states have hired mercenaries, including Afghanistan, Angola, Colombia, Congo-Brazzaville, the Democratic Republic of the Congo, Ethiopia, the former Yugoslavia, Haiti, Kashmir, Liberia, Papua New Guinea, Rwanda, Senegal, Sierra Leone, Sudan, the United Arab Emirates, and Vatican City;[3] and "accusations of mercenary employment" surround almost every recent conflict "from Chechnya to Bosnia, to Kashmir to Angola to Colombia."[4] However, criticism has surrounded the use of mercenaries for security purposes, and many observers oppose the use of private military personnel—even those associated with highly respected private security companies—to promote stability: for example, former United Nations Secretary General Kofi Annan remarked that "the world may not be ready to privatize peace,"[5] as there is no "distinction between respectable mercenaries and non-respectable mercenaries."[6]

As to criminals: historically, in many parts of the world, "non-state governance from below" has been commonplace, where national government authorities no longer monopolize policing functions, and instead criminal groups without official sanction attempt to identify and guard against emerging risks. These criminal groups may be "not entirely parasitic," as they may provide desired services, introduce "elements of order and dispute resolution," and serve as "a source of social stability and depoliticisation."[7] In recent decades, where "criminal networks take over law enforcement functions and monopolize violence at the local level, as well as engage in distributive and service-providing activities normally associated with the state, a local dependence on international networks of organized crime can develop. . . ."[8] Throughout much of West Africa, for example, transnational organized crime now controls many critical security functions. Thus many "parts of the upperworld need the underworld"[9] to survive and thrive. Globally, many marginalized populations have their security provided by criminal groups, to such an extent that these organizations pose the possibility of becoming "proto-states" in the future, replacing many of the state's political, military, and economic functions.[10] In transforming into an alternative form of "parallel state"—or "states-within-states"[11]—criminal groups may challenge national government legitimacy and provide needy populations, especially in weak states, with many benefits, including social advancement, security, and prohibited goods and services. However, trusting criminals to provide stability can be risky.

RELATIVE SUCCESS OF ARMED NONSTATE GROUP CONTROL ATTEMPTS

As with armed nonstate groups, the major types of armed nonstate group control attempts are not all equally successful in promoting stability. Moreover, the findings pertaining to governance dilemmas that elicit armed nonstate group action suggest that such attempts are unlikely to maximize all four stability functions simultaneously; and the findings pertaining to armed nonstate group responses to governance dilemmas suggest that such attempts are unlikely to achieve simultaneously the desirable combination of commitment, support, continuity, and adaptability. Thus caution needs to surround any attempt to identify any particular type of armed nonstate group control attempt as optimal.

Patterns Linked to Governance Dilemmas Eliciting Armed Nonstate Group Action

When considering governance dilemmas that elicit armed nonstate group control attempts, key patterns stand out. From a conceptual perspective, the most effective stability promotion occurs in a governance dilemma when (1) the security needs of all or part of states' citizenry remain unfulfilled, and (2) an armed nonstate groups attempts to address the second essential stability function—fulfillment of basic survival needs to the affected population:

> Whether violent or nonviolent, groups reap three main benefits from providing public goods through their social welfare aims. First, the creation of a social welfare infrastructure highlights the failure of the state to fulfill its side of the social contract, thereby challenging the legitimacy of the state. Second, nonstate social welfare organizations offer the population an alternative entity in which to place their loyalty. Third, a group that gains the loyalty of the populace commands a steady stream of resources with which it can wage battle against the regime.[12]

Conversely, the least effective stability promotion occurs in a governance dilemma when (1) multiple factions are warring over control within a state, and

(2) an armed nonstate group attempts to address the third essential stability function—cessation of internal violent conflict:

> The strategic culture of armed groups . . . has several common precepts: the conflict and the suffering entailed are constant conditions and not anomalies; the political and legal system is corrupt and is rigged to favor the elite; the gang or organization provides the only real protection, governance, and economic opportunity for the community; the use or threat of violence is everyday business, to be employed as a routine tool, not as a last resort; the support, submission, or passive acceptance of the population is essential to an armed group's ability to operate and continue.[13]

So given that turf protection is a primary goal of armed nonstate groups, that violent coercion is often a primary means of achieving this goal, and that eradicating violence is counter to many of these groups' cultural values, armed nonstate group control attempts have a considerably greater potential to help out with the second stability function (dealing with basic survival needs) than with the third stability function (focusing on cessation of internal violent conflict). This finding confirms the more general proposition that "the emergence of paramilitary bands in weak and divided societies often results in a sharp increase in civil violence,"[14] even with gains in other stability areas. The chaos in Somalia exemplifies the least conducive stability pattern.

An empirical evaluation of the evidence from the twelve cases confirms these patterns. Among governance dilemmas, the winner is where there is an inept central state government, as this opens the door to effective armed nonstate group action; and among essential stability functions, the winner is provision for basic survival needs to the population, as in virtually every case studied where armed nonstate groups enhanced stability, this needs provision was promoted and yielded certain important benefits. In contrast, the loser among governance dilemmas is where multiple internal factions are warring over control, as this fosters violence and turmoil; and the loser among stability functions is the absence of internal violent conflict, as in most of the cases armed nonstate groups initiated, perpetuated, or failed to end violence within the affected area, causing those protected to pay a price for their security. The case evidence reveals mixed results regarding the other two types of governance dilemmas that elicit armed nonstate group control attempts associated with the other two stability functions: a governance dilemma when (1) nobody is effectively in charge within a given territory and lawlessness prevails, and (2) armed nonstate groups attempt to address first essential stability function—promotion of rules and order; and a governance dilemma when (1) unsanctioned outside forces have seized power and are severely oppressing large numbers of people, and (2) an armed nonstate group attempts to address the fourth stability function—preclusion of unwanted disruptive external coercive intervention. Providing for basic survival needs under an inept regime thus is best for armed nonstate group stability promotion.

Patterns Linked to Armed Nonstate Group Responses to Governance Dilemmas

Key patterns emerge when evaluating armed nonstate group responses to governance dilemmas. From a conceptual perspective, armed nonstate group responses appear especially likely to be effective in enhancing stability when they exhibit high internal commitment, external support, predictable continuity, and strategic adaptability. This combination would entail high coercive strength and willingness to use one's capabilities; high support from the mass public, high outside funding and ties to state or other groups; highly consistent status quo orientation, high internal unity and duration of existence; and high openness to power sharing and highly realistic expectations about one's limitations. Despite problems in some dimensions, the Yakuza in Japan exemplifies many of these qualities. In contrast, armed state group responses appear especially likely to be ineffective in enhancing stability when they exhibit low internal commitment, external support, predictable continuity, and strategic adaptability. The Islamic Army of Aden in Yemen highlights these deficiencies.

From an empirical perspective, the evidence from the case studies seems to confirm these contentions. Because only major armed nonstate group control attempts were included in the twelve case studies, all exhibited high internal commitment in terms of coercive strength and willingness to use capabilities to pursue goals. However, a more informal examination of global post–Cold War instances where armed nonstate group control attempts lacked either coercive strength or willingness to apply it reveals that they not only had a negligible impact on stability, but also they largely failed to achieve any of their significant security objectives. In terms of external support, the cases demonstrate a general (though not invariable) relationship between stability promotion and armed nonstate group control attempts exhibiting the combination of high mass public approval and significant and diversified outside funding and ties to states or other nonstate groups. In terms of predictable continuity, the case evidence reveals a rough but positive link between stability promotion and armed nonstate group control attempts exhibiting highly consistent status quo orientation and high internal unity and duration. Finally, in terms of strategic adaptability, despite the subjective and intangible nature of openness to power sharing and realistic expectations about one's limitations, a consistent pattern was still discernible: the most stabilizing cases are those where public-private linkages and modest security goals—indicating openness to working with the state—associate with armed nonstate group responses to governance dilemmas.

Responses involving strong, willing, and unified armed nonstate groups with high domestic and international support and constrained status quo goals would thus be ideal candidates for stability promotion. The control attempts to be avoided at all costs are those associated with armed nonstate groups for whom the use of violence appears to be an end in itself, not a means toward an end, because it can be an intrinsic source of empowerment and identity. These disruptive, uncooperative groups following unprincipled "thuggism" may want violence, conflict, and instability to continue indefinitely.[15] While some armed nonstate groups certainly "do act with the intent of improving their communities or for some perceived public good," these more unruly groups "pursue less noble objectives such as increasing profit margins or eradicating a rival group; to this end, they benefit by the deepening of the roots of violence, which in turn increases their recruiting pool."[16] It would seem fruitless to focus one's time and effort on considering as stability enhancers any armed nonstate groups that are avowed enemies of the state, that appear to enjoy brutality as an end in itself, or that relish the promotion of instability for their own purposes.

Broader Power-Sharing Implications

The relative success of armed nonstate group control attempts, in terms of potential for power sharing between states and nonstate groups, requires broad historical reflection beyond this study's cases. Across time, some states have appreciated private groups providing protection and fulfilling basic survival needs to people living inside the state's borders when it is unable to do so. In these cases, because the central state governments are experiencing inadequacy in this crucial stability function, they do not necessarily see armed nonstate groups filling the void as a challenging to state power or a wresting away of state authority. Often in such circumstances, the government regime has largely given up on trying to maintain order and providing protection in what it considers to be highly dangerous and volatile areas. In contrast, because of the fluidity in power of armed nonstate groups, the historical record for predicaments when multiple factions are coercively competing for power reveals that the most common outcome of armed nonstate group control attempts is chaos and instability.

Given the severe security deprivation experienced by the least fortunate and most marginalized populations in both developed and developing societies, it is fortunate that both the governance dilemma and essential stability function where armed nonstate group control attempts tend to work best are such important ones. Receiving help with basic survival needs might well be the stability function that people experiencing security deprivation would choose as their highest priority, as it addresses their security welfare more directly than abstract and distant governance or peace objectives. Moreover, private provision for basic survival needs is so common today that it may be seen as nothing out of the ordinary.

Historical reflection on the nature of armed nonstate group responses to governance dilemmas reveals that, over time, the attributes surrounding control attempts most coveted by armed nonstate groups—and most vital to their success—have revolved around internal commitment, external support, predictable continuity, and strategic adaptability. Armed nonstate groups have faced many bottlenecks and shortfalls, including scarcity of food, weapons, and safe havens, as well as intense internal splits and grandiose demands for sole total control over ever-expanding areas. When these problems have proven to be insurmountable, not only has instability resulted, but also the groups themselves have begun to fall apart at the seams.

What is fascinating about these findings is that the attributes of control attempts that maximize stability happen to be the same attributes that armed nonstate groups tend to desire most on their own. What group would eschew high internal commitment, external support, predictable continuity, and strategic adaptability? The key to discriminating between promising and unpromising armed nonstate groups thus revolves around not these attributes themselves but rather the ends to which these groups apply these attributes.

CONDITIONS WHEN ARMED NONSTATE GROUPS ENHANCE STABILITY

This study's case evidence allows specific conditions to be identified when armed nonstate groups seem most and least likely to enhance stability (summarized in Figure 6.2). These conditions challenge the notions that states are always the best providers of stability, that armed nonstate groups always degrade this provision of stability, and that "only impotent, failed or otherwise deficient states would permit such nonstate actors to exist."[17] The conditions identified are (1) a legacy of state ineffectiveness or injustice, (2) customary authority being located outside of the central state government, (3) supportive armed nonstate group relationships with the state government, (4) positive ties between an armed nonstate group and the local society, (5) unified direction within an armed nonstate group, and (6) the specter of more dangerous forces gaining control. It is evident that in limited circumstances armed nonstate groups promote stability—at least occasionally, best in conjunction with the state—better than states do by themselves. The implications are that sometimes it would be wise from a security standpoint to allow contraction of state authority and to accept some kind of power sharing with armed nonstate groups.

Where there is a legacy of state ineffectiveness or injustice, an armed nonstate group seems most likely to enhance stability if violence is rampant in designated area, if government defense and law enforcement efforts have failed to manage the chaos,[18] and/or if the central government intentionally treats a whole society—or a particular group of people—unfairly. These circumstances conducive to armed nonstate groups having a positive security impact relate to a scenario in which there is an urgent need for stability, and the central state government seems unable or unwilling to manage ongoing turmoil. The vacuum of decent authority seems most likely to occur in marginalized areas—or among marginalized people—in both weaker and stronger states.

When customary authority is located outside the central state government, an armed nonstate group seems most likely to enhance stability if there is a societal tradition of tribal, clan, or armed nonstate group authority, if the affected population has little national government loyalty and sees the centralized government as largely irrelevant, and/or if little infrastructure or communication and transportation technology exist to facilitate national rather than local rule. This scenario enhancing private stability increases both the legitimacy and the effectiveness of armed nonstate groups assuming a key role in security governance. This set of circumstances seems most likely to occur within traditional premodern societies.

When there are supportive armed nonstate group relationships with the state government, an armed nonstate group seems most likely to enhance stability if it has some form of representation in or linkage to the government, if

Figure 6.2. Conditions when armed nonstate groups enhance stability

Legacy of state security ineffectiveness or injustice

Violence rampant within designated area

Failed efforts by government defense and law enforcement to manage the chaos

Intentionally unfair treatment of the whole society, or a particular societal group,
by the central state government

Customary authority located outside of central state government

Societal tradition of tribal, clan, or armed nonstate group authority

Little national government loyalty from the affected population, which sees the centralized
government as largely irrelevant

Lack of infrastructure or communication/transportation technologies to facilitate national
rather than local rule

Supportive armed nonstate group relationship with the state government

Some form of representation in or linkage to the government by the armed nonstate group

Tolerance of or flexibility by a state toward the armed nonstate group or a state's
leverage over it

Incorporation of status quo elements in the armed nonstate groups' goals

---

Positive armed nonstate group ties to the local society

Legacy of past goodwill or ethnic, tribal, racial, or religious ties

Desire for local autonomy among much of the affected population

High domestic public opinion receptivity to and enthusiasm for the armed nonstate group

---

Unified direction within an armed nonstate group

Few internal disagreements within the group

Key commonalities in background or belief among group members

Reliable funding and/or outside support for the group, facilitating achievement of its goals

---

Specter of more dangerous outside forces gaining control

Unambiguous presence of menacing outside forces in the area

No existing effective government restraint of menacing forces in the area

Possession by the armed nonstate group attempting security control of will and ability to
manage external dangers

the state regime is tolerant or flexible toward the armed nonstate group or has leverage over it, and/or if an armed nonstate group's goals incorporate status quo elements. The net effect of these conditions is to make an armed nonstate group not be in a totally antagonistic zero-sum relationship with the central government regime. This absence of deep permanent enmity, most likely to emerge in countries without major state-society tensions, could eventually allow power-sharing relationships between states and armed nonstate groups to emerge more smoothly.

When positive ties exist between an armed nonstate group and the local society, the potential for stability promotion seems greatest if high receptivity exists toward an armed nonstate group among the affected population. These ties could involve ethnic, tribal, religious, or racial linkages, or a legacy of goodwill from actions taken in the past. If an armed nonstate group is deeply unpopular with the civilian population, as is the case with the Revolutionary United Front in Sierra Leone, then the prospects for political reintegration are dim:[19] public memory of past atrocities or mistreatment usually persists across generations; and because armed nonstate groups operate in a bottom-up fashion, focusing on the local level, their machinations can sometimes be more visible to the mass public than to the central state government. An armed nonstate group seems most likely to enhance stability if the affected population already desires local autonomy, and/or if significant public enthusiasm exists for the group. Thus stability is aided by a positive internal reputation and approval of goals and methods in the eyes of the people. This pattern seems most likely to emerge if the armed nonstate group emerged directly from the affected part of the society, has key commonalities with the affected public, or has become sensitized to societal norms.

In terms of a unified sense of direction, an armed nonstate group seems most likely to enhance stability if few internal disagreements exist within the group, if the members share key internal commonalities in backgrounds or beliefs, and/or if the group has access to reliable outside funding and support so as to develop sufficient ability to provide protection for the people to carry out their objectives. This situation highlights the need for group cohesion, common purpose, and steady financial support in order to have a positive stability impact. Often this may necessitate the emergence of high-quality political leadership in the armed nonstate group,[20] guiding its goals and methods of achieving them. This level of togetherness (noted in Chapter 3 as being not universal because of occasional incoherence and divisiveness within these groups) appears most likely to emerge when armed nonstate groups have well-defined, well-thought-out goals.

When facing the specter of more dangerous outside forces gaining control, an armed nonstate group seems most likely to enhance stability if the menacing outside forces are unambiguously threatening the area, if the government cannot restrain them effectively, and/or if the armed nonstate group attempting security control displays a clear will and ability to manage the threat. This predicament reflects a clear and present danger, with an armed nonstate group representing the sole means of safeguarding against the external threat. Indeed, "targeting violence at the primary opponent . . . can produce positive dividends by demonstrating the commitment of the group to the cause, reinforcing the framing of the problem by clearly identifying 'the enemy', and making it clear that the group aims to protect the community."[21] This situation seems most likely to emerge on a national level within a developing society with high xenophobia and a history of outside attack or oppression, but on a community level can occur any time an outside force threatens and the existing state authority cannot or will not manage it.

Together these six conditions imply that having an inept state in a setting where nonstate authority is widely accepted is a perfect opportunity for a cohesive armed nonstate group—one that can restrain disruptive forces, has managed not to alienate the affected population, and can work with the state government—to take charge and enhance stability. Given the mass public's growing emphasis on receiving effective protection and survival needs rather than on the identity or character of the stability provider, a tacit sense of legitimacy can emerge for armed nonstate stability enhancers under these conditions. With the unorthodox nature of many ongoing security threats resisting the application of traditional government military force, a more flexible and versatile means of protection may be worth considering. Armed with evidence of the reluctance or inability of many central state governments to manage turmoil in marginal or hard-to-protect areas, private provision of security under such circumstances may be appropriate. Rejecting the global proliferation of armed non-state groups capable of providing protection, not taking advantage of their stability-enhancing potential—or, worse, treating them as if they were only disruptive and merited extermination—may be unwise. In such circumstance, few options for promoting order may be available, making advisable for stability purposes a transitional and local use of armed nonstate groups that understand and operate well in the global security setting, and that are especially well tuned to the bottom-up human security needs of the mass population. When choosing this security path, states must guard against (1) treating armed nonstate rule as an intrinsically permanent solution and (2) ignoring negative regional security spillover effects.

This analysis also indirectly highlights the conditions under which armed nonstate groups would be either unnecessary or detrimental for stability. These conditions include the presence of an effective and just central state government that provides protection to the entire population of the country; a long tradition of authority and coercive power being vested exclusively in the state; armed nonstate groups that are uninterested in cooperating with the state and may be overtly antagonistic toward it; armed nonstate groups that lack ties with or support from the local society and may be viewed as unwanted intruders; armed nonstate groups that have internal and external divisions impeding coherent movement and predictable behavior; and a national and regional atmosphere of peace and tranquility devoid of any significant violent disruptive outside forces that need to be restrained. Together these conditions, several of which would make state power sharing with armed nonstate groups unwise, appear to be increasingly uncommon. Thus the circumstance conducive to both the need for and the availability of armed nonstate groups as stability enhancers are—for better or for worse—on the rise.

ADDITIONAL LESSONS FROM THE CASE STUDIES

Lessons emphasizing the importance of poverty, the youth bulge, traditional tribal rule, societal militarization, ideological conviction, a rural setting, drug revenues, and a menacing adversary in areas where armed nonstate groups exert security governance control have also emerged from the case studies, and are displayed in Figure 6.3. The insights highlight how little many onlookers understand about the circumstances surrounding unorthodox state sovereignty-eroding activity. These extra findings help flesh out comprehension of how armed nonstate groups affect stability and what challenges security policies face.

First, in contrast to a common belief that the key trigger to armed nonstate groups seizing power is weak/fragile/failed national state governments, this study's findings indicate that what is equally crucial in many parts of the world is the presence of abject poverty. The case patterns demonstrate that state weakness/fragility/failure is neither a necessary nor a sufficient condition for armed nonstate group stability promotion. As the World Bank asserts, "if noth-

Figure 6.3. Additional lessons from the case studies

Poverty as important as state weakness for vulnerability to armed nonstate groups

Although the rich often receive private protection, armed nonstate groups may arise and provide protection in the poorest areas.

This protection may not be the result of free choice by the people affected.

Youth bulge as relevant to stability as mature older population

Having many uneducated or unemployed young men in a population can foment societal disorder.

Youth appear to fill the ranks of armed nonstate groups as eager recruits willing to fight and die in pursuit of these groups' goals.

---

*Affected states are as unprepared for any functioning central government
as they are for democracy*

Traditional, long-standing tribal authority is commonly preferred by much of the mass public to central government rule.

There is often rejection of both modernity and remote ruling infrastructures with which no sense of connection exists.

Societal militarization as influential as civil society norms to level of violent disruption

Weapons availability can be devastating in the face of disruptive armed nonstate groups promoting strife and chaos.

Societal militarization increases the scope and intensity of destabilizing violent destructive operations.

Public desperation can facilitate strong conviction as much as fatalistic acceptance

Improved communication can link together frustrated people in a common cause more easily than in the past.

The emergence of charismatic leaders among alienated populations makes it easier for armed nonstate groups to rise to power.

Remote rural areas are as conducive to armed nonstate groups as are dense urban areas

Jungle, mountainous, and desert areas make monitoring, perpetrator apprehension, and imposition of law and order very difficult.

Many urban ghettos are inaccessible to the central state government because of the chaotic violence occurring there.

(continued)

Figure 6.3. (*continued*)

---

*Addictive-drug revenues are as critical to most armed nonstate groups
as they are to criminals*

Addictive drugs are the single best-selling product in the world and involve
almost every country.

The revenues from the global drug trade are staggering and fund many armed nonstate group
activities.

---

*A menacing adversary is as crucial as ideology or benefits are to armed
nonstate groups' popularity*

This pattern follows the classic adage, "the enemy of an enemy is a friend."

The fear and hatred of the enemy image can be used to distract followers from any armed
nonstate group failings.

---

ing is done about fighting grinding poverty, then lasting peace and stability are but a distant dream."[22] The internal link between poverty and instability involves the inability of people without the means to survive to feel secure; and the international link between poverty and instability is that "poor states are threatening to rich states because the weaknesses of poor states could be globalized, thereby destabilizing the entire international system."[23] Although often the richest segments of a population tend to receive protection from private security providers, in the form of armed home security firms, private military companies, and gated communities, in numerous cases armed nonstate groups arise and provide some level of protection in areas where the poorest people live. This form of protection may not be the result of free, open choice by those people affected. Often discrimination by the central state government against the affected population has reinforced poverty patterns, along with the absence of meaningful opportunity for advancement: "contributing to the prevalence of private armies in the province is a lack of job opportunities and education, and the sense among constituents that the current local political system is unfair."[24] For example, in Colombia, Russia, Uganda, and Yemen, armed nonstate groups have arisen in parts of the country harboring the poorest and most disadvantaged population; while in the United States and Jamaica, such groups have arisen in the poorest parts of major cities (Los Angeles and Kingston). In a related manner, economic inequality played a major role in the emergence of the FARC in Colombia and the Lord's Resistance Army in Uganda, and economic decline was a key element in the cases involving the Chechens in Russia, the Islamic Army of Aden in Yemen, and the posses in Jamaica.

Second, in contrast to a common assumption that the stability of ruling authority depends principally on older, more mature segments of a country's population, this study's findings indicate that in many areas the demographic element of the "youth bulge" also plays a major role. The National Intelligence Council in the United States has noted that "lagging economies, ethnic affiliations, intense religious convictions, and youth bulges will align to create a 'perfect storm' for internal conflict."[25] Large numbers of young men without education or any prospects for employment can often be a recipe for disaster when it comes to a stable, orderly society: the risks of political violence increase with "a large youth bulge, that is, an expansion of the 15 to 25 age cohort relative to the overall adult population of a society, especially where political institutions are weak."[26] Indeed, "the populations of several youth-bulge states are projected to remain on rapid growth trajectories"; and "unless employment conditions change dramatically" in youth-bulge states such as Afghanistan and Yemen, "these countries will remain ripe for continued instability and state failure."[27] Youth appear most likely to fill the ranks of armed nonstate groups as eager recruits willing to fight and die in pursuit of these groups' goals in such societies, and young people seem to be most vulnerable and manipulable when exposed to strong, charismatic armed nonstate group leaders. Illustrating this pattern are the Chechens in Russia, the Islamic Army of Aden in Yemen, the posses in Jamaica, and the Taliban in Afghanistan.

Third, in contrast to a common premise that many countries are not yet ready to implement fully functioning democratic government, this study's findings indicate that many societies are not yet ready—and may not be ready for some time—for any form of functional central state government. Traditional tribal authority and strong clan identification not only exist in several of the cases studied—and have existed for centuries—but also are preferred to any form of central government by a significant proportion of the mass public. Often "tribal allegiance, clan difference (defined in negative terms) and exclusive cultural identity (affirmed outside the framework of true democracy) cause conflict."[28] In these cases there is explicit rejection of both modernity and remote ruling infrastructures with which the people feel no sense of connection. In instances such as the Chechens in Russia, Executive Outcomes in Sierra Leone, the gangs in Somalia, and the Islamic Army of Aden in Yemen, a long-standing pattern of widespread government corruption has intensified this resistance to the reemergence or imposition of a strong central government. Afghanistan, Somalia, and Yemen especially exemplify unpreparedness for a strong central government, and it is no coincidence that all are home to predominantly Muslim populations and considered potential safe havens for violent terrorists.

Fourth, in contrast to a common understanding that weapons availability has little effect on the emergence of ruling authority, this study's findings indicate that militarization of a society—incorporating the spread of arms and military training among the population—can be at least as influential as implanting civil societal norms in determining the level of violent societal disruption. Widespread weapons availability can be devastating when taken advantage of by uncooperative, disruptive armed nonstate groups: for such groups, possessing such capabilities creates not only the abstract potential for an increased scope and intensity of their dangerous, destructive operations, but also creates the increased pragmatic probability that operations will turn out to be even more cataclysmic. These findings are reinforced by Chapter 2's discussion of militarization promoting instability and Chapter 4's discussion of militarization negatively affecting the global security governance shift. Militarization can also hurt the cultural values of a society, causing it to believe that violence is a natural way to deal with grievances and that civil discourse is less likely to be worth the effort or to be effective as a means of resolving disputes. Generally, "instability is most likely in countries where the opportunities for armed conflict are greatest; in societies where the infrastructure and capital for organized armed conflict are more plentiful and accessible, the likelihood for civil conflict increases."[29] Societal militarization also can reduce protest against an unstable, coercively imposed order guided by a "might makes right" mentality. These patterns appear with the Chechens in Russia, Executive Outcomes in Sierra Leone, the FARC in Colombia, the gangs in Somalia, the Islamic Army of Aden in Yemen, the Lord's Resistance Army in Uganda, the Mara Salvatrucha in the United States, and the posses in Jamaica.

Fifth, in contrast to a common view that public desperation creates a sense of fatalism associating with passive acceptance of exploitative predicaments, this study's findings indicate that such desperation can also translate into strong conviction to form an armed nonstate movement and can increase people's receptivity to armed nonstate group recruitment efforts. Improved communication technologies have allowed people with common frustrations to find each other and combine efforts in a common cause more easily than in the past. When charismatic leaders emerge, the coalescence and rise to power of armed nonstate groups becomes that much easier. Terrorist and insurgent recruits, in particular, appear to be true believers who engage in simple black-and-white thinking, who share a sense of humiliation and injustice, and who feel disenfranchised and alienated from society:[30] among those with common gripes, they may or may not rationally believe that supported armed nonstate groups can actually improve their plight. The Chechens, Hezbollah, the Irish Republican Army, the Lord's Resistance Army, the Mara Salvatrucha, and the Taliban exemplify this pattern.

Sixth, many analysts contend that the politically marginalized settings most conducive to the rise of armed nonstate groups are dense urban areas rather than rural areas: "although civil wars, agrarian or rural based rebel movements still persist in a select subset of countries around the world, violence and 'warfare' are more likely to unfold in cities, especially capital cities."[31] In contrast, however, this study's findings indicate that both rural and urban settings can equally facilitate armed nonstate group control attempts. For example, to avoid confrontation with their opponents, "guerrilla warfare typically begins in rural areas, mountainous regions or in remote areas that are beyond the central government's control."[32] Just as in many countries urban ghettos are inaccessible to the central state government because of their chaotic violence, so remote rural areas can make it difficult for law enforcement officials to respond effectively to the emergence of armed nonstate groups because of relatively impenetrable jungle, mountainous, and desert areas that make apprehension of disruptive forces nigh impossible. The FARC, the Islamic Army of Aden, and the Taliban illustrate the rural rise of armed nonstate groups; while the Somali gangs in Mogadishu, the Mara Salvatrucha in Los Angeles, and the Jamaican posses in Kingston illustrate the rise of armed nonstate groups in ungovernable parts of major cities.

Seventh, in contrast to a common premise that international drug trafficking funds primarily transnational criminal organizations, this study's findings indicate that addictive-drug revenues are a major source of funding for most of the major armed nonstate groups. This revelation is unsurprising, given the pervasiveness of such an enticing activity: the global illicit drug trade nets between $420 billion and $1 trillion a year, making illicit drugs the largest sector of the global black market and the single best-selling product in the world;[33] and most states of play a part in the global market for prohibited drugs, with "the global explosion of demand and supply" so monumental that "now, no country is isolated enough to delude itself or its critics into imagining that it has no part in the world drug trade."[34] The incredibly lucrative nature of drug trafficking makes it appealing to groups of all stripes. For armed nonstate groups without much outside funding and/or without much food, water, or high-demand nonrenewable resources within areas they control, drug sales can provide the means of obtaining basic survival needs from abroad. The Chechens, the FARC (which produces and processes drugs as well as sells them), Somali gangs (who export the legal but highly addictive narcotic *qat*), Hezbollah, Mara Salvatrucha, Jamaican posses, Taliban, and Yakuza all reap significant profits from global drug running.

Eighth, in contrast to a common belief that an armed nonstate group's internal ideology or benefits provision is the key to mass popularity, this study's findings indicate that the presence of a menacing mutual state or nonstate adversary can be equally important in generating loyalty and commitment to the group. This pattern supports the old adage that "the enemy of an enemy is a friend." Because hatred or fear of menacing outsiders can overshadow all other emotions, the enemy image can provide a scapegoat for venting frustration and for distracting attention away from armed nonstate group shortcomings.[35] The more oppressive, vicious, and unjust the menacing outsiders, the greater the chances for an armed nonstate group to exploit hatred and resentment of them for its own purposes and to attract popular support simply due to this opposition. Particularly when facing an illegitimate or disliked regime, or when other, more disruptive forces are vying for power, the impact can be far greater than from positive appreciation of either what the armed nonstate group stands for or what the group can provide. Serving this unifying purpose are the Russian government for the Chechens, the Revolutionary United Front for Executive Outcomes, the paramilitary groups for the FARC, rival clans for the Somali gangs, Israel for Hezbollah, the British government and the Protestant Ulster Volunteer Force for the Irish Republican Army, Western powers for the Islamic Army of Yemen, the Ugandan government for the Lord's Resistance Army, rival gangs for the Mara Salvatrucha and the Jamaican posses, and the United States and independent Afghan warlords for the Taliban.

CONCLUDING THOUGHTS

This analysis of the relative stability success of armed nonstate groups and armed nonstate group control attempts, along with the findings about conditions when armed nonstate groups most promote stability, forms a platform from which to develop policy discrimination and prioritization in dealing with global security upheaval. This discussion points to exactly when policy initiatives opening up or closing down armed nonstate group security control attempts make the most and least sense. Despite the limitations of the evidence from these twelve case studies, some consistent, revealing patterns emerge: (1) certain types of armed nonstate groups are better suited than others to promoting stability; (2) certain types of armed nonstate group control attempts—considering both governance dilemmas that elicit armed nonstate group action and armed nonstate group responses to those dilemmas—are more likely to be successful than others in promoting stability; and (3) certain background conditions are more likely than others to promote armed nonstate group success in promoting stability.

The additional lessons highlight some worrisome and difficult global circumstances that can erode both the power of states and the stabilizing potential of armed nonstate groups. Among these patterns, perhaps the most destabilizing—regardless of whether central state governments or armed nonstate groups are in control—are poverty, the youth bulge, societal militarization, and drug revenue dependence. Together these provide the rationale for disruptive violence, the recruits most eager to undertake this violence, the means by which the disruptive violence can be undertaken, and the funding for expansion of these violent operations. Even the most propitious changes in security governance may be insufficient to contain the full range of violent disruptions created by these problem areas.

It is a daunting task to address these deficiencies in a global security setting that seems so conducive to global instability. Many lessons revolve around unfortunate circumstances that are largely systemic and cannot easily be changed in the short term. Many observers prefer to avoid focusing on the international-system roots of the problem because they are so intractable. In this regard, "recognizing the systemic factors that make state-sponsored militias ubiquitous in many parts of the developing world calls into question the international community's policies aimed at fostering state building; the current tool kit of aid, assistance, and intervention does little to alter the conditions that ultimately lead states to devolve violence."[36] The national, regional, and global patterns of high economic inequality, high unemployment, high birth rate among the poorest segments of the population, high small arms availability, high illicit substances profits, and high perceived outside threat are not likely to change soon.

As long as evidence continues to mount that the global security setting resembles the Wild West, parties of all sorts will feel empowered, in the absence of special restraints or incentives, to take unilateral coercive action without hesitation in pursuit of their own ends. This Wild West security setting is filled with pockets of anarchy, incorporating multiple conflicting core values that create cross-national disparities in what is deemed legitimate and effective in security governance. Whereas central state governments are supposed to cater to the full range of values represented by their citizenry, armed nonstate groups usually have to concern themselves only with a limited area or niche population. This anarchic setting incorporates minimum incentives for security transparency and maximum incentives for political manipulation of threat, and that combination can cause the mass public to be confused or conflicted about armed nonstate groups. A feature inherent in the Wild West setting is fluidity in who is most powerful at any time, with no fixed long-term hierarchy, which rewards nimble adaptive parties (armed nonstate groups) and punishes those relying on fixed, formulaic responses (central state governments).

Although often the origins of armed nonstate groups seem to be local frustration and repression or private within-group lust for money and power, the global security setting seems equally culpable. This systemic context affects both armed nonstate group evolution over time and evolving within-group and cross-group linkages across national boundaries. A key obstacle to considering armed nonstate groups as stability enhancers is the systemic incentives allowing, and in some cases encouraging, disruptive violent stability-reducing behavior. Neither the United States nor other Western states created—or should be held accountable for—this volatile international system in which they now find themselves. Nonetheless, they must find an effective way to manage armed nonstate groups in the context of a less-than-optimal security setting in order to improve the protection of their citizenry and the stability of the world as a whole. Ultimately, any recommendations to have armed nonstate groups play a constructive role in security governance will need to be framed within the confines of these troublesome systemic parameters, rather than denying their existence or hoping they will disappear.

7 PRIVATE COERCIVE STABILITY PROMOTION COMPLEXITIES

ANY EFFORT TO INCORPORATE private coercive forces in the global provision of stability is likely to face daunting complexities. This discussion covers the dilemmas surrounding clashing societal values, the tensions between coercive force and stability, the challenges and risks surrounding private coercive stability promotion, and the needed rethinking of the framing of stability promotion. Identifying these problem areas clarifies the hurdles that need to be overcome in order to successfully manage the impact of armed nonstate groups on stability.

DILEMMAS SURROUNDING CLASHING SOCIETAL VALUES

It is odd to suggest that people who rely on the threat and use of violence could be the best choice for promoting international stability. To some observers, this idea might seem perversely akin to "letting the lunatics run the asylum" and raises serious questions, such as, "Can thugs be transformed into law-abiding citizens"[1] whose behavior is conducive to stability? Indeed, there is enduring conflict between the spread of armed nonstate groups and democratic ideals that see "control over the use of collective violence as an inalienable right of the citizenry,"[2] who may with private security governance forfeit the customary accountability to the will of the people.[3] In this regard, any form of power sharing between central governments and such groups (which might often be covert) would seem, on the surface at least, to impede the functioning of any meaningful form of checks and balances. Furthermore, there is a critical tension underlying the question of whether armed nonstate group "structures, which in individual cases may have a stabilizing effect, can be used as an interim solution or as building blocks in the (re-)establishment of statehood; or whether such a strategy will ultimately prevent the creation of an effective statehood because it strengthens militant actors and adversely affects the prospects of sustainable development."[4] These tensions appear particularly worrisome if the goal is a stability that requires reconstituted authority structures that people accept as legitimate.[5]

Underlying these concerns are basic value clashes within societies between (1) individual freedom versus collective order, (2) right to choose versus obligation to obey, (3) tolerance of diversity versus enforcement of uniformity, (4) open global exchange versus restricted national protectionism, and (5) facilitation of transformation versus preservation of authority.[6] Figure 7.1 summarizes these divisive value clashes and the direction toward which armed nonstate groups are pushing them. Ultimately, these clashes reflect armed nonstate groups' major influence on the type of stability promoted.

Figure 7.1. Impact of armed nonstate groups on clashing societal values

DIRECTION OF ARMED NONSTATE GROUPS' IMPACT ON VALUE CLASHES
Formal, centralized, standardized, $\longrightarrow$ *Informal, fluid, varied, receptive* *static, top-down values*   *bottom-up values*
Collective order vs. Individual freedom
Armed nonstate group activity increases the pressures within states to downplay collective order in favor of the local security freedom of individual communities.
Obligation to obey vs. Right to choose
Armed nonstate group activity increases the pressures within states to downplay obedience to political authority in favor of promoting a sense of security choice.
Enforcement of uniformity vs. Tolerance of diversity
Armed nonstate group activity increases the pressures within states to downplay state-mandated uniformity in favor of diverse security governance arrangements.
Restricted national protectionism vs. Open global exchange
Armed nonstate group activity increases the pressures within states to downplay protectionist restrictions on goods and services in favor of their efficient, free global flow.
Preservation of authority vs. Facilitation of transformation
Armed nonstate group activity increases the pressures within states to downplay preserving existing political authority in favor of facilitating security change.

States and international organizations witnessing intensifying global chaos have a choice to make: do they care more about the reestablishment of collective order, providing societal protection; or the preservation of principles of individual freedom, providing a sense of openness and lack of restraint within a society? Democratic values emphasizing freedom and political self-determination are at the root of this thorny trade-off. In today's highly interconnected world, having an area within a state that desperately wants some level of autonomy over its own security affairs but is subordinated into a collective national order not fulfilling its needs is a frequent yet volatile predicament. Even though historically the escalation of internal societal tensions usually has led to order trumping freedom, such as during the Taliban rule in Afghanistan, in the future as armed nonstate group control attempts increase (and as state provision of effective security decreases), pressures within states will intensify to downplay the collective order of the country as a whole in favor of the local freedom of individual communities to chart their own courses so as to achieve their own protection goals.

The value clash between the right to choose and the obligation to obey opens up a fundamental question: do individual citizens, who may or may not understand complex relevant issues, have the right to decide their security governance system? Given the subjectivity of the effectiveness of state versus armed nonstate group security control, and given the emotions and irrational affinities associated with mass public preferences about the best kind of security protection, it would appear to be difficult for any single governance authority to satisfy all major parties and generate consistent obedience and compliance. This difficulty seems particularly acute in countries composed of diverse multiethnic societies with sharp differences in core values; countries stressing rugged individualism and an independent voice by the citizenry; and countries where the central state regime does not or cannot provide the quality of security protection needed to merit obedience to its authority. The rise of the Mara Salvatrucha in Los Angeles illustrates the benefits and dangers of allowing segments of the public to decide their own security governance system. A new balance may need to emerge between individual citizens' right to privacy (linked to the right to choose) and the national strategic infrastructure's protection from violent disruption (linked to the obligation to obey). The clandestine nature of much subnational and transnational armed nonstate group activity means that, without some form of government eavesdropping or wiretapping, the ability to monitor, apprehend, and prosecute disruptive violent members of these groups may be extremely limited. If power-sharing arrangements were to develop between states and cooperative armed nonstate groups, the public right to privacy may need to be violated frequently in order to ensure that armed nonstate groups are conforming to the terms of the power-sharing agreement; and if more effective restraining action were to occur against hostile, violent, disruptive uncooperative groups, then outside tracking of their every move would be essential to impede their operations. Together, citizens and national government officials in affected countries need to decide where this balance lies, in terms of what appropriately fits with prevailing cultural norms, and if and how the balance differs from the status quo. Proliferating armed nonstate group control attempts intensify the pressures within states to downplay obedience to a monolithic political authority in favor of promoting a sense of choice about exactly what is best for the security of the mass public.

The value clash between tolerance of diversity and enforcement of uniformity, with regard to stability, represents a critical cultural divide about whether homogeneity is always a virtue and heterogeneity is always a vice. Indeed, "there is a fundamental tension between the greater organization that states represent and human diversity," and "it was assumed that people—the very entities the state was designed to protect—in the long run would recognize that the authority which possesses the power to protect is the authority with which their loyalty must lie."[7] Unfortunately, the reality in many countries is that loyalties still run strongest to local tribal and ethnic identities, not to central state governments. Attempts to transform identities and allegiances so that they align more with the state rather than with deep subnational or transnational ties have often proven to be unsuccessful and can cause ominous frictions to emerge. The predicaments of the Acholi people in Uganda and the Chechans in Russia illustrate this challenge. As armed nonstate group control attempts increase, the pressures within states intensify to downplay state-mandated uniformity in favor of adopting the type of security governance appropriate to the human diversity evident in multicultural societies, with the result often being a loyalty shift downward.

The value clash between open global exchange and restricted national protectionism opens up controversies about the security outcome of an international free-market economic system. There is a basic trade-off in today's interdependent world between the efficiency of the free global flow of goods and services and the inescapable vulnerability to disruption deriving from armed nonstate group involvement in that flow. Built-in limits exist on states' ability to deter illicit cross-border transactions "if they wish to maintain open societies and keep their borders open to high volumes of legitimate cross-border exchange."[8] Indeed, "the inescapable predicament facing border control strategists is that the massive volume of cross-border trade and travel requires that borders function not simply as barriers against CTAs [clandestine transnational actors], but as filters that do not impede legitimate border crossings."[9] Order-oriented societies emphasize restriction of what goes in and out of a country, undertaking protectionist policies that safeguard not only the affected people but also the proprietary property rights of innovative domestic corporations; while freedom-oriented societies emphasize openness to the widest range of incoming and outgoing flows regardless of who controls them or what impact they have on society. The flow of illicit drugs out of Central and South America and out of Central Asia highlights this dilemma. As armed nonstate group control attempts expand, the pressures within states intensify to downplay protectionist efforts at restricting the global flow of goods and services, as inherent limits exist on state deterrence of illicit cross-border transactions, in favor of the encouragement of the efficient, free flow of goods, service, and people without encumbrance in a globalized world.

Finally, the value clash between facilitation of transformation versus preservation of authority represents a critical debate between approaching security from a status quo versus non–status quo perspective. The traditional security emphasis (preserving existing state authority structures and the integrity of national boundaries in the face of disruptive turmoil generated by armed nonstate groups) seems intrinsically problematic in a rapidly changing world: the legitimacy of existing structures, regimes, and boundaries can be arbitrary when looked at from a broad historical perspective;[10] and a focus on this kind of stability can lead to dysfunctional (and unjust) outcomes resulting from pressures for continuing adaptation and movement.[11] The tensions between the IRA and the United Kingdom exemplify this challenge. Yet if one abandons preservation of existing political authority in favor of allowing significant political change, the result can be continuous violent turmoil. In many societies, the option of slow, gradual, incremental, evolutionary positive change is not feasible, so any policy other than preserving existing authority opens up the floodgates to the potential of radical changes that can dramatically transform the area. Nonetheless, as armed nonstate group control attempts rise, the pressures within states intensify to downplay preserving existing political authority in favor of allowing political transformation, affording adaptation in existing security governance systems.

As is evident from the five societal value clashes, armed nonstate groups are consistently pushing societies away from an Orwellian "Big Brother" kind of formal, centralized, standardized, and static top-down government control, and—in the case of the more promising cooperative groups—toward a more informal, fluid, varied, and receptive bottom-up control: freedom rather than order, choice rather than obedience, diversity rather than uniformity, openness rather than protectionism, and transformation rather than regime preservation. Instead of moving upward toward larger, more impersonal, and all-encompassing units of authority, this represents adaptation in the opposite direction—devolving authority downward so that it can become more personalized, localized, and tuned to particular cultural needs and traditions. Going in this direction creates considerable unpredictability: both motivation and behavior can change over time, and identities and allegiances are more likely to morph in response to changing events and interaction with other forces.

Is the direction that armed nonstate groups seem to be pushing societies beneficial or detrimental to stability? As armed nonstate groups engage in more control attempts, the pressures within states intensify to downplay justice in favor of stability because of (1) the ambiguities surrounding globally accepted notions of fair play, (2) the differences among local traditions and customs; (3) the empowerment of localized private authorities to gauge justice in differing ways, and (4) armed nonstate groups' emphasis on achieving success in the delivery ends—basic survival needs and protection—rather than on maintaining fairness in the delivery means. The outcome may be a nontraditional kind of stability, more micro than macro in scope and more transitory than durable in time span. As a consequence, if one cares first and foremost about the survival needs of an affected population, then it may be wise "to delay democracy in favor of stability."[12] Otherwise, tensions can escalate in the wake of violent conflict between "what are legitimate demands for justice" and "the requirements of political stability."[13] After all, an emphasis on justice promoting fairness in treatment of individuals and groups can lead to inadvertently facilitating violent chaos in response to the many changes necessitated, especially in dysfunctional states. An important underlying is that Western enlightened democratic principles in rhetoric may stress justice for the people but in reality may not be the best way to fairly and equitably provide their security protection. If stability encompasses more than simple continuity of the political regime, as Chapter 2 argues, then one may have to be willing to do what works within a given societal context to fulfill essential stability functions, regardless of whether the form of what emerges is consistent with existing security governance norms or broad fairness principles developed in a foreign security environment. Prioritizing protection of the people thus often necessitates significant sacrifices in lofty justice ideals. Illustrating the common popular preference for a safe, unjust, but stable system over a just but chaotic system is the immediate aftermath of the 2003 Iraq War. After the major military fighting ended, many Iraqis expressed a preference for the stable yet unjust Saddam Hussein regime over the violent chaos involving looting and a disruption of basic social services.[14] The ultimate answer to the question about the desirability of armed nonstate groups' directional push on stability appears to depend on which stability functions one emphasizes and whether one focuses on country-level stability (linked to state security) or community-level stability (linked to individual security). If one assumes that significant societal pressures for transformation are behind the global shift in security governance, then the direction armed nonstate groups are pushing the societal value clashes is one that would accommodate movement away from a global system of state control, which many consider to be stifling, outmoded, and ineffective.

Are global rules and security governance norms degenerating and disappearing, or are they just transforming in ways that differ from traditional patterns and thus are not immediately recognizable? If one focuses on the value clash between order and freedom, is it possible that what is happening is simply redefining order in such a way that parts of the system not directly connected to central state governments now have more freedom to pursue their own means of providing their own security? Empirically, it indeed does appear that redefinition of acceptable authority, rather than erosion of any particular kind of authority, is at the heart of the global shift in security governance. Under this somewhat optimistic approach, current trends may not be moving the world headlong into destructive chaos but rather fostering more pluralism, diffusion, and openness in the sources of authority, thus allowing the particular variety of security authority put into place to be more precisely tuned to the nature of the particular instability predicament encountered by the affected population.

Western security-policy makers need to figure out how to effectively address the challenges posed by armed nonstate groups while avoiding the sacrifice of cherished, enlightened societal values. If willingness existed to forgo democratic processes and cross-border openness, along with broader liberal internationalist principles, then gaining ground in both power sharing with cooperative armed nonstate groups and containing violent disruptions by uncooperative armed nonstate groups would be a lot simpler. In this situation, for facilitating cooperative groups, collusive public-private arrangements could be forged that might be effective in providing protection but would be nontransparent and illegitimate in the eyes of the public; and for impeding uncooperative groups, draconian measures could be implemented that violate all civilized norms. However, the pervasiveness of democratic values limits the feasibility of such arrangements and measures. For this reason, effective state action toward either type of group seems hindered less by the behavior or offensive or defensive abilities of armed nonstate groups and more by the self-imposed constraints under which Western states claim to be operating: these constraints include adherence to the rules of domestic and international law, consistent due process deliberation, noninterference in other countries' internal affairs, respect for personal privacy, the need for cross-national consultation, and an aversion to harming innocent people based on belief in the sanctity of human life.

TENSIONS BETWEEN COERCIVE FORCE AND STABILITY

Perhaps the element most objectionable to many observers about armed nonstate groups playing a role in stability promotion is their presumed reliance on coercive power (linking to Chapter 3's discussion of violence and armed nonstate groups). Heated controversy surrounds the tensions between coercive force and stability, summarized in Figure 7.2. The concerns expressed about having stability based on force rest on grounds of both effectiveness and morality.

There is an image paradox surrounding coercion in today's global security setting. On one hand, the application of brute physical force is seen as the most intuitive way of resolving disputes, universally understood and not requiring any kind of sophisticated communication system among disagreeing parties. Often, following the principles of "satisficing," physical force is the first idea of how to respond to a challenge, a knee-jerk reaction that in many ways seems natural and appropriate. On the other hand, such force is seen as primitive and barbaric, reflecting the failure of more delicate instruments of power, bypassing meaningful resolution of any underlying tensions, and allowing superior might alone to control outcomes. This paradox raises significant questions about the utility and desirability of using force to achieve durable stability.

Figure 7.2. Tensions between coercive force and stability

Centrality of coercion to Westphalian stability

Coercive states with monopoly on instruments of violence are supposed to use force to maintain social order.

States are supposed to coercively suppress subnational violence when inhabitants compete over scarce resources.

State-initiated violence suppression is supposed to eliminate internal fears about individual and group security.

The social contract demands citizen loyalty to the state and payment of taxes in return for this protection.

But today more military weapons are in the hands of private citizens than in the hands of national governments.

But today much of the mass public is highly dissatisfied with security protection from their state governments.

Effectiveness tensions between force and stability

At the top of the international hierarchy, the link between military power and global status may no longer hold.

At the bottom of the international hierarchy, coercion's inability to provide order has led to failing and fragile states.

Benefits from a decisive military victory in warfare are declining, and costs of modern warfare are escalating.

Force can achieve short-term gains but not long-term durable stability.

Force alone cannot control the hearts and minds of the people.

Use of force can trigger a violent escalating action-reaction cycle.

Morality tensions between force and stability

Force is intuitive but appears to be primitive and barbaric.

Reliance on force for stability flies directly in the face of Western enlightened democratic principles.

Force is more difficult to employ today because of the recent growth in universal humanitarian values.

Force is associated with violations of human rights, national and international law, and prevailing justice norms.

Mutual respect and trust—essential to preventing exploitation—cannot derive from force alone.

Diplomacy and negotiation are always preferable to coercion.

As suggested in Chapter 4, Westphalian stability is based on the concept that the coercive state with its monopoly on instruments of violence would use force to maintain social order. The underlying assumption is that, through coercion, a state can suppress the subnational violence that might ensue when those within national territory compete over scarce resources. This state-initiated violence suppression is supposed to eliminate internal fears about individual and group security within a country. The social contract has citizens remaining loyal to the state and continuing to pay taxes in return for state protection.

However, for the first time since the emergence of the nation-state, "more military weapons are in the hands of private citizens than in the hands of national governments."[15] Indeed, "the steady concentration of power in the hands of states, which began in 1648 with the Peace of Westphalia, is over, at least for a while" in part because of the ability of armed individuals and armed nonstate groups to undertake physical coercion.[16] Moreover, many members of the mass public are dissatisfied with the level of security protection they receive from their central state governments.

The appeal of applying physical force has continued over the centuries despite its apparent recent empirical record of futility, raising questions about its strategic value. At the core of these questions is the need to evaluate the apparent irrationality of the persistent heavy reliance on and frequent use of force in a world posing so many obstacles blocking its ability to achieve stated goals:

> Can political and military violence be *strategic*, and is it satisfactory to understand it primarily in such terms? When, and for what ends, can armed force be successfully and legitimately used? When one considers armed conflict, the 20th century is structured by a striking paradox: even as it was a particularly terrible one for war, during much of it war was also widely seen as futile and illegitimate. In this world paradoxes abound: the long-assumed equation between military capability and strategic effect, and between material power and security—where more of one implies more of the other—no longer holds.[17]

For those at the top of the international hierarchy, there appears to be a receding link between military might and global status. For those at the bottom of this hierarchy, the inability of state coercion to maintain and restore order has contributed to the proliferation of failing and fragile states. Moreover, for central state government armies to attain large-scale physical force using state-of-the-art weaponry is becoming prohibitively expensive, as the cost of modern military equipment is skyrocketing; for many players today not endowed with huge budgets, defense resources for this purpose are exceedingly scarce.

Today even decisive military victory in warfare seems to have reduced payoffs.[18] Military force, designed to kill humans and destroy property, can certainly achieve victory in battle and determine short-term outcome, but it faces significant limitations when asked to achieve long-term political stability through undertaking missions with unclear objectives, with humanitarian goals, or with a primary thrust of providing social services to civilians. Military force also cannot by itself instill civil society or change a political system toward democracy. Many of today's global conflicts center on competing attempts to control the hearts and minds of the people, and force alone cannot attain this objective. Whereas uses of military force in the distant past were often followed by long-term occupation of subjugated areas, recent confrontations often reflect a widespread naive expectation that a quick, decisive victory followed by a speedy withdrawal are sufficient to achieve long-term political ends.

Aside from utility concerns, objections have escalated concerning the morality of using brute force in international relations, especially for stability purposes. Even though possession and application of a certain threshold of coercive force may be necessary in certain situations, reliance on force for stability flies directly in the face of Western enlightened democratic principles. It is widely recognized that "hard military threat and use are more difficult to employ today than was the case in the past, in part because of the relatively recent growth in popular respect for universal humanitarian values."[19] An assumption persists that any use of physical force to provide stability will automatically involve a callous "might makes right" mentality entailing severe human rights violations, flagrant disobedience of national and international law, and significant deviation from prevailing justice norms. Moreover, abiding mutual respect and trust—essential for the morally desired progressive movement toward nonexploitative international relations—cannot be derived from force alone. Finally, diplomacy and negotiation are frequently deemed to be always preferable—in terms of producing fruitful and potentially legitimizing avenues of conflict resolution—to coercion.

Both armed nonstate groups and states resort to force to promote stability, with state coercion generally more accepted nationally and internationally. However, autocratic central state governments' reliance on coercion for stability can receive heavy criticism, and even some democracies find themselves relying on coercion more than they would like to manage groups that cannot seem to resolve their differences through civil discourse. At the same time, the use of force by armed nonstate groups can elicit praise when aimed at preventing the intrusion of violent outside elements so that internal peaceful processes of civil society promotion, economic reconstruction, and human rights protection can flourish. In practice, either states or armed nonstate groups can attempt to exert security governance over affected populations—at least temporarily—through the threat or use of force, but unless this coercive control yields substantial security benefits to the people, then instability is likely to follow. In any case, in order to maximize efficient stability provision, rational incentives exist for either public or private rule to minimize the amount of force needed over time to maintain control. As armed nonstate group control attempts increase, the pressures within states seem likely to intensify to downplay reliance on coercive power in favor of allowing the will of the people to flourish.

Although Chapter 3's analysis shows that armed nonstate groups do not invariably need coercive violence as the means to achieve their ends, when these groups do employ force, it can trigger coercive retaliation. Once this reaction occurs, areas under armed nonstate group control can become safe havens for disruptive thugs,[20] fostering regional chaos and a violent escalating action-reaction cycle[21] in which extreme brutality can foster emotional overreactive coercive responses.[22] Armed nonstate group "violence often produces an escalatory cycle of tit-for-tat measures wherein it becomes difficult to de-escalate the violence and enter into political negotiations."[23] Furthermore, private groups possessing coercive power seem likely to become agitated and more prone to violence if the state reaction to security governance deficiencies is to crack down on them in such a way as to restore central state government control. Indeed, armed nonstate groups "are more likely to challenge than to support any steps which would strengthen security governance through government, i.e. the (re-) establishment of the state's monopoly of the use of force."[24]

PRIVATE COERCIVE STABILITY PROMOTION CHALLENGES AND RISKS

Even with the recognition that armed nonstate groups can sometimes enhance stability, several key challenges still remain to be overcome, outside of the predictable handicap associated with the inertia of the Westphalian state system. At the same time, having armed nonstate groups participate in stability promotion carries significant risks, outside of the expected dangers of central state governments seeing their national sovereignty eroded. Failure to address these challenges and risks ensures instability.

Armed Nonstate Group Stability Promotion Challenges

The core private coercive stability promotion challenges involve channeling armed nonstate groups so that their activities reap maximum stability benefits for the affected population. When armed nonstate groups act together in "marriages of convenience," these challenges can become more complicated. Figure 7.3 summarizes the three clusters of major challenges—policy inconsistencies, identity transformations, and threat misperceptions—for armed nonstate group stability provision in today's world.

In the matter of policy inconsistency, there seems to be a contradiction between encouraging the spread of armed nonstate forces to provide stability and discouraging their spread because of the widespread desire to eradicate sources

Figure 7.3. Armed nonstate group stability promotion challenges

---

Policy inconsistencies

Armed nonstate groups providing stability but also promoting chaotic disruption

Armed nonstate groups' stability efforts spreading arms and drugs and human rights abuses

Stable predictability within a society undercutting progressive governance, reflecting globally upheld values

---

Identity transformations

Blurring identities associated with the transformation of some armed nonstate groups into quasi-states

Tension between effectiveness and nonuniversal availability of armed nonstate group protection to the mass public

States outsourcing stability functions to armed nonstate groups versus these groups initiating on their own

---

Threat misperceptions

Misreading by outsiders of states' intentionally created ungoverned spaces as undesired anarchic zones

Misidentification by government personnel of armed nonstate groups as incompetent, dangerous, or unworthy

Exaggeration by states and the mass public of the internal and external threat from armed nonstate group control of chaotic disruption. The multiplicity of overlapping tensions surrounding the use of armed nonstate groups for stability purposes makes resolution of this contradiction difficult, as having simultaneous policies of supporting some armed nonstate groups and opposing others can be internally and externally confusing and promote an image of incoherence. The behavior promoted by some of the most well-publicized armed nonstate groups are problematic: sometimes the stability promoted by these groups ensures the continuation of illicit activities, such as the proliferation of arms and drugs that potentially erode the foundations of civil society; and sometimes armed nonstate group protection allows the perpetuation of human rights abuses, including the exploitation of women and children, or prevents the emergence of any kind of responsive rule that takes into account the changing desires of the people. This predicament reinforces the critical choice between achieving effective authority within a society and attaining a progressive form of governance reflecting globally upheld values.

There are blurring identities associated with the transformation of some armed nonstate groups into "proto-states" or into official legitimate entities within a relatively short period. For example, in Brazil and Colombia, armed nonstate groups "may interact directly with the state in identifiable social networks, providing financial or narcotic kick-backs to security forces, which in turn provide armed groups with weaponry and a modicum of unconstrained maneuverability in their respective communities;"[25] and in Lebanon, Hezbollah holds seats in parliament, yet the United States labels Hezbollah a terrorist group. Often such identity confusion occurs when, following warfare, efforts occur to disarm, demobilize, and reintegrate armed nonstate groups back into society. Identity ambiguities also exist with regard to tensions between the increased effectiveness of protection from armed nonstate groups and the non-universal availability of protection—owing to its private nature—to the mass public. As well, there is a critical identity distinction between states outsourcing stability-enhancing functions to armed nonstate groups versus these groups launching their own control attempts, with no convincing pattern of which is more likely to have positive outcomes. Although outsiders might attach more legitimacy to state-initiated power sharing, ambiguity can often dominate in this scenario, because armed nonstate groups may establish control on their own, but then through a variety of informal means states may tacitly acknowledge these groups' right to rule and establish cooperative relationships with them.

Threat misperception can occur in situations when, for instance, a state intentionally creates ungoverned spaces[26] that are misread as anarchic zones, thus undermining the state's interests. Moreover, government soldiers and state government officials may overestimate the extent to which armed non-state groups are incompetent, dangerous, or unworthy of security governance. The international community has a common misconception that only failed states or ungoverned spaces attract armed nonstate group rule and constitute potential threats; in reality, "not all cases in which private actors have assumed statelike functions, however, involve chaos or failure."[27] Armed nonstate groups also may cause the mass public to distort its perception of the level of internal and external threat, and states may exaggerate the threat these groups pose, often for purposes of finding a scapegoat for government incompetence, even when clear evidence exists that no such threat exists.[28] Overall, having armed nonstate groups participate in security governance can cloud systematic threat assessment, prioritization, and management.

Armed Nonstate Group Stability Promotion Risks

Private coercive stability promotion risks encompass the possible dangers of negative security outcomes arising from involving armed nonstate groups in stability promotion. The principal risks are (1) opposition from states and international organizations, (2) confounding of existing international law and global security governance norms, (3) retarding of nonsecurity public goods provision, (4) errors in distinguishing stabilizing from destabilizing armed nonstate groups, (5) contradictory impacts of armed nonstate groups, and (6) misallocations in dividing authority between states and armed nonstate groups. Figure 7.4 outlines these concerns, which warn against indiscriminate support for armed nonstate groups being used as stability enhancers.

Established states and international organizations would presumably be upset if armed nonstate groups were formally or informally recognized and accepted as legitimate providers of stability in an increasingly large proportion of the world. In the minds of many state officials, "when the state is already weak, the sharing of governance tends to undermine rather than strengthen state authority and legitimacy."[29] Most state officials seem hesitant to be open to positive contributions from these groups, and given that "the inimical attitude of states toward armed groups has manifested itself throughout history," the dysfunctional consequence has often been that "while some states have negotiated with armed groups, most states have been reluctant to embrace discussions":[30]

Figure 7.4. Armed nonstate group stability promotion risks

Opposition from states and international organizations

Formal global bodies contest armed nonstate groups' recognition and acceptance as legitimate stability providers.

Most states are hostile to armed nonstate groups and have been reluctant to talk with them.

States are often fearful of conferring authority to armed nonstate groups.

Confounding of existing international law and global security governance norms

It is difficult to incorporate armed nonstate groups properly into the formal and informal international system rules.

If incorporation into an international legal framework is improper, the wrong message (violence pays) can be sent.

In contrast, leaving armed nonstate groups outside the legal framework can foster anarchic violence.

Retarding of nonsecurity public goods provision

Other important services traditionally provided by state governments are not maximized.

Economic progress can be stunted and unpredictable without public enforcement of property rights.

Power may revert to patrimonial networks based on clan or tribal solidarity, thwarting social development.

Errors in distinguishing stabilizing from destabilizing armed nonstate groups

Armed nonstate group motivations and behavior are hard to assess in deciding if they might help or hurt stability.

Armed nonstate groups in control may lack power, proper values, or appropriate protection incentives.

Low competition among groups and high barriers to entry play a role in worsening this predicament.

Contradictory impacts of armed nonstate groups

Positive impacts on provision of basic survival goods/services may combine with negative impacts on human rights.

Positive impacts on internal security may combine with negative impacts on external regional or global security.

Positive contribution to short-term stability may generate negative impacts on durable long-term stability.

(*continued*)

Figure 7.4. *(continued)*

> *Misallocations in dividing authority between states and armed nonstate groups*
>
> The line may be fuzzy between where the authority of the state ends and that of an armed nonstate group begins.
>
> Because of this ambiguity, public-private contention over the scope of authority between the two may emerge.
>
> Dangers may escalate if key elements are ignored in the division of control over violence, resources, and rule making.

[S]tates, in large part, exhibit a reluctance to develop negotiation channels with armed groups. States (and other agencies) around the world share a concern that engaging armed groups diplomatically can end up lending legitimacy to the groups and their grievances, or strengthening the groups' negotiating positions. The unwillingness to initiate channels of communication can prolong conflicts and undermine post-conflict settlements if states do not address the long-term grievances that fueled the conflict as well as such consequences of conflict as the loss of life and property.[31]

Justifying this diplomatic recalcitrance are skeptical state assumptions, such as that armed nonstate groups never negotiate in good faith; that they use negotiations to stall for time, resupply, or gain a tactical advantage; that "they only understand force"; or that they are inherently untrustworthy and cannot be counted on to keep their part of the deal.[32] State motivations for this rigid position may not be completely devoid of self-interest, as "perhaps refusing to negotiate with armed groups is based on a statewide campaign to preserve the hegemonic status of states in the international community."[33] From the state and international organization perspective, although armed nonstate groups "may offer a minimum of stability on the local level, they ultimately prevent the establishment of sustainable state structures—financed, implemented, or monitored by the international community."[34] Moreover, state governments and international organizations can feel that "negotiating with armed groups may actually negatively impact humanitarian conditions or legitimize the group's illegal acts."[35] From a pragmatic standpoint, armed nonstate groups operating locally may have agendas that conflict with those of central governments acting nationally. Even when facing continuing opposition from state governments and international organizations, armed nonstate groups "can protect communities in spite of international failure to recognize this."[36]

When considering the risk of confounding existing international law and global security governance norms, it is difficult to incorporate armed nonstate groups properly into the formal and informal rules governing the way the international system operates. The dominant view here is that, when considering armed nonstate groups collectively, "they represent unique long-term challenge to governments, Western policymakers, and the precepts of international law."[37] Unquestionably, "a key difficulty in addressing armed non-state actors is that legal and normative frameworks governing the use of force—international humanitarian law (IHL) and international human rights law (HRL)—are still understood primarily on the state level."[38] Illustrating this dilemma on a local level is an armed nonstate group control of an area—regardless of the perceived benefits—depriving the affected population of the democratic right to decide whether that group has the right to rule. Often "concerns over legitimacy lead states to deny legal status to non-state armed groups" because the result can be that this denial "hinders the protection of vulnerable groups during conflicts."[39] However, if this incorporation into an international legal framework is done improperly, "the international community runs the risk of sending the wrong message ('violence pays') by devoting too much attention or by granting privileges to armed non-state actors who have already benefited from war and shadow economies; this may not only trigger increasing demands by these actors but also seriously harm the credibility and legitimacy of external actors vis-à-vis the general public ('moral hazard' problem)."[40] In contrast, leaving armed nonstate groups completely outside the legal framework can foster anarchic violence.

Armed nonstate group stability promotion does not necessarily maximize other important services traditionally provided by state governments. For example, often "for those living without the protection of a state and its enforcement of property rights, economic progress will certainly be stunted"; and under these circumstances "power will likely revert to patrimonial networks based on clan or tribal solidarity, thwarting ambitions for social development and equality."[41] Significant unpredictability in public goods provision is also associated with this global "shift in ownership"—the combination of declining state and rising nonstate authority.[42] As discussed in Chapter 2, these deficiencies can raise questions about whether ensuring fulfillment of the essential stability functions should always take precedence over all other dimensions of good governance. However, global perceptions of insecurity reinforce the view that survival needs consistently deserve the highest priority.

It is exceedingly tough to assess either motivations and intentions or actual behavior of armed nonstate groups in order to decide which of them are the most promising candidates for power sharing. This introduces the risk of errors in distinguishing stabilizing groups from destabilizing ones. Armed nonstate groups controlling areas are not necessarily those best equipped to enhance stability because of inherent power limitations, unsavory internal values, or the lack of incentive to provide effective protection. For example, armed nonstate groups that appear promising and are consequently integrated into political structures and granted special liberties and privileges may use the opportunity to undermine the processes of stability and progressive reform.[43] They may deceptively manipulate external state support for unsavory private ends, or play factional politics at the state level in a way that subverts state authority to their own ends and fosters instability. A relationship of trust can all too quickly transform into a relationship of betrayal. Wrong choices about armed nonstate groups may arise because of an ineffective central state government combined with low competition among armed nonstate groups—in terms of which is best suited to provide protection for an affected population—resulting from high barriers to entry. In other words, out of the available security providers in a particular area, there frequently turn out to be few decent choices, particularly if the population needing security protection is marginalized. In determining who takes on security governance functions, the risks of costly errors may escalate because no "invisible hand" operates automatically to maximize security utility in either the short run or the long run. Escalating risks can then sometimes elicit troublesome foreign coercive intervention.

The contradictory impacts of armed nonstate groups make it difficult to ensure entirely beneficial results. First, these groups' positive impacts on fulfillment of basic survival needs may combine with negative impacts on human rights (particularly the rights of women and children). These groups' abuses can make them difficult to accept as political allies and can undermine the international legitimacy of the states in which they operate. Armed nonstate groups can be seen sometimes "engaging in 'uncivil' activities while at other times providing key public goods"[44] (like security); unsavory groups can provide for basic survival needs and local stability while simultaneously being nasty to humanitarian groups pushing global governance norms. Because armed nonstate groups "do not recognize international norms, the rule of law, or the idea of human rights, and they are willing to kill those who oppose them,"[45] there have been "rising complaints about human-rights abuses lodged against private police by citizens" in many societies.[46] Second, as the case studies confirm, these groups' positive impacts on internal security often combine with negative impacts on external regional or global security.[47] The risk of involving them includes the triggering of undesired flows—such as of illicit arms, drugs, and refugees or sex slaves—across national boundaries.[48] Even within a country, armed nonstate groups may be exclusionary, protecting one particular ethnic or sectarian group while ignoring the needs of others. Indeed, "as state structures collapse and borders become more porous, these countries [weak and failing states] often export violence as well as refugees, political instability, and economic dislocation to states in their vicinity; this risk is compounded when weak, vulnerable, or collapsed states are adjacent to countries with similar characteristics that possess few defenses against spillovers," as "weaknesses in one state can thus encourage the rise of an entire bad neighborhood."[49] For risks to be minimized, maximizing local stability cannot simultaneously maximize regional instability. Third, in a similar fashion, because the positive impacts of armed nonstate groups on short-term stability may produce negative repercussions on long-term stability, risk minimization would necessitate the discovery of more durable means of stability promotion. Many instances of armed nonstate group rule are ad hoc, with few trappings of permanency; however, in some circumstances such nonstate rule may be "less transitory, more significant, and more resistant to intervention than is commonly assumed."[50] Thus the risks are that the kind of stability promoted by armed nonstate group rule may be limited—temporary, local, and only for designated protected group members and supporters—rather than broad, durable, and regional.

In terms of the risk of misallocating authority between states and armed nonstate groups, there is rarely a clearly defined demarcation between where the authority of the state ends and the dominion of an armed nonstate group begins. Areas requiring explicit demarcation include who controls violence, who controls resources, and who controls rule making.[51] In making the decision about violence control, risks could be amplified if the division of authority ignores either the capacity or the willingness of the security providers to manage existing turmoil. In making the decision about resources control, risks could be maximized if the division of authority ignores the propensity of certain kinds of security providers to use financial and natural resources to promote inequality or overexploitation. Finally, in making the decision about rule-making control, risks could be escalated if the authority division ignores the degree to which laws formulated by security providers correspond in either their formulation or their implementation to the popular will of those affected. Failure to properly demarcate authority between states and armed nonstate groups can lead both to forgo a mutually beneficial "symbiotic"[52] relationship.

Confusion underlying the division of authority between states and armed nonstate groups may undercut the ability to hold either party tightly accountable for their actions. Privatized security has been consistently attractive over the centuries because it often saves the rulers money and because it allows for the responsibility-avoiding escape route of "plausible deniability" (a concept first mentioned in the seventeenth century). With this end in mind, state governments began authorizing privatized security forces as early as the thirteenth century, when privateering first emerged; large private armies were widespread in the fourteenth and fifteenth centuries; and mercenaries were commonplace in the eighteenth century.[53] Even today, "the absence of effective regulatory frameworks poses significant problems for establishing the legitimacy for international actions, as well as for encouraging ownership by local authorities."[54] Armed nonstate groups "are subject to limited accountability, domestically and internationally, and therefore are inclined to take greater risks; they are generally secretive, repressive, and distrustful of outsiders, and they tolerate Western media only when they can use them for their own propaganda purposes."[55] In a more sinister way, armed nonstate groups may be "used as a subterfuge to avoid blame for violence commissioned by the state."[56] Without tighter accountability, armed nonstate groups could inflame factional tensions within states, subverting elements of state control for their own purposes. Because of ambiguity over accountability, the risks of severe public-private contention could soar over differences about their scope of authority if left totally unmanaged.

When these six clusters of risk are taken to their extreme, the result can be the total obliteration of responsible, overarching security authority. Illustrating this extreme outcome is a country completely controlled by an armed nonstate group, Aruba, which emergence "the world's first independent mafia state" in 1993.[57] This event represents a nonstate thrust intended to allow transnational criminals to become respectable local power elites, to worm their way into legitimate commercial and governmental activities, and to gain covertly international acceptance so as to secure their survival protection, social status, and business success:[58]

[T]his process of merging reaches its logical conclusion when organized criminals actually seize control of the state, an entire country effectively being run as a criminal enterprise. In parts of Latin America, the Caribbean, Eastern and Southern Europe, South-East Asia and Sub-Saharan Africa this is precisely what has occurred. It has led in some cases to the privatization not just of specific utilities and public companies but of key elements of governance, ranging from the police or military to the presidency itself. In such cases the criminals either operate under unofficial license from the civil authority or are indistinguishable from it. . . . This entails neutering political obstacles such as an independent judiciary and a free press. It constitutes a model of governance based on the acquisition of power as a means of self enrichment.[59]

In 2012, Bulgaria, Guinea-Bissau, Montenegro, Myanmar, Ukraine, and Venezuela have been accused of becoming "mafia states," where "high government officials actually become integral players in, if not the leaders of, criminal enterprises, and the defense and promotion of these enterprises' businesses become official priorities."[60] This taking over of state functions—sometimes referred to as "the black hole syndrome"[61]—represents "the dark side of state displacement." In combining "socio-economic decay and state retreat," dilapidated major urban areas in advanced industrial societies and devastated parts of the developing world can provide comfortable niches within which illicit disruptive activity can thrive without interference.[62] Inside weak states, the organs of government are "eminently purchasable," and if these organs fall into the hands of criminals, mercenaries, terrorists, and warlords, the frequent result is that "government and crime become indistinguishable or identical."[63]

NEEDED RETHINKING OF THE FRAMING OF STABILITY PROMOTION

The framing of stability promotion needs rethinking if global instability is to be reduced. To accomplish this, four focus changes are warranted, stressing stability ends rather than means. These are summarized in Figure 7.5. This rethinking entails a focus on the promotion of order by the ruling authority, not on whether the state is promoting it; a focus on the provision of security needs within the affected society, not on whether the state is supplying it; a focus on the deterrence or resolution of violent internal conflict, not on whether the state is managing it; and a focus on the constraint of unwanted coercive foreign intervention, not on whether the state is rebuffing it. For some observers, the

Figure 7.5. Needed rethinking of the framing of stability promotion

Focus on promoting order by the ruling authority, not on how it is fostered

Do not focus on how it came to power, its leadership, or its institutionalization.

Do not focus on whether the ruling authority is representative or responsive.

Do not focus on whether the ruling authority has the traditional attributes of sovereignty or absolute territorial control.

Do not focus on whether nonstate groups take part in the ruling authority, but rather on its overall effectiveness.

Focus on providing security goods and services within the affected society, not on how they are supplied

Do not focus on whether civil society exists.

Do not focus on whether the needs provider is legitimate.

Do not focus on internationally held ideas of exploitation, inequality, and injustice.

Do not focus on adherence to global security norms, but instead on supplying essentials in a particular affected society.

Focus on deterring or resolving violent internal conflict, not on how it is managed

Do not focus on the mode of violence reduction within an affected society.

Do not focus on the avowed intention of the conflict manager.

Do not focus on the justification of each warring party.

Do not focus on whether coercion is used to enhance stability, but instead on success in quelling internal conflict.

Focus on constraining unwanted coercive foreign intervention, not on how it is rebuffed

Do not focus on whether a society makes decisions by itself or on the motivations of the intervening foreign force.

Do not focus on the level or type of external security dependence.

Do not focus on the distinctiveness of a society's identity.

Do not focus on the quality of international diplomacy, but rather on insulation from outside coercive interference.

---

process of security governance is as important as the outcome, with complete human rights protection and democratic decision making absolutely essential for acceptability. In contrast, this study's notion of stability promotion places primary importance on the effective delivery of security protection and basic survival needs in the many dire and urgent predicaments affecting much of the world's people, considering how unwise it would be to wait until the mode of delivery is globally standardized and approved. Thus the suggested rethinking moves away from a static process-oriented model of stability, often Western and state-centric, toward a more fluid, outcome-oriented approach.

First, it is advisable to renew focus on the promotion of order by the ruling authority, not on how it is fostered. There should be less emphasis, at least initially, on how an authority came to power, its leadership, or its institutionalization; on whether the ruling authority is representative or responsive; on whether the ruling authority has the traditional attributes of sovereignty or absolute territorial control; and on whether nonstate groups take part in the ruling authority. Instead, the focus should be on effectiveness in protecting the people. The rationale for this includes the variety of values and traditions of political authority among different countries, the need to have differentiated control infrastructures that work in the context of local customs, and the wide assortment of global stability challenges.

Second, it is advisable to renew focus on the fulfillment of basic survival needs in the affected society, not on how they are supplied. There should be less emphasis, especially at the outset, on whether fully functioning civil society exists; on whether the provider is legitimate; on forestalling foreign notions of exploitation, inequality, and injustice; or on adhering to global security governance norms. Instead, the focus should be on effectiveness in supplying security needs within a particular affected society. The logic for this is that, even if some basic protection needs are common to all people, different cultures prioritizes those needs in distinct ways, and security provision, at least initially, should conform to citizens' expected norms. The result may be that the mode of stability provision in one society may end up looking ineffective, illegitimate, or even repulsive in other societies.

Third, it is advisable to renew focus on the deterrence or resolution of violent internal conflict, not on how it is managed. There should be little emphasis on the particular mode of violence reduction within an affected society, on the nature of the avowed intention of the conflict manager, on the level of justification of each warring party, or on the presence or absence of coercion. Instead, the emphasis should be on success in quelling internal conflict. Armed nonstate groups are used to employing violence "to deter people from collaborating with the rival actor"[64] when dealing with menacing opposing forces, so they could apply similar tactics to enhance stability. Once again, the reasoning behind this reflects global variation in ways of appropriately managing internal conflict;

and according to some analysts, despite the continuing carnage, it may even on occasion be wisest to let a violent conflict continue and "burn itself out" in order for disputes to be meaningfully resolved.[65]

Fourth, it is advisable to renew focus on the constraint of unwanted coercive foreign intervention, not on how it is rebuffed. There should be little emphasis on whether a society makes decisions to prevent such outside interference by itself; on the motivations of the unwanted foreign force coercively intervening; on the level or type of external security dependence; on the distinctiveness of a society's identity; or on the quality of international diplomacy. Instead, the focus should be on ability of the security authority to insulate a society from unwanted outside coercive interference. The reason for this is the disparity among countries in their tolerance of or desire for outside assistance by force and for the homogenizing pressures of globalization, and in their willingness to admit to the international community their inability to solve their problems on their own.

CONCLUDING THOUGHTS

This discussion of complexities surrounding armed nonstate group stability promotion underscores the fact that powerful Western states and international organizations do not have all the answers regarding how this could work best and cannot apply a standard template that would function well everywhere. Significant challenges and risks surround this security governance transformation, and considerable rethinking of the many modes of stability promotion is essential. This rethinking seems most likely to be successful if it approaches the resolution of stability dilemmas in a bottom-up fashion, through extensive observation and analysis of local communities, and through discovery of what key local leaders think will work best to achieve more protective predictability in the future. Trial-and-error experimentation to determine what works best would be too slow and costly; even without this, there probably will be missteps along the way to achieve this wide variety of stable solutions. Developing local sustainable authority and limiting the role of central state governments may be essential parts of successful policies;[66] and, in this process, armed nonstate group assistance may play a vital role.

Few states have ready solutions to the special pragmatic and moral problems surrounding the use of coercive force to achieve durable stability. At the heart of this thorny set of concerns is the natural tendency of violence to elicit more violence in a cycle of endless conflict. When considering that the West's reliance on foreign government military force is often the primary means it uses to strengthen ineffective state regimes as part of its standard response to global instability, it is no wonder that there are so few success stories.

Because of the significance of private coercive stability promotion challenges and risks, the tensions between coercive force and stability, and the depth of rethinking required about stability promotion, any forward moves need to be undertaken cautiously. Changes in the ways stability is pursued should be implemented gradually wherever possible, with attentiveness to their societal impacts. Beginning this transformation in areas where the prospect for success is highest seems wise, before attempting any form of power sharing in areas where risks and dangers are greatest. In many countries, addressing these issues and considering private groups to promote stability constitute a new kind of initiative, so there would be no wealth of past experience to guide this security transition.

Perhaps the most worrisome element of considering armed nonstate groups as stability enhancers is the set of deep and divisive societal value clashes that such a move could unleash. These clashes could highlight gaping differences that prove extremely difficult to resolve among citizens in an affected society, as well as among observers across societies. There is little domestic or international consensus about the prioritization of individual freedom versus collective order, right to choose versus obligation to obey, tolerance of diversity versus enforcement of uniformity, open global exchange versus restricted national protectionism, or facilitation of transformation versus preservation of authority. Furthermore, the level of emotion tied to these value trade-offs is high, making calm civil discourse difficult. Despite this intensity of feelings, more public discussion between government officials and the mass public within and across countries would be a helpful prerequisite to any smooth security governance transformation.

In this study's attempts to avoid the pitfalls identified, there is a danger that readers might conclude that the pursuit of stability must be characterized by complete value neutrality, devoid of promotion of any core beliefs deemed admirable. Indeed, much of what appears in this chapter smacks of moral relativism, shying away from imposing one's convictions on other societies. However, pursuing stability in and of itself does embody a key value—that maximizing predictable continuity and security protection of the people is central to the functioning of international relations in an anarchic world. This study takes the stance that stability promotion deserves the highest policy priority relative to other security and nonsecurity goals. Because stability as defined here focuses on outcome rather than on process, this focus does not demand or expect that the mode utilized to achieve protection functions will look the same across societies, or that the stability-promoting processes emerging in other societies will look like what promotes stability in Western democracies. Thus diversity would be expected in means rather than ends. The notion of "one size fits all," that a single mode of stability promotion can work for every global predicament, seems inherently flawed and dangerous in terms of its security consequences. Pursuing stability can fit into a variety of cultural contexts if flexibility is maintained about how this crucial end is achieved; yet this quest provides a unifying focal point around which success and failure can be judged.

8 CONCLUSION
Policy Guidelines

GIVEN ALL OF THE MISCONCEPTIONS surrounding armed nonstate groups and their impact on stability, it is not surprising that most states and intergovernmental organizations have undertaken policies toward these groups that have either failed to accomplish their objectives or completely backfired. Over time many of these authorities have seemed determined to continue applying the same tired strategies despite unambiguous evidence of malfunction. To address this problem, this discussion presents both what should and should not be done with regard to shifting security governance challenges, following a utilitarian metric that deemphasizes stability provider identities and global governance norms. The analysis identifies contrasting strategies for stability promotion vis-à-vis cooperative and uncooperative armed nonstate groups, useful particularly in addressing persistent and large-scale instability. In both instances, concrete steps toward designated objectives as well as broader security implications within today's international system are highlighted.

WHAT NOT TO DO TO PROMOTE STABILITY

Of the many strategies undertaken that have not worked to promote stability, two failing options stand out: blanket support for central state governments, and blanket opposition to armed nonstate groups. Their common thread running is a persistent unwillingness or inability to discriminate meaningfully among differing states or armed nonstate groups to determine which actually merit—in terms of stability promotion potential—support or opposition. The faulty underlying assumption behind this is that states inherently help stability and armed nonstate groups inherently hurt stability.

Avoid Blanket Support for Central State Governments

The most widely promoted idea by both academic scholars and government policy makers is to reinforce the prevailing global norms of state sovereignty.[1] Indeed, "the slew of existing programs to build state institutions and capacities—funded by government and intergovernmental organizations—attests to the common assumption that strengthening states is the primary solution for a range of global and local ills."[2] Many analysts contend that "the establishment of competent government—or, more specifically, of coherent political systems and disciplined [government] military and policing forces—is the key to engendering and maintaining civil peace" and to restraining global perpetrators of violence.[3] Despite mounting global evidence of states' inability to manage security threats, the most common remedy proposed is "an 'ideal type' of modern statehood—with full internal and external sovereignty, a legitimate monopoly on the use of force, and checks and balances that constrain political rule and authority."[4]

Exemplifying the universality of attempts "to strengthen legitimate government and the rule of law to alleviate pressures that lead to instability"[5] is that "the U.S. government's latest *National Defense Strategy* calls on the U.S. military to strengthen the sovereign capacities of weak states to combat internal threats of terrorism, insurgency, and organized crime."[6] In the post-9/11 world, American foreign policy essentially demands that states have to ensure that their territory is not used by armed nonstate groups that might endanger U.S. interests, with the implied threat that those states not doing so may be subject to severe negative sanction. This dictum ignores both (1) whether a given state has the capacity to monitor or control such subversive activities and (2) whether an armed nonstate group deemed dangerous to the United States is providing security protection to the local population.

The logic behind resolving internal turmoil through strengthening central state governments centers largely on fears about terrorism. The dynamics are that "the more that states fail to produce public goods—public health services, education, social welfare services—and become dependent upon programs from nongovernmental organizations and private, volunteer organizations to provide these functions, the greater the probability that some assistance will be provided by organizations sympathetic to extremists, or that those programs will be exploited by terrorists; therefore . . . programs that help governments build capacity to provide these public goods would eventually reduce the scope of terrorist exploitation."[7] Furthermore, "it is presumed that strengthening and professionalizing [government] security forces eliminates zones of lawlessness where terrorists find succor and diminishes the need for 'dirty tricks' like the mobilization of nonstate actors to attack opposition."[8]

However, this common "strengthening the state" approach to managing instability seems fundamentally flawed: "approaches to violence that begin with the Weberian assumption that the state is an entity with a monopoly on the legitimate use of violence start in the wrong place,"[9] highlighting the outmoded nature of state-centric assumptions that many experts cling to in seeking to address global chaotic disorder. This typical means of "managing" armed non-state groups—"military strengthening of regimes in power so that sovereignty or government authority is no longer in question"[10]—appears to be grossly mismatched with the current global instability predicament, where many central state governments seem incapable, regardless of outside aid, of finding ways to address the wide range of security threats they face. In recent decades, strengthening states has not automatically increased compliance of disruptive armed nonstate groups or overall national stability.

There are several reasons why a focus on strengthening the state is misplaced and why persisting in this government assistance policy makes little sense in promoting stability. First, such an approach does not address the root causes of the internal security governance problems. If structural issues cause government ineptitude, then aiding the state will do little. For example, "to date the response by the Central American governments to combat the escalation in gang violence through the strengthening of weak, corrupt, and failing criminal justice and judicial institutions has been little more than bandages on a bullet wound."[11] Similarly, in many countries strengthening the central government may require too dramatic a transformation to be successful:

> If . . . the governing style and methods of the ruling group are at the root of the problem, strengthening the state would require instigating more profound social and political change. Such states might not be salvageable through the usual institutional reform mechanisms. To change the character of such a state, if it is to be attempted at all, would be risky and expensive, with uncertain chances of success.[12]

The dominant posture that every state government can be fixed and made functional ignores these impediments, not to mention the fundamental problem in many developing countries that state boundaries were arbitrarily determined by colonial powers in the first place.

Second, the historical record of relying on exclusive state government authority, or attempting to strengthen central state governments and reinforce their position as the sole coercive authorities, is spotty in attaining or maintaining lasting stability. Somalia is a depressing showcase in this regard. Numerous circumstances exist where "states themselves are a major contributor to insecurity at the human and global levels":[13] for example, a comprehensive 2004 study "indicated that nearly all women joined armed groups to shield themselves from violation of their physical and mental integrity by state actors."[14] At least one analyst contends that "the cost of allowing the state to monopolize violence is the terrible barbarity of twentieth century wars and totalitarianism."[15] The bottom-up "Arab Spring" turmoil in North Africa and parts of the Middle East begun in 2010 has highlighted strong national governments' inability to promote lasting stability, instead fostering a kind of temporary "pseudo-stability based on repression" that can explode at any moment.[16] The tendency toward debilitating corruption and unwarranted violence seems as rampant within many state governments and state armies and police forces as within many armed nonstate groups—indeed, "some state behaviours are so outrageous as to constitute intolerable crimes against humanity and require that limits be placed on Westphalian sovereign immunity."[17] Even with outside assistance, national government law-enforcement organizations within slow moving bureaucracies may be no match for wealthy, ruthless, and agile transnational armed nonstate groups benefiting from corrupt central state government officials including "diplomats, judges, spies, generals, cabinet ministers, and police chiefs."[18]

Third, not only has external assistance usually failed to strengthen the state sufficiently so that it can reclaim effective security governance and promote stability, but also it has fostered the potential for significant boomerang effects. In particular, often one of the aims of an outside coercive assistance effort is to cut off sources of funding to disruptive armed nonstate groups; but "if a targeted violent non-state group directly or indirectly operates or funds a social welfare organization, traditional . . . policies could backfire" by risking poverty, despair, and radicalization of the affected population:[19]

> Social welfare can create lasting loyalties not easily supplanted by reassertions of state control. Forcibly stopping a group from dispensing needed social services can backfire. Even if such government action does not bolster the terrorist group's standing with the population, it almost certainly will result in increased

popular hardship. This alone can further undermine the legitimacy of the state, creating a vacuum violent non-state terrorist groups can and will exploit over time.[20]

American and Israeli efforts to hamper Hezbollah in southern Lebanon run this risk. Furthermore, outside assistance in strengthening state sovereignty can backfire by inadvertently reducing democratic processes within the state regime (where, for example, a state like Colombia can respond more to American antidrug pressures than to the will of the Colombian people). This outcome in turn can lead to the emergence of more antigovernment groups that seek to overturn the status quo.

Avoid Blanket Opposition to Armed Nonstate Groups

As discussed in Chapter 3, the most widespread view of armed nonstate groups is that they are violent illegitimate "spoilers" triggering chaos wherever they appear. In the post-9/11 global security environment, there are also those in the West who inappropriately equate every rising armed nonstate group with a potential terrorist threat.[21] For these reasons, a common policy—second in popularity only to propping up the state—is to focus on constraining all armed nonstate groups as a means of attaining stability. Since this perspective sees these groups as incapable of enhancing stability, their proliferation would be deemed to be inherently destabilizing. If complete containment is impossible, the prevailing policy is to, at the very least, remove armed nonstate groups from any position of meaningful power and influence.

The logic underlying this approach is that armed nonstate groups always provide a threat to stability and constitute a primary cause of instability within countries. Thus, impeding these groups' operations would be the key to providing long-term security in affected countries. Rather than being open to integrating these groups into some kind of ad hoc governance structure, the goal instead would be to isolate them as much as possible, reducing their attractiveness to the mass population, bottlenecking their sources of support, and capturing or killing their leadership.

However, there are several reasons why this indiscriminate focus on undermining armed nonstate groups seems misplaced. First, the pervasive, firmly held policy of states refusing to open a dialogue with any armed nonstate group—particularly with terrorists, warlords, rebels/insurgents, or criminals—makes little sense in today's world. As the eventual dialogue between the IRA and the United Kingdom showed, sometimes negotiation between states and antagonistic armed nonstate groups can yield positive results for both parties. In circumstances where "nonstate actors have already replaced state agents as the providers of protection in the local communities, then trying to remove them will only add to the impetus for short-term predation and further endanger human lives."[22] In other words, whether a ruling force can call itself a "state" or a "national government" should not be the primary or exclusive determinant of whether they receive a place at the bargaining table, are eligible for global aid, or receive any form of legitimate international recognition. Perhaps the most obvious reason not to pursue the indiscriminate eradication of armed nonstate groups is that they often provide basic services to local communities, successfully eradicating efforts to hurt human security. In cases where private security's quality, cost, and availability are more appealing to the mass public than public government security, as is evident in the growth of private security services and gated communities across the globe, there appears to be no reason to "bite the hand that feeds you."

Second, the threat from armed nonstate groups seems overstated—"the world is populated by armed groups that do not pose direct challenges to the Weberian state."[23] In many situations, armed nonstate groups' focus is more local than global, and in neither their state aspirations nor their behavior is there any sign that they want to lock horns with the central state government authority. As evident in Chapter 3's discussion of the different types of armed nonstate groups, several would prefer to fit into existing formal power structures—often though not always covertly—than to overturn them. The Yakuza in Japan illustrate this point. Treating all armed nonstate groups as being equivalent to extremist transnational terrorists, inherently violent and anti–status quo, is wrongheaded. So assuming that the mere presence of armed nonstate groups constitutes an inherently destabilizing societal force makes little sense, even from the narrow perspective of the central state government.

Third, the historical record is bleak in terms of managing undesired armed nonstate groups within a country. For example, in the widely publicized case of the war in Afghanistan, as discussed in Chapter 5, outside attempts to contain and restrain the Taliban show that their success has been mixed, with the Taliban extremely difficult to uproot or marginalize permanently. Within the last few decades, there have been few instances where either states or intergovernmental organizations have been effective in long-term removal or constraint of an armed nonstate group exerting territorial control: the usual result, owing to persistent inattention to root causes, is that such efforts temporarily curtail the groups' activities, only to have them resurface later.

WHAT TO DO TO PROMOTE STABILITY

Because of the failure of these commonly used blanket strategies, a dramatically different approach to stability promotion seems warranted. Fearing that any option besides support for state sovereignty would lead to complete global anarchy, where civil order has completely broken down and there is "no security and no legitimacy except in certain arbitrary instances," many observers witnessing global instability simply "cannot envisage alternative forms of authority"[24] that would be viable and effective. Excuses abound as to why any other option would be inferior or dangerous. Nonetheless, a variety of other possible management approaches do exist. As discussed in Chapter 3, the choice for stability promotion is not a simple binary one between failed and corrupt states on one hand and aggressive or illegal armed nonstate groups on the other hand. Instead, the international community could decide to address the root causes of instability, such as economic inequality or political oppression; it could turn to the myriad intergovernmental or nongovernmental humanitarian organizations and civil society groups to help provide for basic survival needs to deprived populations; or it could rely on multinational corporations to foster the kind of global economic integration that could promote global stability.

Of the variety of options available, perhaps the most promising option is the one most overlooked: the possibility of power sharing between states and armed nonstate groups. The reason for the lack of widespread discussion about this option is that it requires a different constellation of authority from what is commonly accepted today. As Chapter 3's discussion of the comparative advantages of the options demonstrates, armed nonstate groups appear to be the only choice where a coercive backdrop can be guaranteed in order to facilitate secure bottom-up provision of human security essentials. In all twelve cases studied in this book, the affected people living in vulnerable areas needing effective security governance would not have been able to have their basic survival needs fulfilled without the presence of an authority possessing considerable force. It is an unfortunate commentary on the current state of global anarchy that such a coercive backdrop seems essential for any improvement in most of the areas of the world with the greatest instability.

The Need for a Discriminating Mix of Public and Private Control

The new constellation of authority would replace the blanket policies prevalent today with a more discriminating mix of public and private control.[25] What this book advocates are policies that emphasize careful discrimination between circumstances where central state governments could and could not promote stability, and where armed nonstate groups could and could not promote stability. Across the board "it is simplistic to state unequivocally that non-state armed groups should be part of the solution to human security and development problems," for "this depends on the armed groups themselves and the human security efforts in which they and the state are engaged."[26] Thus, there would need to be painstaking assessment of which of the two would have the advantage under differing conditions, with the unambiguous goal being to impartially evaluate public and private players on the basis of their capacities to exercise effective and legitimate authority in the pursuit of stability. Such a discriminating policy would require that seemingly contradictory measures would need to be taken toward different kinds of states and armed nonstate groups, depending on their capacity to enhance stability, rather than a uniform policy toward each: it would be especially important to discriminate among the major types of armed nonstate groups and their control attempts, introduced in Chapter 3. Such discrimination would also require an open mindset that does not automatically equate armed nonstate groups with security threat and total state security control with stability—it would require explicit recognition that "limited statehood" does not inescapably imply the absence of governance or the provision of basic security needs to the people.[27]

This discriminating mix of public and private control is not totally innovative, as it harkens back to colonial times when principles of indirect rule were based on using promising local nonstate groups to partner with colonial administrators. Under this system, much day-to-day governance of localities was left in the hands of traditional rulers:

> Indirect rule, then, was devised as a form of governance by colonial powers to cope with the task of ruling over territories and populations largely outside governmental control. They used the prestige and authority of local potentates, so-called chiefs, to strengthen colonial rule by delegating limited powers. This strategy enabled colonial governments to rule over vast territories

and large populations with only small armed forces and limited administrative personnel.[28]

Much like the hard-pressed colonial officials centuries ago, contemporary policy makers in needy states may wish to contract out governance tasks to armed nonstate groups that provide security for local communities. In doing so, these state officials may encounter dilemmas similar to those evident in colonial times, including conflicts between the local and central government agendas, local players who manipulate external support for private ends, and armed groups taking advantage of external support to exploit local communities who no longer constitute the final arbiters of whether these groups have the right to rule. However, if one chooses carefully the armed nonstate groups involved in the mix of public and private control, as well as the joint stability management terms, such dilemmas could be minimized.

In addition to restraining measures aimed at uncooperative armed nonstate groups, this alternative security governance approach would support more flexible power sharing between states and cooperative armed nonstate groups, depending on what arrangement maximizes stability. Power sharing could include using groups that are willing to work with the state to collect reliable information not available through other means; using partnerships with these groups to demonstrate effective control to adversaries; and using success in these public-private alliances to convince local populations to provide broader support to the overall stability promotion effort within a country. Although not consistently evident in the case studies, at its best, "power sharing, in particular within a democratic framework, is a means of reducing the potential for renewed violence, as it may harness illegal armed groups' motivations and capacity to resort to violence."[29] This new constellation of authority recognizes the profound "way in which armed groups 'protect' other human security needs amongst their members, notably social or psycho-sociological needs," with the result being that "membership of an armed group may provide not just a means to livelihood and a source of physical protection, but an alternative unit of solidarity and identity."[30] Since there already has been some unofficial negotiation between armed nonstate groups' illicit networks and central state governments, this suggestion is not quite as radical as it initially sounds; moreover, despite preexisting prejudices, in some recent cases "governments seem increasingly willing to rely on the cooperation and resources of non-state actors."[31] In addition to direct participation in security governance, this power sharing could even involve armed nonstate groups actively participating in public debates through think tanks, nongovernmental organizations, journalism, and public-sector jobs.[32]

The rationale for this alternative security governance approach is multifaceted. In many parts of the world, armed nonstate groups are deeply rooted, with strong local community ties, and are in a position to understand security problems and sources of instability better than central state governments that are often distant. For example, for the United States "the escalating role of armed groups in the international security environment of the 21st century should not be seen as only constituting threats to US interests and security," as "in certain cases armed groups may also provide opportunities that, if taken advantage of, will contribute to the attainment of US foreign policy and national security objectives."[33] Since "the state does not necessarily represent the optimum set of political arrangements for meeting people's needs or for ensuring peace and stability, more organic, bottomup forms of governance, for all their shortcomings, might be the best available in a world of increasingly hollow states."[34] At the same time, the reason for advocating a mix of public and private control, rather than a complete transition to private authority, is that even the most promising armed nonstate groups have limitations and handicaps for some stability functions, which states may still provide effectively.

The new constellation of authority would require significant attitude changes among states, armed nonstate groups, and international organizations, summarized in Figure 8.1. Changes in attitude by states would include support for more flexible power sharing with armed nonstate groups, depending on what arrangement maximizes stability; establishment of a new balance between the protective benefits of armed nonstate groups and the legitimacy benefits of states, especially since these groups usually rely on the threat or use of force for governance;[35] promotion of a new balance between the desire for order at all costs and the maintenance of freedom within a society; openness to negotiate and compromise with armed nonstate groups when useful; and willingness to share, at least temporarily, certain security functions. Changes in attitude by armed nonstate groups would include receptivity to power sharing with central state governments; abandonment of antagonistic adversarial relationships with state officials; acknowledgment of their limitations and a commitment to avoid escalating their demands from the state; refraining from oppression or exploitation of people under their control; and readiness to consider violence as a last resort to achieve or maintain control. This change is not

Figure 8.1. Attitude changes for alternative security governance

---

Changes in attitude by states

Support for more flexible power sharing with armed nonstate groups

Establishment of a balance between the protective benefits of armed nonstate groups and the legitimacy benefits of states

Promotion of a balance between the desire for order at all costs and the maintenance of freedom within a society

Openness to negotiate and compromise with armed nonstate groups

Willingness to share, at least temporarily, certain security functions

---

Changes in attitude by armed nonstate groups

Receptivity to power sharing with central state governments

Abandonment of antagonistic adversarial relationships with state officials

Acknowledgment of their limitations and a commitment to avoid escalating their demands from the state

Refraining from oppression or exploitation of people under their control

Readiness to consider violence as a last resort to achieve or maintain security control

---

Changes in attitude by international organizations

Recognition of a wider range of legitimate state and nonstate security providers

Tolerance of cooperating armed nonstate groups undertaking security control attempts

Acceptance of instances where armed nonstate groups provide basic security needs for people in affected areas

Resistance to automatic equating of armed nonstate rule with security threat

Stopping vain attempts to restore central state government control in many circumstances

---

as far-fetched as it might seem, for groups as diverse as the Lord's Resistance Army and the Taliban have been open to discussion with government authorities. Lastly, changes in attitude by international organizations would include recognition of a wider range of legitimate state and nonstate security providers; tolerance of cooperative armed nonstate groups undertaking security control attempts; acceptance of instances where armed nonstate groups provide for basic survival needs to people in affected areas; resistance to automatic equating of armed nonstate rule with security threat; and stopping vain attempts to restore central state government control in many circumstances. Ultimately to foster smooth, legitimate, and effective power sharing, there would need to be a broader, overarching global system framework incorporating both states and armed nonstate groups, promoting stability in the face of two different sets of standard operating procedures.

Built-in incentives can exist for mutual gains to be achieved from rule combining public and private sources. Indeed, "the dynamics of competition between various domestic and international forces provides an incentive for states to rely on nonstate actors instead of maximizing control over violence": under the right circumstances, the participation of armed nonstate groups in security governance does "not constitute an aberration, a dysfunction or result of a failure of will," given how private "militias and state officials routinely co-operate with and mutually reinforce one another."[36] Perhaps in some cases it might be optimal to have "a system of multi-tiered political authority, in which "the state's role in world politics could be diminished to such an extent that there could be considerable doubt in theory and in practice as to whether sovereignty lay with the national government or with other levels of authority."[37] Highlighting the potential tangible benefits from cooperation between states and armed nonstate groups would help facilitate harmonious coexistence of these two different sources of security.

Preconditions for Successful Public-Private Power Sharing

Certain preconditions, summarized in Figure 8.2, maximize the potential for promoting stability of this discriminating mix of public and private control. In terms of stability enhancement origins, promoting stability appears to work best when it is homegrown and tailored to local needs[38] rather than externally developed or imposed; and when the stability functions most actively pursued are those deemed most relevant and meaningful by the affected state and its population (in contrast to those most valued by the stability enhancer). In terms of the stability enhancement mandate, promoting stability seems to work best when it exhibits the right kind of authority balance—"too little authority brings chaos and the loss of legitimacy; too much can crush the civil society that state institutions are intended to protect and nurture";[39] and when such stability promotion precludes the absolute need for the central state government to be totally and exclusively in control. In terms of stability enhancement responsibility, promoting stability appears to work best when such a thrust constitutes a carefully thought-out joint power-sharing effort between public and private groups;[40] and, within state bureaucracies, responsibility is shared across government agencies (rather than centered in a single branch,

Figure 8.2. Preconditions for successful public-private power sharing

---

Stability enhancement origins

If stability enhancement is homegrown and tailored to local needs rather than externally developed or imposed

If the type of stability pursued is that most desired by the affected state and its people

---

Stability enhancement mandate

If stability enhancement has the right authority balance, promoting both its legitimacy and societal freedoms

If stability enhancement does not require the central state government to be totally and exclusively in control

---

Stability enhancement responsibility

If stability enhancement responsibility constitutes a joint effort between public and private groups

If stability enhancement responsibility is shared across government agencies within state bureaucracies

---

Stability enhancement openness

If stability enhancement is flexible about political ideologies, institutional forms, and core values

If stability enhancement is not demanding about socioeconomic outcomes

---

Stability enhancement comprehensiveness

If stability enhancement is proactive rather than reactive

If stability enhancement incorporates both human and state security concerns

---

Stability enhancement prioritization

If stability enhancement is well integrated into security strategy and doctrine

If consensus exists in the stability enhancer about the primacy of stability as a security goal

---

such as defense). In terms of stability enhancement openness, promoting stability seems to work best when it is flexible about political ideologies, institutional forms, and core values (rather than insistent on certain beliefs) and when it is not demanding about particular socioeconomic outcomes (such as equality). In terms of stability enhancement comprehensiveness, promoting stability appears to work best when actions undertaken are proactive rather than reactive, and when this effort incorporates both human and state security priorities (rather than just securing government regime continuity). Finally, in terms of stability enhancement prioritization, promoting stability seems to work best when it is well integrated into security strategy and doctrine (rather than treated in a disconnected manner), and when consensus rather than dissention exists among the decision makers in the stability enhancer about the primacy of stability as a security goal in the affected area and about the chosen means of enhancing stability. Hezbollah in Lebanon provides a model of some of these preconditions, even though not every optimal circumstance for such power sharing has yet been fully realized

The aspiration in using mixed public-private control for security governance is that a wider variety of security protection types would be available to vulnerable populations and that fewer coverage gaps would emerge. With states and armed nonstate groups possessing differing comparative advantages, as detailed in Chapter 3, each ought to be capable of addressing complementary protection holes. Even under this system, however, there is no guarantee that gaps might not surface in some security areas for some affected people.

STRATEGIES TO FACILITATE COOPERATIVE ARMED NONSTATE GROUPS

The strategy of power sharing between states and armed nonstate groups is not applicable universally, for—as the case studies suggest—only certain kinds of armed nonstate groups in certain situations have the potential to enhance stability. As discussed in Chapter 6, certain prerequisites need to be met in order to maximize this potential: a legacy of state security ineffectiveness or injustice; a tradition of customary authority being located outside of the central state government; supportive armed nonstate group relationship with the state government; positive armed nonstate group ties to the local society; a unified sense of direction in the armed nonstate group; and fear of more dangerous outside forces gaining control of the area. Under these conditions, private sources of stability appear to be one of the few available defensive safeguards against rampant and uncontrolled anarchy and violence, and seem to be more readily available and more likely to be effective than central state government security. In addition, because power sharing entails a two-way-relationship, states involved need to recognize the need and be capable of handling this arrangement.

The notion of power sharing is novel for many types of armed nonstate groups. For many private security providers, however, this is not the case:

[T]he accelerated growth of private security forces on a world-wide scale may be the most important challenge to conventional thinking on non-state armed actors, in theoretical if not empirical terms, because it signals the widespread transfer of security functions from the state to civil society. The fact that private police are evident in rich and poor countries alike, democratic and otherwise, further suggests that this shift may be as much about contemporary times and reflective of larger patterns of security re-organization seen in the widespread transfer of policing functions from the public to the private sphere, as it is about poverty, state fragility, and democratic institutions and practices (or lack thereof). To the extent that private police exist alongside public police, rather than in replacement of them, also means that this phenomenon blurs the line between a state and non-state monopoly of the means of violence, thereby challenging the categorical imperative underlying long-standing use.[41]

This pattern often reflects "the forging of new compromises or complicities between state and non-state coercive actors, with such relationships reinforcing a tendency toward oligopoly [rather than monopoly] in the means of violence."[42] Although power sharing is much less common for some types of armed nonstate groups, this example demonstrates the potential for public-private security cooperation. Thus, many states are already engaging in power sharing with armed nonstate groups, to a certain extent, and in most cases without significant complaints from participating central state governments or cries of outrage from affected populations.

Numerous steps need to be taken in appropriate circumstances to promote the kind of public-private power sharing that maximizes stability. These include (1) carefully choosing cooperative armed nonstate groups, (2) fostering a constructive dialogue among states, armed nonstate groups, and international organizations; (3) encouraging state governments who are open to security assistance to welcome and recognize stability-enhancing armed nonstate groups; (4) delimiting through tacit mutual agreement the division of authority between states and armed nonstate groups; and (5) ensuring that states guarantee noninterference in armed nonstate groups' sanctioned activities in these power-sharing arrangements. Figure 8.3 summarizes these steps, which pose key challenges and radically differ from current policies of both states and intergovernmental organizations toward armed nonstate groups.

In the process, there needs to be considerable care to ensure that the resulting power sharing is real—involving security governance compromises on

Figure 8.3. Facilitating cooperative armed nonstate groups

Carefully choose armed nonstate groups appropriate for security governance

Make sure that sufficient trust, coherence, and credibility exist between states and selected groups.

Encompass only those groups whose internal security benefits outweigh any regional security costs.

Include only those groups whose short-term stability benefits outweigh any long-term stability costs.

Foster a constructive mutual dialogue about the shift in security governance

Encourage reinforcement of humanitarian norms through such engagement by official bodies.

Stimulate positive resocialization of selected groups through these efforts.

Move incrementally toward functional recognition of benefits by both states and selected groups.

Welcome and recognize stability-enhancing armed nonstate groups

Have states initiate power sharing to maximize their perceived legitimacy and ensure serving of the public interest.

Solidify their ties in a local community to encourage selected groups to promote its sustainability and productivity.

Highlight benefits to selected groups from providing stability and security protection to the people.

Delimit division of authority between states and armed nonstate groups

Increase awareness and acceptance by both parties of their physical, political, economic, and cultural authority boundaries.

Be aware that authority division may not conform to political demarcations accepted by states or the international community.

Have a fluid process to determine who controls what, as these authority boundaries may change over time.

Guarantee noninterference from states in sanctioned armed nonstate group activities

Keep those groups helping with local security from becoming victims of unwanted disruptive intervention by the state.

Make the principle of noninterference apply not only to states but also to intergovernmental bodies.

Instill no requirement or expectation of any kind of formal recognition of this power sharing.

both sides—and not a façade. Often "non-state armed groups of various types would be allowed to continue to exist and sometimes prosper, as long as they were willing to pay at least lip service to the bureaucratic process and abstained from actively working against the central government."[43] Illusory power sharing, where one side or the other is not really trying to cooperate and where no genuine power sharing is present, can be more dangerous that no power sharing at all, for it deceives those affected (and sometimes those participating) about what is going on and eliminates any possibility for accountability for security governance missteps.

Carefully Choose Armed Nonstate Groups Appropriate for Security Governance

States that are open and receptive to power sharing must discriminate carefully to determine which armed nonstate groups to approach as potential partners in security governance, because some of these groups would have no interest or capacity to promote stability. Although within power-sharing arrangements both state governments and armed nonstate groups are likely to have some internal corruption, this arrangement would work only if sufficient trust, coherence, and credibility developed between the two parties so as to make tacit agreements meaningful. An error in judgment about a potential armed nonstate group partner could be disastrous, for a group could become more disruptive, violent, and destabilizing once it attains a power-sharing relationship with a central state government. The ideal outcome of a successful public-private power-sharing relationship would be to have armed nonstate groups harmoniously partnering with state governments to provide stability.

In choosing appropriate cooperative armed nonstate groups for power sharing, there is a need to overcome previously mentioned difficulties in distinguishing stabilizing from destabilizing groups, associated with challenges in discerning their motivations and behavior. If an inappropriate and uncooperative armed nonstate group were in control of an area, it would need to be restrained or uprooted. In addition, in light of previously mentioned risks, cooperative armed nonstate groups ought to be selected only if their positive impact on internal security outweighed their negative impact on regional security; and if their positive contribution to short-term stability outweighed any negative impact on long-term stability. If an armed nonstate group was directly or indirectly responsible for helping to foster instability, then its possible inclusion in any security governance arrangement would necessitate that it possess great skills or advantages in restoring stability to the affected area. Careful scrutiny of these balances seems particularly vital when dealing with an armed nonstate group with a legacy of horrific violence—"what are the prospects of reintegrating an armed group that abducts and press-gangs children and adolescents and that is also responsible for massive human-rights abuses?"[44]

Foster a Constructive Mutual Dialogue about the Shift in Security Governance

To move toward an integrative power-sharing arrangement involving state governments and armed nonstate groups, a second step must be taken: fostering a constructive mutual dialogue among representatives from states, armed nonstate groups, and international organizations:

> In these settings [local political contexts], political power is typically personalized, factionalized, and underwritten by nonstate armed groups, some of which are supported by neighboring countries. The desired transformation entails a political effort to enable local leaders and social groups to arrive at a national compact—an agreement on power sharing and the rules of the game—and to jump-start local institutional building and economic development, while managing the policies of neighboring powers to prevent destabilizing interventions. Success requires an intensive engagement—both in terms of leadership time and resources—and therefore should be undertaken selectively in the service of genuine strategic priorities.[45]

Such engagement by official bodies could on occasion reinforce humanitarian norms:

> Engagement is a mechanism by which non-state armed groups can participate in humanitarian norm building. Unlike customary laws, which apply to armed groups through the territorial state, the group consents to the norms of special agreements when negotiating. If an armed group is involved in negotiating the conduct that it will eventually adhere to, it could "create a sense of ownership over the law" and lead to greater compliance. Humanitarian provisions that protect the armed groups' members may also encourage compliance with the laws of war.[46]

The underlying thrust is to maximize the affected population's security.

The purpose of this dialogue would be to figure out how to move incrementally and peacefully toward functional state–armed nonstate group power-sharing arrangements. If done right, "the situation is often one of mutual interchange in which both . . . gain advantages from collaboration or, at the very least, tolerance."[47] Such arrangements would need to determine how to process dynamic change over time in the domains controlled by states and armed nonstate groups. The participants in this dialogue would be respected leaders among relevant parties who appear to have the greatest potential to possess a broad vision of shared security governance possibilities. To facilitate the dialogue between states and armed nonstate groups, "unofficial back channels such as outside non-governmental organizations (NGOs) may sometimes help bring NSAGs [non-state armed groups] and state governments to the negotiating table."[48] In the process, conditions would need to be specified as to when armed nonstate groups have the most acceptable and beneficial impacts on stability, as well as implicitly when states would find it most acceptable and beneficial to allow certain of their traditional security functions to be undertaken by these private groups. However, states need to constantly monitor participating armed nonstate groups' behavior so as to ensure that any positive talk is not accompanied by disruptive actions. Similarly, each side should monitor the other to ensure that each practices what it preaches.

Welcome and Recognize Stability-Enhancing Armed Nonstate Groups

A third step in power sharing, after dialogue has begun, is for central state governments open to security governance assistance to welcome and recognize stability-enhancing armed nonstate groups within their countries, acknowledging those that are already providing essential stability functions; and to invite in to power-sharing arrangements those that are not yet participating in stability promotion efforts. The initiative for these arrangements usually should come from the state (exceptions being if the central state government is nonexistent or is too inept or corrupt) in order to maximize these steps' perceived legitimacy and to ensure that the outcome will serve the public interest. Outsiders cannot believe that armed nonstate groups coercively forced states to accept power sharing unwillingly if these arrangements are to function properly.

Ideally, this approach could free the state from security responsibilities it is having trouble fulfilling. Indeed, "rather than trying to replace militias by rehabilitating and augmenting state security services, the international community must focus on recruiting the services of tribes, ethnic groups, and village strongmen" to help out in this regard, as "solidifying their ties in a local community encourages them to form a vested interest in the community's sustainability and productivity."[49] Instead of a struggling central state government having to rely on the sometimes inconsistent provision of foreign security aid by humanitarian groups and intergovernmental organizations whose will, capacity, and understanding of local traditions are often suspect, such a regime could look internally for help from those groups that may already have a deep comprehension of the local culture and may already be plugged into the societal infrastructure in ways that can enhance stability.

Figuring out the appropriate avenues to be used by states to officially welcome and recognize cooperating armed nonstate groups would entail finding the best ways to reinforce these groups' realization of benefits to themselves from providing stability to the people living in areas they control. Such reinforcement efforts could lead to constructive resocialization of armed nonstate groups:

> In the context of established institutional arrangements (e.g. electoral system, modes of power-sharing) and through political practice spoilers are successively socialised into accepting certain norms and rules of the game. Armed non-state actors undergo processes of collective learning which may change their strategies and, eventually, their preferences and their character. This medium- to long-term strategy may work again primarily for those armed actors with political ambitions who have to address certain long-term expectations of their followers.[50]

However, states would need to be careful in these welcoming and recognizing processes to specify that the kind of private autonomy being offered is limited rather than total.

Delimit Division of Authority between States and Armed Nonstate Groups

A fourth step in implementing power sharing is to delimit, through tacit mutual agreement, the division of authority between states and cooperative armed nonstate groups. Both parties need to become aware and accepting of the physical, political, economic, and cultural boundaries of their authority. In all likelihood, these lines of authority would not be immediately apparent and instead would be the product of extensive negotiations between the two parties. For a successful power-sharing outcome, both participating states and cooperative armed nonstate groups would need to be willing to be flexible and compromise on key issues. All participating parties should take care to communicate effectively to avoid the previously identified risks of public-private contention, mutual condescension, or a pervasive sense that key elements have been ignored. Within agreeable, well-demarcated power-sharing relationships between states and armed nonstate groups, both would need to recognize and accept their power limitations. Ideally, states would benefit from receiving assistance in providing security in difficult-to-manage areas, and armed nonstate groups would benefit from operating in an environment they find to be both predictable and hospitable.

Although the territorial boundaries of armed nonstate group authority may not conveniently conform to those of political demarcations previously defined by the state or accepted by the international community—in some cases, the lines of control may even cross national boundaries—external respect for the lines of jurisdiction is essential for power-sharing success. These authority boundaries may change over time, but the key is having a process in place to determine adjustments in who controls what. As population concentrations, resource availability, and security needs change over time, the division of authority could be reconsidered and renegotiated. However, if too much ambiguity persists about the shared control between central state governments and armed nonstate groups, if dividing lines of authority are too fluid, or if no procedure is in place through which new agreements can be reached when circumstances transform, such power sharing is doomed to failure.

Guarantee State Noninterference in Sanctioned Armed Nonstate Group Activities

The fifth and final step of this power-sharing process is for central state governments to ensure that cooperative armed nonstate groups have a confident sense of noninterference from the state. No such power-sharing arrangement can work if armed nonstate groups accept the invitation to help with local security provision, only to find themselves constantly the subject of unwanted and disruptive snooping and intervention by the state into how these groups undertake sanctioned activities to supply security to the local citizenry. While armed nonstate groups would possess constrained autonomy, the central state government needs to leave well enough alone in the areas designated for private control if the power-sharing arrangement is to work smoothly. Given that this private coercive stability promotion works in a bottom-up fashion contrasting with the top-down state control, government officials need to exhibit patience in temporarily tolerating such issues as "the reluctance of commanders to hand over [or substantially reduce] their full weapons stockpiles" or to terminate on-going corrupt practices;[51] and these groups' more-than-occasional sluggishness and nonlinearity to take meaningful steps to stabilize their local communities. Furthermore, this principle of noninterference would need to apply not only to states—including both the central government within the country where the armed nonstate group has received license to operate and outside states—but also to intergovernmental organizations. Despite this noninterference, this power sharing does not need any kind of formal recognition, instead just tacit local acceptance of its existence.

There need be no intrinsic humiliation or sense of sovereignty loss in this kind of power sharing or reaching out by states to armed nonstate groups. In-deed, it would be inappropriate to portray this power sharing as inherently a loss of state sovereignty, for often noninvolvement of an armed nonstate group might simply mean that a designated area remains ungoverned or inadequately governed. Under the right circumstances, central state governments might eventually develop a compelling relationship with armed nonstate groups where complementary security governance strengths are accepted and appreci-ated, and where each party realized that its security responsibilities are those it accomplishes best. However, the state pledge of noninterference needs to be contingent on armed nonstate group compliance with the mutually-agreed-upon terms of authority, including provision of stability to the affected popula-tion in an acceptable manner.

Security Implications

What would such power-sharing arrangements between states and armed nonstate groups look like in the long run? Typically, in most countries there would be areas where the state had ceded security governance—not all forms of control—to armed nonstate groups, and allegiance by local citizens living in these areas would often be more toward the local groups than to the cen-tral state governments. The nature of this ceding of control would probably remain tacit rather than formal and not necessarily be transparent to outsid-ers: in most cases, the area controlled by the private group would not become a legally recognized autonomous zone; and the private group would not be fully reintegrated back into mainstream society and would not become a le-gally recognized governing authority or even an official political party of any kind. However, unlike tribal enclaves all over the world, armed nonstate groups performing security governance roles would not have to fear constant state-initiated attempts to eradicate them, and states involved in power sharing would be able to reallocate scarce resources to other areas. The mass public would not necessarily immediately see huge changes in their protection, as the primary transformation would be in security authority control. The power sharing between states and armed nonstate groups would not, in all probability, involve equal responsibilities on each side. An uneasy truce would exist between states and these groups operating within its boundaries, with both parties wary of exceeding their authority on issues of overlapping jurisdiction. Despite fluctuating ties and interactive networks with other groups, armed nonstate groups pursuing stability would focus on internal local security concerns, shunning most foreign security-policy issues that would remain the prerogative of the state. Thus, despite the increasingly transnational spread of armed nonstate groups, global negotiations and diplomacy would largely remain interstate, as is the case today.

Some fundamental thorny questions emerge about the security implications of power sharing between states and armed nonstate groups. First, would the world be a lot safer than it is today with such power sharing? Local communities that previously had no effective government security might view such power-sharing arrangements as increasing the chances that they have access at least to some form of stability-enhancing protection. Second, would global violence decrease from the current level if such power-sharing arrangements were commonplace? Given that armed nonstate groups frequently resort to force to maintain order, this move toward civility does not appear to be particularly likely, at least in the short run. Third, would the people now protected by armed nonstate groups perceive that their plight had improved? Although members of the mass population would probably be safer, they might be more fearful, and there is the possibility of greater human rights violations as well. Finally, can states go too far in power-sharing efforts toward cooperative armed nonstate groups—"is there a breaking point where an 'over-facilitation' of former combatants' interests will jeopardise the overall economic wellbeing of a country and perpetuate cycles of underdevelopment, grievance and insecurity?"[52] Without clear state limits on accommodation to private power sharing, problematic human security impacts on the country as a whole could proliferate.

The security implications of changing to this new constellation of authority are not modest ones. Ultimately the whole playing field in international relations would undergo change as a result of this shift in security governance. Top-down reform would have to occur to cope with the bottom-up governance changes wrought by armed nonstate groups. States would need to dramatically expand their perceptions of who has the right to use force and for what purpose. International organizations might have to consider the possibility of giving armed nonstate groups some form of representation. The concept of sovereignty would require considerable expansion. Notions of legitimacy would require rethinking and revision, along with the currently state-centric principles of international law on which the acceptability of many actions is based: certain kinds of violence have become more legitimate than others, and certain kinds of perpetrators of violence can do so with more impunity than others.[53] Notions of predictability and permanence might recede in popularity in favor of notions of adaptability and flexibility. Mass public security expectations would transform regarding the level, type, and source of security anticipated. The comparative attractiveness of being a state government official versus an armed nonstate group member could change dramatically. Outside perceptions of stability in a power-sharing area would likely differ more sharply than they do of states today.

Perhaps most important, our ways of classifying key security players in international relations may undergo significant change. Instead of assuming that all central state governments promote stability, this alternative approach to security governance would force a distinction between state regimes possessing and those not possessing the capacity and will to be stabilizing. Instead of lumping all armed nonstate groups together as being threats to the state and threats to the stability and security of vulnerable populations, this alternative approach to security governance would induce a discriminating policy split between cooperative armed nonstate groups and uncooperative groups. Instead of viewing stability in monolithic terms, this alternative approach to security governance would separate the stability functions that states and armed nonstate groups can and cannot promote. Finally, instead of viewing the international system as being most functional when top-down control is evident, emphasizing increased centralization and a larger scope of authority, this alternative approach concludes that bottom-up security governance, emphasizing local control and a smaller scope of authority, could be just as effective, if not more so, under some circumstances.

STRATEGIES TO IMPEDE UNCOOPERATIVE ARMED NONSTATE GROUPS

If careful assessment reveals that an armed nonstate group is uncooperative and disruptive, then public-private power sharing should not be pursued. This inappropriateness could be a function of an armed nonstate group's refusal to play ball with existing state authorities, its antagonistic relationship with the local society, its internal divisiveness or promotion of factionalism within a society, or its central position in fomenting the very instability and turmoil that needs to be addressed. In these situations, however, uncooperative armed nonstate groups should not be ignored, and there should not necessarily be reversion to strengthening the central state government as the means of promoting stability. Instead, as with more conventional counterinsurgency policies, the focus should be on undermining, containing, and minimizing the disruptive impact of threatening uncooperative armed nonstate groups.

Because disruptive armed nonstate groups can be extremely clever and resilient and can adjust quickly to changing circumstances and countermeasures, taking advantage of the combined resources of defense and law-enforcement institutions—utilizing both police and military forces—provides the best chance for containing unruly corrupt or violent subnational and transnational activity. Utilizing these combined resources should result in at least a delay and possibly a long-term reduction in violent disruptive activities by these groups. Although the containment efforts may not always be successful, this combined institutional strategy should not be difficult to achieve because of the recent fusion of criminal justice and national security concerns, especially in Western advanced industrial societies.[54]

In order to maximize stability, concrete steps impeding uncooperative armed nonstate groups ought to include better (1) intelligence on disruptive armed nonstate groups; (2) early warning through preventative measures; (3) negative and positive sanctions to minimize violence; (4) bottom-up local responsibility to provide protection against the human security dangers; and (5) target-centered threat protection from disruptive armed nonstate groups. These unorthodox prescriptions consider both the feasibility and desirability and the short-term and long-term impacts of these disruptive groups thwarting stability promotion. Figure 8.4 summarizes these steps, which are for uncooperative groups almost as markedly different from current policies as are the strategies recommended earlier for dealing with cooperative groups.

Intelligence on Disruptive Armed Nonstate Groups

A cornerstone of impeding uncooperative armed nonstate groups to promote stability is improving intelligence on them and their disruptive activities. This thrust requires recognizing that traditional forms of intelligence have not been and will not be sufficient in the future:

Figure 8.4. Impeding uncooperative armed nonstate groups

Intelligence on disruptive armed nonstate groups

Improving knowledge about these groups' strength, funding, goals and intentions, and susceptibility to countermeasures

Understanding better how these groups transform and the trajectory of particular groups in the near future

Relying more on nongovernmental intelligence networks and on cross-agency and cross-national intelligence sharing

Early warning through preventative measures

More carefully tracking illicit cross-border transactions, group containment efforts, and protection of vulnerable areas

Insulating states from the entrance of these groups rather than dealing with them after they have already taken root

Finding globally acceptable ways to undermine norms that promote the development and flourishing of these groups

Negative and positive sanctions to minimize violence

Isolating disruptive violent groups diplomatically, militarily, or economically through a variety of stronger multilateral sanctions

Strengthening the armed forces and the police to protect citizens in the face of dangers from these groups

Using creative positive incentives to get these groups to see the benefits to themselves in constructive transformation

Bottom-up responsibility to protect against human security dangers

Enhancing awareness that security is everyone's business, with local communities working to oppose these groups

Expanding local accountability, preparedness, and vigilance to help with monitoring and enforcement

Promoting decentralized civic engagement, fostering resilient communities that look locally for protection

Target-centered threat protection from disruptive armed nonstate groups

Emphasizing victim protection from existing vulnerabilities because identifying the culprits for disruptions is usually futile

Applying "target-hardening" techniques, determining what can be done to reduce existing vulnerabilities

Focusing on high-risk targets including those most exposed and susceptible to the threat from these groups

In particular, the intelligence communities of states have struggled to understand the motivations, interests, and ethno-national, religious, and resource-based grievances of new groups. Intelligence networks have also struggled with how to gain internal access to these groups in order to monitor their plans and activities from within the organization, particularly when group identity is centered on religious or ethno-national loyalties.[55]

Bureaucratic inertia and complacency frequently impede recognition of these deficiencies in standard operating procedure.

As to the most important kinds of intelligence to be collected, states and international bodies need to have much better specific knowledge about the strength of the perpetrators of disruption, their goals, plans, and intentions, and the actual impact upon them of implemented countermeasures.[56] Because many of these groups rely on illicit drug funding, there is a need to follow the money trail more carefully. Since so many armed nonstate groups are in a state of flux, there is a pressing need to know more about how they transform, the trajectory of particular groups in the near future, and the resources needed to achieve this transformation. There also should be more careful tracking of rapidly changing new technologies useful to these groups for recruiting, training, and equipping new members and facilitating, distorting, or concealing their illicit cross-border transfers. Beyond expanded and refocused intelligence collection, more disruptive counterintelligence operations toward armed nonstate groups may merit consideration, even though such efforts could risk devastating consequences if detected. Special circumstances, however, may warrant their consideration.

As to the best sources of information for this purpose, nongovernmental intelligence networks stand out. Because disruptions usually arise in a bottom-up fashion from local communities, on-the-ground intelligence would seem most helpful. Such networks may include the armed nonstate groups themselves, as due to "marriages of convenience" and collusive arrangements such groups often have considerable knowledge of each other's operations. Human intelligence (rather than technical intelligence gathered through electronic means) seems most vital,[57] as the often concealed nature of armed nonstate group activities makes them difficult to discern even at close range or with great observational detail. Given this bottom-up approach, source credibility would require careful background investigation. In utilizing these information sources, the expanding global scope of armed nonstate group control attempts requires a transnational intelligence thrust, making cross-national intelligence sharing essential and overcoming barriers caused by distrust. Moreover, secure sharing of intelligence among relevant agencies within states is essential to track elusive transactions. When relying more on unorthodox intelligence sources while simultaneously expanding the sharing of information collected, care should be taken, through careful cross-checking, to avoid corrupt and disreputable parties whose cooperation may risk significant leaks.

Early Warning through Preventative Measures

Given how subtly entrenched uncooperative armed nonstate groups are within societies, it appears crucial for stability promotion to stress better early warning through preventative measures. Responding too late to uncooperative armed nonstate groups is a persistent problem: for example, especially in the war in Afghanistan, "US stability and security operations to date have been primarily reactive, rather than pro-active, in seeking resources and strategies to inhibit establishment of terrorist strongholds in failing states."[58] The logic behind the necessity of this change is straightforward: "unable to control the battlefield through overwhelming violence or technological advances, Western warriors are systematically disadvantaged; because they are *reacting* to insurgency challenges, states are all but unable to regain the military initiative."[59] This early-warning approach would use precautionary policies to minimize armed nonstate group expansion, isolate such groups in terms of their links with both states and cooperative armed nonstate groups and disrupt armed nonstate groups' well-connected nodes,[60] and keep these groups away from vulnerable areas. Some specific positive initiatives to improve the speed of attending to critical instability lapses include (1) improvement of early-warning capabilities in affected areas, pushing for "for increased attention to what precipitates, escalates, and feeds conflicts"; (2) strengthening of rapid political and economic responses to preventing "the escalation of crises, and thereby avoid the need for expensive peace operations"; and (3) refinement of rapid security assistance, thereby enhancing operational effectiveness.[61] Underlying this strategy would be an emphasis on insulating countries from the entrance of armed nonstate group tentacles rather than—as is often the case today—dealing with them after they have taken root inside a country and formed a network of interconnections with other groups and government officials. Most generally, internationally acceptable ways need to be found to challenge and undermine norms that permit and promote the development and flourishing of uncooperative armed nonstate groups: in order to accomplish this, covert links between these disruptive groups and any state officials need to be identified and—to the extent possible—interrupted.

For security-capable advanced industrial societies, there are two principal components of this early-warning strategy. First, a unilateral internal thrust to safeguard one's own national borders against armed nonstate group violent intrusion seems essential. Improvements could include doing more cargo inspections closer to their point of origin; undertaking new technologies to provide electronic border filtering that discriminates between the legitimate and illicit crossing of goods, services, and people; and identifying and facilitating low-risk frequent travelers.[62] Some coordination—though not always complete harmonization—should occur among neighboring states' unilateral safeguarding of national borders, particularly if a common transshipment state is right next to a primary receiving state (as with Canada and the United States) for illicit cross-border transactions. Second, a multilateral external thrust appears crucial to improve the defenses of other countries without strong security capabilities, so that they can develop early-warning systems, avoid becoming safe havens, and nip their own problems in the bud before they spread elsewhere. On occasion, even the most needy recipients may require convincing about the value of this external defensive assistance and the utility of sidestepping worries about sovereignty to receive it. Although the first priority is protecting the security needs of the citizens living within one's own country, doing so without shoring up others' defenses against violent intrusion would appear to be relatively fruitless in an interdependent world.

For developing countries lacking a capable security apparatus, there is a need for openness to outside monitoring and possibly enforcement in tracking and apprehending members and activities of uncooperative armed nonstate groups and in preventing these areas from becoming safe havens for disruptive parties. Many of these states are justifiably wary of cultural imperialism and outside—particularly Western—influence, but this external assistance does not need to intrude on their sovereign right to make their own security decisions or on their distinctive cultural traditions. Thanks to technological advancements, much of the tracking can be accomplished remotely, precluding the need for the entrance of foreign security personnel to make the system work. However, such monitoring may require societal sacrifices concerning the right to privacy.

Negative and Positive Sanctions to Minimize Violence

Once better intelligence and early-warning systems are in place, sterner negative sanctions and stronger positive incentives need to be applied to improve prospects for stability. Threat targets should attempt to isolate disruptive violent groups diplomatically, militarily, or economically through a variety of multilaterally applied positive and negative sanctions.[63] Both types of sanctions need coherent integration in this effort to restrain uncooperative armed nonstate groups, for in such cases "a comprehensive strategy vis-à-vis spoilers, combining coercion and co-option," has served as "key ingredients in the set of policies that have brought high levels of stability."[64]

The usual emphasis in responses to disruptive, uncooperative armed nonstate groups has been on negative sanctions. These have typically fallen under the categories of (1) beefing up law-enforcement units' ability to confront the perpetrators of violence, (2) increasing monitoring and vigilance regarding violent activities, and (3) escalating penalties, especially for the severest acts of violence. Certainly "strengthening the armed forces and the police further is an essential part of restoring citizens' lives to safety" in the face of armed nonstate group dangers,[65] especially when these groups possess more coercive power than states. Many analysts believe that "deterrence remains a viable strategy for meeting their challenge."[66]

The negative sanctions imposed on uncooperative armed nonstate groups should include (1) placing every kind of pressure possible on the group's support system—financial interdiction, negative public affairs campaigns, direct attack, and deception; (2) keeping the pressure on for a sustained period; (3) working to establish or restore the integrity and legitimacy of political, economic, and social institutions tainted by armed nonstate group ties; (4) changing countermeasures continually to keep these groups off balance and to keep pace with their own changes in behavior; (5) fostering international cooperation to dismantle armed nonstate group networks[67] through concerted multilateral rather than unilateral action; and (6) enlisting the aid of third parties, such as host governments and international law-enforcement organizations. A flexible and versatile toolbox of approaches needs to be available for simultaneous use, utilizing both positive and negative incentives to confront these disruptive armed nonstate groups on all fronts: seek to deny them financial support and safe havens; attempt to interfere with and jam their use of advanced technologies; make unavailable or interfere with their modes of transport; pressure third parties not to support them; create a generally inhospitable environment for them; conduct aggressive intelligence operations against them; take action to disrupt their operations as much as possible, especially apprehending leaders and key operatives; visibly harden security to deny its objectives by making it physically much more difficult to achieve their goals; showcase one's victories against them; and mount one's own strategic communication campaigns. A special target of these negative sanctions might be societies whose cultural norms support widespread violence in a manner conducive to the emergence and thriving of uncooperative disruptive armed nonstate groups. Overall, those selecting negative sanctions need to keep in mind that armed nonstate groups "have fundamentally different perspectives from states on the issues of victory and defeat," as many of these groups appear to be willing to engage in protracted conflict with no decisive outcome[68] or to persist in undertaking disruptive activities when logically they should have given up the effort.

However, it would be foolhardy to address uncooperative armed nonstate group violence through force alone, as this thrust could easily lead to a spiraling, bloody action-reaction cycle and to state neglect of needed accompanying social measures and justice reform.[69] Moreover, while "confronting a VNSA [violent non-state actor] force with yet another force (e.g. using soldiers to stop suicide bombers) can work in the short-term," in the long term this approach can "play directly to the strengths of asymmetric confrontations" initiated by armed nonstate groups.[70] Particularly within transitional developing societies, a danger exists that state responses to armed nonstate groups could become overly militarized—reversing any progress toward civil society—due to intense pressures (1) from the government security establishment itself to utilize in a familiar and traditional way its capabilities and (2) from the mass public for immediate decisive government action against lawlessness.[71] Indeed, if a state always responds to the threat of uncooperative armed nonstate groups with the "heavy hand" of coercion, that could easily constitute a form of state failure, because as the state realizes that "it can no longer count on the fabric of shared values to hold it together, the basis of state authority in such situations then shifts to the unstable solution of coercion."[72] Historically, the first one to use violence in this action-reaction cycle has usually been the state, and often afterward violent conflict ensues.[73]

Because of these coercive limitations, more creativity is needed in developing positive sanctions and incentives to get uncooperative armed nonstate groups to transform constructively in ways that enhance stability. To move in this direction, key roadblocks need to be overcome. Many disappointments in dealing with disruptive groups are due to "the initial failure to formulate and implement an effective reintegration strategy—one able to transform 'insurgent' and other non-state armed groups into viable political entities; from political 'spoilers' to groups and key individuals that are prepared to eschew armed struggle and participate in peaceful political intercourse."[74] Managing such shifts successfully is not easy, and it requires surmounting the obstacle that these groups "may be less likely than states to be deterred, influenced by sanctions, or persuaded by the traditional incentives of negotiation attempts."[75] Such shifting efforts can be risky, particularly if undertaken by parties outside of the affected area: if it is known that such outside parties are trying to meddle and strategically influence the security governance of a particular area, local and global resentment can develop even if the motives of outside parties are noble and even if the outcome turns out to be temporarily stabilizing. Thus, while negative sanctions run the risk of triggering a mutual tit-for-tat cycle of violence, positive sanctions run the risk of perceived illegitimacy, potentially labeled by cynical observers as intrusive unwarranted outside manipulation that ignores local traditions.

With these roadblocks in mind, positive transformation efforts might require careful identification of the conditions under which armed nonstate groups see it in their best interests to participate in security governance, undergirded by isolating precise tipping points[76]—including those related to splits within and among these groups—necessary to shift their behavior in this direction. On the broadest level, this approach necessitates discovering ways to reshape the surrounding security environment to maximize compliance by armed nonstate groups. Because armed nonstate groups' orientation toward stability is not fixed, policies might try to shift the position of strong disinterested groups by encouraging them to recognize the utility of stability promotion through "a realization that non-violent strategies can be rewarded," as "mediators can also introduce norms into the negotiation and persuade all parties to a conflict that complying with these norms will benefit everyone involved."[77] Facilitating this forward movement can be the recognition by certain armed nonstate groups, such as maritime pirates, that "a basic level of law and order may be necessary for pirates to ply their dangerous trade."[78]

Most fundamentally, this transformation effort would need to affect the perceptual framework used by armed nonstate groups. First, to provide a springboard to begin positive transformation, perhaps the greatest focus of positive incentives for armed nonstate groups and their potential victims alike should be to try to end passive fatalistic acceptance of the global inevitability of violence. Second, to promote willingness to negotiate with states, it seems important to find ways to reduce armed nonstate groups' zero-sum competitive perceptions of confrontations with states, with such an effort deemed successful "when they decide that cooperation yields vastly greater benefits to both than antagonism."[79] Third, to enhance the potential for compromise, it appears crucial to minimize any extreme emotional perceptions by these groups, involving, for example, either "back to the wall" desperation or smug arrogance, in response to emerging predicaments they see as crises. Because the emotions surrounding violence—and the recruitment of new personnel for violent armed nonstate groups—are often associated with human rights abuses, demonization of enemies, severe unemployment, and easy weapons access, their minimization seems especially vital.

Bottom-Up Responsibility to Protect against Human Security Dangers

Enhancing bottom-up local responsibility seems essential for protecting against the human security dangers associated with disruptive, uncooperative armed nonstate groups. Since these groups' stability impact begins at the bottom, it makes sense that constraining uncooperative groups would also start there. This focus would help to overcome mass public ignorance of the scope and scale of the human security dangers involved,[80] for preparedness works best with "a population that acknowledges that security must become everyone's business."[81] Specifically, "if local communities can be convinced to turn against those who perpetrate barbaric acts of violence," then the chances increase that citizens who work with or support disruptive armed nonstate groups can be identified and rooted out.[82] Local accountability, preparedness, and vigilance— often of a "neighborhood watch" variety—need substantial improvement to help with monitoring and enforcement, for the scope of the threat is beyond the capacity of any central state government alone to manage, no matter what the size and strength of its police force. Because dangerous, uncooperative armed nonstate groups are often attracted to precisely those areas where state security governance is least effective, this local bottom-up responsibility seems particularly important.

Central to this effort is the promotion of civic engagement and civil society. One hopeful trend is the recent proliferation of resilient communities that look locally for protection rather than relying on outside facilitation.[83] To be most effective, local responsibility should be decentralized and sensitive to the community norms of distinctive cultural settings. However, because local municipal responsibility for civil defense can potentially create large differentials between the best and worst protected areas—often corresponding to socioeconomic disparities—universal minimally acceptable levels of protection would need to be firmly established for overall effectiveness.

Target-Centered Threat Protection from Disruptive Armed Nonstate Groups

To manage uncooperative armed nonstate groups in a way that promotes stability, more concerted target-centered threat management should be pursued. Given the largely covert and intertwined nature of armed nonstate group activities, it is likely to prove futile to concentrate on isolating the culprit in each instance of disruptive violent activity. For that reason, security analysis needs to move away from its traditional focus on identifying armed nonstate group initiators of violent disruption and move toward a target-centered threat management approach[84] emphasizing victim needs and designed to increase protection of vulnerable individuals and institutions. This target-centered approach assesses vital interests and protection priorities, emphasizing assets within targets at risk for violent disruption; level of vulnerability to damage or loss, incorporating threat targets' anticipation and preparation for the risk of violent intrusion; and the probability and magnitude of damage or loss, including the risks of occurrence and impact if they were actualized.

Target-centered management of armed nonstate groups necessitates critical application of "target-hardening" techniques, determining what makes certain targets vulnerable and how to reduce their vulnerability. This approach would focus on vital high-risk targets, including those most exposed and susceptible to disruptive armed nonstate group threat. By emphasizing more what a threat target cares about and can do something about, its security regarding incoming dangers could be improved even if they prove to be elusive. However, uncooperative armed nonstate groups are likely to shift targets constantly depending on relative safeguards and vulnerabilities, so priorities for target hardening would need to be constantly reevaluated.

Security Implications

Key security implications emerge from pursuing these particular avenues of dealing with uncooperative, disruptive armed nonstate groups. First, cross-national coordination and harmonization of positive and negative countermeasures would need to improve dramatically, with states sacrificing their sovereign right to choose what they want to do on behalf of overall constraint of these groups. Second, to have these countermeasures persist over time and be perceived as credible by armed nonstate groups, participating states may occasionally need to short-circuit democratic processes. Third, to increase the likelihood that the violent, disruptive armed nonstate groups have no covert links to government officials making security decisions about them, there would have to be a significant increase in the extradepartmental scrutiny of such officials, accompanied by a willingness to weed out those who have developed—or who are vulnerable to developing—such ties. One promising idea along these lines would be creating "coalitions of the honest" among law-enforcement officials, judges, police, intelligence analysts, and policy makers who are less likely to have been penetrated or captured by disruptive armed nonstate groups.[85] Finally, to maximize inhospitable environments for uncooperative, disruptive armed nonstate groups and to minimize the likelihood that safe havens for them would emerge, states would have to be more open to outside monitoring and apprehension of threats located within their borders.

Even though applying the full array of forceful countermeasures may constrain violent disruptions from uncooperative armed nonstate groups, some important dangers deserve consideration. For instance, in improving intelligence on disruptive armed nonstate groups, policies may divert information gathering from other important security threats. In developing better early warning through preventative measures regarding the armed nonstate group threats, there may be problematic misestimates about the most central security concerns, and money and manpower could be devoted to ominous possibilities that never materialize. In imposing stronger positive and sterner negative sanctions to minimize violence, the risk exists of being seen as engaging in intrusive cultural imperialism, forcing foreign values of integrity and civil discourse onto settings with sharply different interpretations about what is legitimate and effective. In enhancing bottom-up local responsibility to protect against human security dangers associated with disruptive uncooperative armed nonstate groups, there is the possibility of promoting anarchic vigilantism that disrupts the society stability for most citizens even further. Finally, in pursuing target-centered threat protection from disruptive armed nonstate groups, an unintended side effect of hardening potential targets could be to increase the fear pervasive in target societies and decrease the individual freedom of citizens to the point where they consider the "cure" to be as bad as or worse than the "disease."

In the long run, what would the impact of such countermeasures against uncooperative, disruptive armed nonstate groups look like? There would be extensive monitoring of these groups' activities, restrictions on their freedom of action, rewards when they positively changed their behavior, and punishments when they overstepped their designated bounds. Unlike current policies toward armed nonstate groups, there would be more careful discrimination about when such countermeasures were applied and more focus on the net stability impact. A long-term struggle would exist between states and uncooperative armed nonstate groups, with one set on disruption and the other set on using every means at its disposal to constrain the other's activities. Over time, states would find their domestic and foreign policies increasingly intertwined with policies toward uncooperative armed nonstate groups.

As Chapter 7 highlights, it is tricky to figure out how to promote power sharing with some armed nonstate groups while undertaking hostile countermeasures toward others. The likelihood of simultaneously needing to undertake these contrasting policies seems high, given the wide global variety of armed nonstate groups. For such a dual approach to function successfully, there would need to be considerable (but not necessarily complete) transparency in the criteria utilized to select an armed nonstate group for power sharing in security governance.

CONCLUDING THOUGHTS

For any study this broad and iconoclastic, there is a need at the end to step back and reflect on what results could be misconstrued, what findings and lessons are really most central, and what new challenges are likely to emerge. So this section examines the importance of not taking global security governance transformation too far; broadening and transforming the framing of global security governance; reorienting relevant academic scholarship and government policy making about global security governance; and preparing better for future global security governance challenges. Standing pat—using status quo modes of analysis and relying on standard operating procedures—does not make sense, given the ongoing transformation in the global security setting.

Do Not Take Global Security Governance Transformation Too Far

It is crucial that nobody takes too far this study's counterintuitive findings about the stabilizing value of armed nonstate groups. Such groups acting by themselves generally cannot provide durable long-term stability, and they should not be looked to as a stand-alone solution to global turmoil. These groups seem particularly deficient at ending violent conflict and at perpetuating peace. However, their greatest strength is in the human security area, specifically their ability to provide for basic survival needs and protection to the affected population in a timely manner. Moreover, in power-sharing arrangements, they can sometimes possess special advantages over states regarding stability promotion. The admittedly narrow conditions under which these groups can enhance stability confirm that relying on armed nonstate groups is not a panacea. As a result, this study advocates neither working across the board to eliminate state security governance nor working actively to promote armed nonstate group security control. Nonetheless, the recent combination of apparent state ineffectiveness and potential armed nonstate group success demands a substantial reorientation toward global stability maximization that reverses conventional wisdom. In the long run, armed nonstate groups could perhaps best provide a stabilizing transition or bridge to a more solid system of security governance. What is being proposed here is both pragmatic and utilitarian in light of the transformed global environment: moving away from long-accepted, state-centric global security governance norms while simultaneously moving toward a slimmed-down goal of supporting a variety of players with coercive potential—whether state or nonstate—that can engage in the effective fulfillment of basic survival needs and that can garner acceptance locally as legitimate security providers.

It is equally important that nobody derives from this study the notion that it would be inevitably necessary for some outside force to intervene to make authoritative choices and provide support in order for armed nonstate groups to be involved in stability-enhancing power-sharing arrangements with states. In contrast, many of these arrangements could be developed and resolved locally. There can be little expectation that the United Nations and other intergovernmental organizations, which consistently uphold the broader spectrum of global norms of state security governance, would be willing (or able) to step in to facilitate this shift. The United States would also not be a prime candidate for this supportive intervention, for American foreign security policy currently demands that countries ensure that their territory is not used by armed nonstate groups that might potentially threaten American interests, with an underlying assumption that all states need to be held responsible—whether or not they possess the requisite security capacity—for control and surveillance of their territory.

Lastly, it is critical that nobody assumes that this study is ready to discard completely traditional global security governance norms focusing on stability management through central state governments and international organizations. These widely accepted sources of authority and security have indeed been falling short in their performance in recent decades, but they still can make important contributions to the mix of protection provided to the people. For that reason, this book advocates greater flexibility in these global governance norms—and the institutions associated with them—in being willing to widen the permissible sources and the methods utilized in pursuit of global stability promotion.

Broaden and Transform the Framing of Global Security Governance

Unlike the customary narrow interpretation of the social contract between a government and its citizenry—in which citizens are loyal and obedient in return for state protection in an internationally recognized territory—this study suggests that in some situations armed nonstate groups are just as or more likely as central state governments to fit this arrangement. Sweeping generalizations such as "violent non-state groups offering social welfare services undermine the state by attacking the social contract"[86] do not seem helpful in this regard. Indeed, maintaining a security environment that is predictable and causes affected people to feel more secure can often directly serve the interests of armed nonstate groups. Especially if one focuses on human security concerns, these groups are often well situated to provide protection and fulfill basic survival needs to marginalized areas that many central state governments either cannot reach because of limited capacity or intentionally abandon as hopeless or worthy of negative discrimination.

In considering different kinds of privatized protection, we must find ways to get beyond the conclusion that "whether they enhance or detract from 'security' depends on who is doing the reckoning."[87] We need better metrics for gauging the security performance of states and armed nonstate groups and for determining the attainment of acceptable levels of stability for the affected population. We need to develop better understanding of the differences in these metrics across cultures. Last, we need improved comprehension of the fluidity of stability measures across time, accompanied by a willingness to consider the impact on these measures of dramatically changing security predicaments.

Perhaps the most fundamental question raised by this study's analysis of global security upheaval is, Whose protection is most critical for global stability?[88] Traditionally, a skew toward central state government security interests—protecting and maintaining the existing political regime—has led to some understandable reluctance to allow armed nonstate groups to have any significant role in security governance. However, if—as this study contends—priority needs to go to human security, emphasizing societal protection and fulfillment of basic survival needs to citizens, then it makes sense to move in the direction of states engaging in power sharing with armed nonstate groups. Prioritizing protection of the people requires openness to any effective means of doing so. If one begins with the challenge of maximizing protection of the people and providing for their basic survival needs, and continues with the willingness to consider any source that could fulfill these tasks most effectively, then public-private power sharing seems like an inevitable conclusion. In today's globalized world, it is difficult to deny the vital roles that subnational and transnational groups are already playing in providing stability and their potential to help even more in the future.

Reorient Relevant Academic Scholarship and Government Policy Making

For academic scholars, the research implications of this study are the need (1) to replace state-centric analytical models of international security; (2) to distinguish effective from ineffective armed nonstate group security governance; (3) to analyze broader implications of security function transfer from state to society; and (4) to assess more carefully armed nonstate group impacts back on the states themselves. Most broadly, if in the future "security policies are made and implemented by a growing number of public and private actors at different levels of analysis, we might be required to reconsider the underlying assumptions of security studies."[89] The opportunity costs of turning to armed nonstate group stability promotion require rigorous assessment—systematically comparing the costs and benefits of armed nonstate groups to that of alternatives such as international organizations, humanitarian groups, or global or regional governmental peacekeeping operations. Basic frameworks for analyzing global security governance need fundamental reconceptualization. Because armed nonstate group security control attempts exhibit so much variation, this reorientation needs to analyze circumstantially differentiated assessments of outcomes rather than simply presenting universal, overarching theoretical propositions.

For responsible officials, there is a need for significant reorientation of policy guidelines pertaining to global security governance. This reorientation includes the need (1) to improve understanding of armed nonstate groups "to help distinguish who is part of an armed group, who is assisting them, who is engaging only in political dissent, and who can work effectively locally [for and] against the armed group networks";[90] (2) to promote appropriate power sharing and to decide when to support, ignore, or oppose armed nonstate groups; (3) to stop vain attempts to restore potentially inept central state government control or to obliterate potentially valuable armed nonstate groups in many circumstances; (4) to refine national security governance structures' standard operating procedures in such a way as to more effectively take into account armed nonstate group security control attempts; (5) to integrate differing responses to different types of armed nonstate groups into a coherent security policy; (6) to promote mutual tolerance between states and cooperative armed nonstate groups; (7) to find better ways to gauge fulfillment of the security needs of marginalized peoples living in marginalized areas, identifying the full spectrum of possible solutions when these needs are not being met; (8) to avoid relying on coercive deterrence as the primary strategic reaction to the rise of armed nonstate groups, as it often fails because of members' willingness to die for their cause;[91] (9) to be willing to negotiate and cooperate with armed nonstate groups when useful; and ultimately (10) to consider armed nonstate forces not only as part of the problem but also as part of the solution.[92] It is evident that adaptation needs to occur in the policy realm as armed nonstate groups usurp state stability functions.

Prepare Better for Future Global Security Governance Challenges

For the foreseeable future, global security governance will remain in flux: "the 21st century will see a continuing dialectic between the forces of order and the forces of disorder; within this co-evolution, the limits of state power will become increasingly apparent, while the empowerment of nonstate actors will increase significantly."[93] In many instances, "learning to accommodate those nonstate actors who are actually providing security to local communities is a better alternative than waiting in vain for strong states to replace them."[94] This global receptivity to nonstate sources of security governance ought eventually to expand to encompass not only armed nonstate groups but also, when appropriate, noncoercive groups such as private humanitarian organizations and civil society groups; however, the current scope and intensity of the security challenges within areas where state stability promotion is inadequate necessitates the presence of those with coercive enforcement capabilities. Flexibility and trust—including willingness to take risks with new forms of security governance—seem essential for progress in protecting the people and fulfilling their basis survival needs. For achieving this kind of constructive public-private cooperation, "both the government and the groups themselves will have to demonstrate exceptional levels of political will, sincerity, and constitutional creativity."[95]

Because of the persistence of global instability trends, it is worth questioning the prevailing security mind-set and considering openly how durable stability ought to be pursued, which public and private parties ought to participate in achieving it, and what changes in security governance ought to be promoted. The underlying objective, particularly with persistently ineffective central state governments, needs to be "adapting institutions and attitudes created for a world of [state] sovereignty to deal with the slipperiness of flexible security challenges" posed by armed nonstate groups.[96] If in the future there is little change in responses to the global instability dilemma, there will be little forward progress. What is ultimately at stake is nothing less than the safety of the world's population and the survival of world order.

NOTES

Chapter 1

1. Haywood and French, "Potential Roles," 3.

2. Clunan and Trinkunas, "Conceptualizing Ungoverned Spaces," 20.

3. See, for example, Davis, "Non-State Armed Actors," 221; Stedman, "Spoiler Problems in Peace Processes," 5–53; and Schneckener, "Spoilers or Governance Actors?" 7.

4. Holt, *Against All Enemies, Foreign and Domestic*, 13.

5. See, for example, Cutler, Haufler, and Porter, *Private Authority and International Affairs*; and Higgott, Underhill, and Bieler, *Non-State Actors and Authority in the Global System*.

6. Schear et al., "Fragile States and Ungoverned Spaces," 104.

7. Davis, "Non-State Armed Actors," 223. See Chesterman and Lehnardt, *From Mercenaries to Market*.

8. Cederman, *Emergent Actors in World Politics*, 5, 19–22.

9. National Intelligence Council, *Global Trends 2025*, iv.

10. Patrick, "Weak States and Global Threats," 47.

11. For a discussion of stability operations, see Serafino, *Peacekeeping and Related Stability Operations*; Szayna et al., *Integrating Civilian Agencies in Stability Operations*; U.S. Department of the Army, Field Manual 3-07 *Stability Operations*; Shin, "Narrowing the Gap"; U.S. Department of Defense, *Military Support for Stability*; Bond, "Hybrid War"; and Gray, "Stability Operations in Strategic Perspective."

12. Davis, "Non-State Armed Actors," 241.

13. Kelly, "Criminal Underworlds," 11.

14. Berdal and Serrano, *Transnational Organized Crime and International Security*, 7.

15. Cutler, Haufler, and Porter, "Private Authority and International Affairs," 16; Rapley, "New Middle Ages," 102; and Davis, "Non-State Armed Actors," 239–240.

Chapter 2

1. Goldstone et al., "Global Model for Forecasting Political Instability," 194; and Political Instability Task Force website, http://globalpolicy.gmu.edu/pitf/.

2. Hewitt, Wilkenfeld, and Gurr, *Peace and Conflict 2012*, 6–7.

3. Office of Conflict Management and Mitigation, *2010 Alert Lists*, 3, 16.

4. Kaufmann, Kraay, and Mastruzzi, "Governance Matters VIII," 6.

5. Ibid.

6. Country Indicators for Foreign Policy, "Indicator Descriptions," http://www.carleton.ca/cifp.

7. U.S. Agency for International Development, *Fragile States Strategy*, 1.

8. *Foreign Policy* and Fund for Peace, "Failed States Index 2010," http://www.foreignpolicy.com/articles/2010/06/21/the_failed_states_index_2010.

9. U.K. Department for International Development, *Why We Need to Work More Effectively*, 8.

10. Ghani, Lockhart, and Carnahan, *Closing the Sovereignty Gap*, 6, 14; and Ghani and Lockhart, *Fixing Failed States*, 21, 124–166.

11. Klare, "Deadly Connection," 117.

12. Rice and Patrick, *Index of State Weakness*, 8.

13. Rotberg, "Failure and Collapse of Nation-States," 2–3.

14. Institute for Economics and Peace, *Peace, Wealth, and Human Potential*, 6.

15. Patterson, *Privatising Peace*, 200; and Center for Systemic Peace, "Global Conflict Trends: Measuring Systemic Peace," http://www.systemicpeace.org/conflict.htm.

16. Binnendijk and Johnson, *Transforming for Stabilization*, 90.

17. Schear et al., "Fragile States and Ungoverned Spaces," 113.

18. The distinction between juridical and empirical sovereignty derives from Vinci, *Armed Groups and the Balance of Power*, 11, 27–32.

19. Keohane and Nye, "Introduction," 12; and Schneckener, "Fragile Statehood," 33.

20. Ghani, Lockhart, and Carnahan, *Closing the Sovereignty Gap*, 11.

21. Vinci, *Armed Groups and the Balance of Power*, 13, 39–40.

22. See, for example, Rapley, "New Middle Ages," 95–96.

23. See Williams, *From the New Middle Ages to a New Dark Age*, ix.

24. Cutler, Haufler, and Porter, "Contours and Significance of Private Authority," 361–362.

25. Stillman, "Concept of Legitimacy," 32–56.

26. See, for example, Godson and Shultz, *Adapting America's Security Paradigm*, 34–35.

27. Rabasa et al., *Ungoverned Territories*, 80.

28. Goldstone et al., "Global Model for Forecasting Political Instability," 22.

29. Hall and Biersteker, "Emergence of Private Authority," 5.

30. Bruderlein, "People's Security," 353–366.

31. U.K. Department for International Development, *Why We Need to Work More Effectively*, 5.

32. National Intelligence Council, *Global Trends 2025*, 61.

33. Ghani and Lockhart, *Fixing Failed States*, 3.

34. Hewitt, Wilkenfeld, and Gurr, *Peace and Conflict 2010*, 8.

35. Mandel, *Armies without States*, 29.

36. Cutler, Haufler, and Porter, "Contours and Significance of Private Authority," 369.

37. Schneckener, "Spoilers or Governance Actors?" 7.

38. Davis, "Non-State Armed Actors," 224.

39. Mandel, *Armies without States*, 33.

40. Ibid., 40.

41. U.S. Department of the Army, Field Manual 3-07 *Stability Operations*, D7–D11.

42. Ibid.

43. Ibid.

44. Goldstone et al., "Global Model for Forecasting Political Instability," 10, 19–20.

45. U.S. Department of the Army, Field Manual 3-07 *Stability Operations*, D7–D11.

46. Goldstone et al., "Global Model for Forecasting Political Instability," 10, 19–20.

47. Ibid.; and U.S. Department of the Army, Field Manual 3-07 *Stability Operations*, D7–D11.

48. U.S. Department of the Army, Field Manual 3-07 *Stability Operations*, D7–D11.

49. Schear et al., "Fragile States and Ungoverned Spaces," 111.

50. Ghani, Lockhart, and Carnahan, *Closing the Sovereignty Gap*, 9.

51. U.S. Agency for International Development, *Fragile States Strategy*, v.

52. Patrick, *Weak Links*, 9.

53. Ghani, Lockhart, and Carnahan, *Closing the Sovereignty Gap*, 4.

54. Williams, *Violent Non-State Actors*, 6.

55. Ricks, "FM-3-XX."

56. Schneckener, "State Building or New Modes of Governance?" 240.

57. U.S. Government Accountability Office, *Military Operations*, 21.

Chapter 3

1. Krause, "Armed Groups."

2. For a discussion of the definitional parameters surrounding armed nonstate groups, see Vinci, *Armed Groups and the Balance of Power*, 4.

3. See Cederman, *Emergent Actors in World Politics*, 17–19.

4. Schneckener, "Spoilers or Governance Actors?" 8.

5. Davis, "Non-State Armed Actors," 221–222.

6. Schneckener, "Spoilers or Governance Actors?" 7, 14–16; and Shultz and Dew, *Insurgents, Terrorists, and Militias*, 270.

7. Schlichte, "With the State against the State?" 59.

8. Vinci, *Armed Groups and the Balance of Power*, 17.

9. Dekmejian, *Spectrum of Terror*, 11.

10. Schlichte, "With the State against the State?" 59.

11. Krause and Milliken, "Introduction," 2.

12. Ibid.

13. Krause, "Armed Groups." See also Pearlman, "Composite-Actor Approach to Conflict Behavior," 217.

14. Krause and Milliken, "Introduction," 1; and Krause, "Armed Groups."

15. Shultz and Dew, *Insurgents, Terrorists, and Militias*, 263.

16. Krause, "Armed Groups."

17. Pearlman, "Composite-Actor Approach to Conflict Behavior," 201.

18. Kalyvas, *Logic of Violence*, 19.

19. Fisman and Miguel, *Economic Gangsters*, 114, 136.

20. Thomas, Kiser, and Casebeer, *Warlords Rising*, 22.

21. Smith, *Penguin State of the World Atlas*, 60.

22. Cockayne and Mikulaschek, *Transnational Security Challenges and the United Nations*, 2.

23. Lawrence and Chenoweth, "Introduction," 4–5.

24. Kalyvas, *Logic of Violence*, 20.

25. Ibid., 62.

26. Thomas, Kiser, and Casebeer, *Warlords Rising*, 10.

27. Kalyvas, *Logic of Violence*, 68.

28. Smith, *Penguin Atlas of War and Peace*, 38.

29. Cunningham, "What Is So Extreme about Extreme Violence?"

30. Krause, "Armed Groups."

31. Reno, "African Warlords."

32. Lawrence and Chenoweth, "Introduction," 2.

33. Karp, "Changing Ownership of War," 174.

34. Vinci, *Armed Groups and the Balance of Power*, 25.

35. Kalyvas, *Logic of Violence*, 61.

36. This complexity is such that calling armed nonstate groups "violent nonstate actors," as is popular in the literature, may be a misleading oversimplification.

37. Thomas and Casebeer, "Turbulent Arena," 4.

38. Lawrence, "Driven to Arms?" 148.

39. Schneckener, "Spoilers or Governance Actors?" 24.

40. Naim, *Illicit*, 2, 8.

41. Edwards and Gill, "After Transnational Organized Crime?" 273–274.

42. Mair, "New World of Privatized Violence," 56.

43. Galeotti, "Transnational Organized Crime," 36.

44. See, for example, Thomas, Kiser, and Casebeer, *Warlords Rising*, 121–156, for a discussion of the wide range of violent nonstate actors.

45. Hammes, "Armed Groups," 444.

46. Mair, "New World of Privatized Violence," 47.

47. See ibid., 48; and Schneckener, "Fragile Statehood," 25–28.

48. Williams, *Violent Non-State Actors*, 4.

49. Naim, "Mafia States," 100–101.

50. Lea and Stenson, "Security, Sovereignty, and Non-State Governance," 18–19; and Williams, *Violent Non-State Actors*, 9, 12, 15.

51. Williams, *Violent Non-State Actors*, 9, 13–14, 16.

52. Lea and Stenson, "Security, Sovereignty, and Non-State Governance," 19; Mair, "New World of Privatized Violence," 48; and Williams, *Violent Non-State Actors*, 16.

53. For one view on this issue, see Mair, "New World of Privatized Violence," 48.

54. Ibid.

55. Curtis and Karacan, *Nexus among Terrorists*, 3–4.

56. Williams, *Violent Non-State Actors*, 15, 17.

57. Oehme, "Terrorists, Insurgents, and Criminals," 81.

58. Shultz and Dew, *Insurgents, Terrorists, and Militias*, 53.

59. Makarenko, "Crime–Terror Continuum," 130.

60. Kaldor, *New and Old Wars*, 9.

61. Thomas, Kiser, and Casebeer, *Warlords Rising*, 55.

62. Menkhaus, "Governance without Government in Somalia," 75.

63. Karen DeYoung, "World Bank Lists Failing Nations That Can Breed Global Terrorism," *Washington Post*, September 15, 2006, A13.

64. Kraft, "Foibles of an Armed Citizenry," 207.

65. Thomas, Kiser, and Casebeer, *Warlords Rising*, 63.

66. Kraft, "Foibles of an Armed Citizenry."

67. Felbab-Brown, "Rules and Regulations in Ungoverned Spaces," 180–181.

68. Mandel, "Fighting Fire with Fire," 62–72.

69. UPI News Service, "Call for Private Forces to Fight Pirates," May 10, 2010, http://www.upi.com/Business_News/Security-Industry/2010/05/10/Call-for-private-forces-to-fight-pirates/UPI-62261273507905/.

70. Diane E. Davis, "Irregular Armed Forces, Shifting Patterns of Commitment, and Fragmented Sovereignty in the Developing World" (September 2009), 14, http://hdl.handle.net/1721.1/51817; and Davis et al., "Public Accountability of Private Police," 197–210.

71. Giustozzi, "Bureaucratic Façade," 85.

Chapter 4

1. For a broad discussion of the context of global anarchy, see Mandel, *Deadly Transfers*, 12–13.

2. Kirchner, "Regional and Global Security," 3.

3. Kaplan, "Coming Anarchy," 44; Hills, "Warlords, Militia, and Conflict in Contemporary Africa," 35–51; Rich, *Warlords in International Relations*; and Thomas and Kiser, *Lords of the Silk Route*.

4. Rabasa et al., *Ungoverned Territories*, 178.

5. International Alert, "Assessment of the Mercenary Issue."

6. Herz, "Rise and Demise," 475.

7. Klare, "Deadly Connection," 117.

8. See Linklater, *Transformation of Political Community*, 155.

9. Hall and Biersteker, "Emergence of Private Authority," 3; and Weber, "Politics as a Vocation," 77–78.

10. Isenberg, *Soldiers of Fortune Ltd.*, 1.

11. Herbst, "Regulation of Private Security Forces," 109; Mandel, "What Are We Protecting?" 335–355; and Mandel, *Armies without States*, 30.

12. Hutchful, "Understanding the African Security Crisis," 212.

13. Tilly, "War Making," 169–191; and Hutchful, "Understanding the African Security Crisis," 212.

14. Diane E. Davis, "Irregular Armed Forces, Shifting Patterns of Commitment, and Fragmented Sovereignty in the Developing World" (September 2009), 6, http://hdl .handle.net/1721.1/51817. See also Tilly, "War Making," 169–191.

15. Scott, *Art of Not Being Governed*, 324.

16. Thomas, Kiser, and Casebeer, *Warlords Rising*, 7.

17. Scott, *Art of Not Being Governed*, 328.

18. Lynch and Walsh, "Good Mercenary," 133.

19. Thomson, *Mercenaries, Pirates, and Sovereigns*, 2.

20. Cutler, Haufler, and Porter, "Contours and Significance of Private Authority," 348.

21. Brauer, "Economic Perspective," 130–146.

22. Risse, "Governance in Areas of Limited Statehood," 2.

23. Pauly and Grande, "Reconstituting Political Authority," 7.

24. Pereira, "Armed Forces," 388.

25. Thomas, Kiser, and Casebeer, *Warlords Rising*, 7.

26. Rapley, "New Middle Ages," 102.

27. For a broader discussion of these issues, see Mandel, *Security, Strategy, and the Quest for Bloodless War*.

28. Musah and Fayemi, *Mercenaries*, 1–2.

29. Carafano, "Contracting in Combat," 1–2.

30. Frederick Forsyth, "Send in the Mercenaries," *Wall Street Journal*, May 15, 2000.

31. See Mandel, "Overview of American Expeditionary Operations."

32. Clunan and Trinkunas, "Conceptualizing Ungoverned Spaces," 25.

33. Risse, "Governance in Areas of Limited Statehood," 1.

34. Kaldor, *New and Old Wars*, 181.

35. Williams, *From the New Middle Ages to a New Dark Age*, 3.

36. Mandel, *Changing Face of National Security*, 21.

37. Toffler and Toffler, *War and Anti-War*, 104, 122; Van Creveld, *Transformation of War*, 197; Hammes, *Sling and the Stone*, 208; and Mandel, *Global Threat*, 11–27.

38. Kaldor, *New and Old Wars*, 9.

39. Williams, *From the New Middle Ages to a New Dark Age*, 41.

40. Hammes, "Armed Groups," 444.

41. Thornton, *Asymmetric Warfare*, 1.

42. Caldwell and Williams, *Seeking Security*, 170.

43. Branscomb, "Nation Forewarned," 20.

44. Reese, *Homeland Security Advisory System*, 5.

45. Ervin, *Open Target*, 24–25.

46. Posner, *Catastrophe*, 171.

47. Davis, "Non-State Armed Actors," 234, 238.

48. Davis, "Irregular Armed Forces," 2.

49. Vinci, *Armed Groups and the Balance of Power*, 1–2.

50. Caldwell and Williams, *Seeking Security*, 2nd ed., 250.

51. Rapley, "New Middle Ages," 96.

52. Schneckener, "Fragile Statehood," 34.

53. Hall and Biersteker, "Emergence of Private Authority," 16.

54. Clunan, "Ungoverned Spaces?" 6.

55. Rapley, "New Middle Ages," 96.

56. Williams, *Violent Non-State Actors*, 5.

57. Ibid.

58. Thomas and Casebeer, "Turbulent Arena," 2.

59. Thomas and Casebeer, "Violent Systems," 8.

60. Silverstein, "Privatizing War," 12.

61. Mandel, *Armies without States*, 98.

62. Thomas and Casebeer, "Violent Systems," 10.

63. Hammes, "Armed Groups," 442.

64. Rapley, "New Middle Ages," 101.

65. Godson and Shultz, *Adapting America's Security Paradigm*, 7.

66. Davis, "Irregular Armed Forces," 15.

67. Mandel, *Armies without States*, 39.

68. Williams, *Violent Non-State Actors*, 7.

69. Mandel, *Armies without States*, 1–24.

70. Adamson, "Crossing Borders," 191.

71. Williams, *From the New Middle Ages to a New Dark Age*, ix.

72. Ahram, *Proxy Warriors*, 2.

73. Rapley, "New Middle Ages," 95–96.

74. Crawford and Miscik, "Rise of Mezzanine Rulers," 123.

75. Davis, "Non-State Armed Actors," 229.

76. Crawford and Miscik, "Rise of Mezzanine Rulers," 123.

77. Ruggie, "Territoriality and Beyond," 143.

78. Cutler, Haufler, and Porter, "Private Authority and International Affairs," 16.

79. Schneckener, "Spoilers or Governance Actors?" 7–8.

80. Rosecrance, Solingen, and Stein, "Globalization and Its Effects," 5.

81. Kirchner, "Regional and Global Security," 4.

82. Shearer, *Private Armies and Military Intervention*, 69–72.

83. Nagle, "Criminal Gangs in Latin America," 13–14.

84. Cutler, Haufler, and Porter, "Contours and Significance of Private Authority," 351.

85. Vinci, *Armed Groups and the Balance of Power*, 6.

86. Hammes, "Armed Groups," 441–442.

87. Thomas, Kiser, and Casebeer, *Warlords Rising*, 7.

88. Crawford and Miscik, "Rise of Mezzanine Rulers," 126.

89. Ibid.

90. Dekmejian, *Spectrum of Terror*, 291–292; and Duffield, "Post-Modern Conflict," 70.

91. See Mandel, *Deadly Transfers*, chap. 3; Williams, *From the New Middle Ages to a New Dark Age*, 28; and Duffield, "Post-Modern Conflict," 65–102.

92. Patrick, "Weak States and Global Threats," 27.

93. Casebeer, "Stories, Identities, and Conflict."

94. For criticism of the "greed versus grievance" approach, see, for example, Davis, "Non-State Armed Actors," 222; and Vinci, *Armed Groups and the Balance of Power*, 6.

95. Vinci, *Armed Groups and the Balance of Power*, 21–22.

96. Program on Humanitarian Policy and Conflict Research, *Empowered Groups*, 25–26.

97. Davis, "Non-State Armed Actors," 222; and Davis, "Irregular Armed Forces," 19.

98. Godson and Shultz, *Adapting America's Security Paradigm*, 13.

99. See Davis, "Irregular Armed Forces," 2.

100. Godson and Shultz, *Adapting America's Security Paradigm*, 14.

101. See Mandel, *Deadly Transfers*, chap. 11.

102. Cutler, Haufler, and Porter, "Private Authority and International Affairs," 16.

103. Grynkewich, "Welfare as Warfare," 355.

104. Davis, "Irregular Armed Forces," 7. See also Linklater, *Transformation of Political Community*.

105. Davis, "Non-State Armed Actors," 234.

106. Brauer and Haywood, "Non-State Sovereign Entrepreneurs," 10.

107. Rapley, "New Middle Ages," 96.

108. Vinci, *Armed Groups and the Balance of Power*, 1–2.

109. Davis, "Irregular Armed Forces," 18.

110. Howe, "Global Order," 4.

111. Davis, "Non-State Armed Actors," 238.

112. Mandel, "Overview of American Expeditionary Operations."

113. Rabasa et al., *Ungoverned Territories*, 30.

114. Patterson, *Privatising Peace*, 118.

115. Mandel, *Armies without States*, 85.

116. Industrial College of the Armed Forces, *Privatized Military Operations*, 16.

117. Kraska, "Militarization and Policing," 1. See also Lutterbeck, "Blurring the Dividing Line," 231–253.

118. Lutterbeck, "Between Police and Military"; and Kraska, "Militarization and Policing," 2.

119. Brauer and Haywood, "Non-State Sovereign Entrepreneurs," 3.

120. Lamb, *Ungoverned Areas*, 18.

121. Thomas and Casebeer, "Violent Systems," 1; see also Program on Humanitarian Policy and Conflict Research, *Empowered Groups*, 50.

122. Cutler, Haufler, and Porter, "Contours and Significance of Private Authority," 334, 338–344.

123. Davis, "Irregular Armed Forces," 18. For discussion of this general issue, see also Volkov, *Violent Entrepreneurs*.

124. Bruderlein, "People's Security," 358.

125. Ibid., 362.

126. The question of armed nonstate groups' effects on trust is raised in Howe, "Private Security Forces and African Stability," 309.

127. Mandel, *Armies without States*, 88.

128. Klare, "Deadly Connection," 119.

129. See Mandel, *Deadly Transfers*, chap. 1.

130. Cutler, Haufler, and Porter, "Contours and Significance of Private Authority," 351.

131. Crawford and Miscik, "Rise of Mezzanine Rulers," 126.

132. Ibid., 124.

133. Klare, "Deadly Connection," 120.

Chapter 5

1. Saeed Ahmed, "How Chechen Rebels Threaten Russian Stability," March 29, 2010, http://www.cnn.com/2010/WORLD/europe/03/29/chechnya.explainer/index.html.

2. Shultz and Dew, *Insurgents, Terrorists, and Militias*, 103–104.

3. Lapidus, "Contested Sovereignty," 26.

4. Nichol, *Stability in Russia's Chechnya and Other Regions of the North Caucasus*, 4.

5. Lapidus, "Contested Sovereignty," 26.

6. Hewitt, Wilkenfeld, and Gurr, *Peace and Conflict 2010*, 137.

7. King and Menon, "Prisoners of the Caucasus," 21.

8. Ahmed, "How Chechen Rebels Threaten Russian Stability."

9. Nichol, *Stability in Russia's Chechnya and Other Regions of the North Caucasus*, 4.

10. Hughes, "Chechnya," 40.

11. Reppert and Shevchenko, "Failure of Chechen Separatism," 135.

12. Ibid.

13. Ahmed, "How Chechen Rebels Threaten Russian Stability."

14. Reppert and Shevchenko, "Failure of Chechen Separatism," 136.

15. Nichol, *Stability in Russia's Chechnya and Other Regions of the North Caucasus*, 5.

16. King and Menon, "Prisoners of the Caucasus," 28, 31.

17. Ahmed, "How Chechen Rebels Threaten Russian Stability."

18. Gorenburg, "Russia Confronts Radical Islam," 40.

19. Shultz and Dew, *Insurgents, Terrorists, and Militias*, 105–106.

20. Matveeva, "Chechnya," 11.

21. King and Menon, "Prisoners of the Caucasus," 31.

22. Shultz and Dew, *Insurgents, Terrorists, and Militias*, 143–144.

23. King and Menon, "Prisoners of the Caucasus," 21.

24. Reppert and Shevchenko, "Failure of Chechen Separatism," 133.

25. Ahmed, "How Chechen Rebels Threaten Russian Stability."

26. Reppert and Shevchenko, "Failure of Chechen Separatism," 138.

27. King and Menon, "Prisoners of the Caucasus," 21.

28. Kramer, "Perils of Counterinsurgency," 63.

29. Bakke, "Turn to Violence," 233.

30. Nichol, *Stability in Russia's Chechnya and Other Regions of the North Caucasus*, 10.

31. King and Menon, "Prisoners of the Caucasus," 21–22.

32. Hughes, "Chechnya," 39.

33. Matveeva, "Chechnya," 4.

34. Nichol, *Stability in Russia's Chechnya and Other Regions of the North Caucasus*, 9.

35. Melvin, "Building Stability in the North Caucasus," 21.

36. Lapidus, "Contested Sovereignty," 44; and Hughes, "Chechnya," 15.

37. King and Menon, "Prisoners of the Caucasus," 21.

38. Mabry, "Soldiers of Misfortune," 40–41.

39. Cleaver, "Subcontracting Military Power," 140–141.

40. Howe, "Private Security Forces and African Stability," 313–314.

41. Cleaver, "Subcontracting Military Power," 140, 141.

42. Reno, "Privatizing War in Sierra Leone," 228–229.

43. Howe, "Private Security Forces and African Stability," 315.

44. Whitelaw, "Have Gun, Will Prop Up Regime," 47.

45. Cleaver, "Subcontracting Military Power," 140.

46. Ibid., 141–142.

47. Ibid., 134.

48. Ibid., 137.

49. Ibid., 139.

50. Howe, "Private Security Forces and African Stability," 307, 310.

51. Cleaver, "Subcontracting Military Power," 139.

52. Ibid., 141.

53. McGhie, "Private Military Companies."

54. Taulbee, "Privatization of Security," 4.

55. Cleaver, "Subcontracting Military Power," 141.

56. Howe, "Private Security Forces and African Stability," 316.

57. Reno, "Privatizing War in Sierra Leone," 229–230.

58. Howe, "Private Security Forces and African Stability," 318.

59. O'Brien, "Freelance Forces," 43.

60. Cleaver, "Subcontracting Military Power," 141.

61. McGhie, "Private Military Companies."

62. Howe, "Private Security Forces and African Stability," 323.

63. Cleaver, "Subcontracting Military Power," 135, 146.

64. Howe, "Private Security Forces and African Stability," 323.

65. Guáqueta, "Colombian Conflict," 73.

66. McDougall, "State Power," 323.

67. Guáqueta, "Colombian Conflict," 73–74.

68. Ibid., 77.

69. Ibid., 73.

70. Boudon, "Guerrillas and the State," 297.

71. Chernick, "FARC-EP."

72. Jojarth, *Crime, War, and Global Trafficking*, 95; and Guáqueta, "Colombian Conflict," 81.

73. Guáqueta, "Colombian Conflict," 74.

74. Bonner, "New Cocaine Cowboys," 42.

75. Kerry, *New War*, 71.

76. MacDonald, *Dancing on a Volcano*, 28–29.

77. McLean, "Colombia," 124, 131.

78. Jojarth, *Crime, War, and Global Trafficking*, 95.

79. Naim, *Illicit*, 70.

80. Sanín, "Internal Conflict," 141.

81. Pereira, "Armed Forces," 398.

82. McLean, "Colombia," 126, 132.

83. Pereira, "Armed Forces," 398.

84. John Holmberg, "FARC-EP," April 13, 2009, http://traccc.gmu.edu/pdfs/student _research/HolmbergFARC_new.pdf.

85. Bolivar, "Local Dimensions of the Colombian Conflict," 25.

86. Boudon, "Guerrillas and the State," 289.

87. Guáqueta, "Colombian Conflict," 100–101.

88. McLean, "Colombia," 124, 131.

89. Pereira, "Armed Forces," 398.

90. Guáqueta, "Colombian Conflict," 73, 78–79.

91. Sweeney, "Colombia's Narco-Democracy."

92. MacDonald, *Dancing on a Volcano*, 124–134.

93. Shultz and Dew, *Insurgents, Terrorists, and Militias*, 62.

94. Menkhaus, *Somalia*, 8.

95. Feldman and Slattery, "Living without a Government in Somalia," 202.

96. Shultz and Dew, *Insurgents, Terrorists, and Militias*, 59.

97. Menkhaus, "Governance without Government in Somalia," 81.

98. Shultz and Dew, *Insurgents, Terrorists, and Militias*, 74–75.

99. Menkhaus, "Governance without Government in Somalia," 87.

100. Rabasa et al., *Ungoverned Territories*, 152.

101. Ibid., 161.

102. Bakonyi and Stuvøy, "Violence and Social Order beyond the State," 366–367.

103. Davis, "Non-State Armed Actors," 240.

104. Menkhaus, "Governance without Government in Somalia," 96.

105. *Foreign Policy* and the Fund for Peace, "Failed States Index 2010."

106. Shultz and Dew, *Insurgents, Terrorists, and Militias*, 57.

107. Menkhaus, *Somalia*, 22.

108. Menkhaus, "Governance without Government in Somalia," 100.

109. Menkhaus, *Somalia*, 19–20.

110. Menkhaus, "Governance without Government in Somalia," 102–103.

111. Menkhaus, *Somalia*, 31.

112. Menkhaus, "Governance without Government in Somalia," 87.

113. Ibid., 93.

114. Feldman and Slattery, "Living without a Government in Somalia," 204.

115. Menkhaus, "Governance without Government in Somalia," 77.

116. Shultz and Dew, *Insurgents, Terrorists, and Militias*, 76.

117. Feldman and Slattery, "Living without a Government in Somalia," 205.

118. Menkhaus, "Governance without Government in Somalia," 86.

119. Feldman and Slattery, "Living without a Government in Somalia," 202.

120. Ibid.

121. Shultz and Dew, *Insurgents, Terrorists, and Militias*, 62–63.

122. Menkhaus, *Somalia*, 18.

123. Ibid., 40–41.

124. Menkhaus, "Governance without Government in Somalia," 88.

125. Janus and Lawrence, *Al Shabaab and the Somalia Food Crisis*, 1.

126. Shultz and Dew, *Insurgents, Terrorists, and Militias*, 85–86, 99.

127. Phillips, "Somalia and al-Qaeda."

128. Menkhaus, *Somalia*, 34.

129. Menkhaus and Shapiro, "Non-State Actors and Failed States," 85.

130. Menkhaus, *Somalia*, 9.

131. Boot, "Pirates, Then and Now," 94. See also Hanson, "Combating Maritime Piracy."

132. Norton, *Hezbollah*, 32–35.

133. Byman, "Should Hezbollah Be Next?" 58.

134. Ibid., 57.

135. Grynkewich, "Welfare as Warfare," 361.

136. Byman, "Should Hezbollah Be Next?" 60.

137. Godson and Shultz, *Adapting America's Security Paradigm*, 13–14.

138. Crawford and Miscik, "Rise of Mezzanine Rulers," 124–125.

139. Gunning, "Hizbollah," 158.

140. Godson and Shultz, *Adapting America's Security Paradigm*, 7.

141. Byman, "Should Hezbollah Be Next?" 59.

142. Council on Foreign Relations, "Hezbollah."

143. Hamieh and Mac Ginty, "Very Political Reconstruction," 104–105. See also Mac Ginty, "Reconstructing Post-War Lebanon," 459–461.

144. Byman, "Should Hezbollah Be Next?" 58.

145. Crawford and Miscik, "Rise of Mezzanine Rulers," 124.

146. Harik, *Transnational Actors in Contemporary Conflicts*, 7–8.

147. Byman, "Should Hezbollah Be Next?" 58.

148. Diane E. Davis, "Irregular Armed Forces, Shifting Patterns of Commitment, and Fragmented Sovereignty in the Developing World" (September 2009), 26, http://hdl.handle.net/1721.1/51817.

149. Byman, "Should Hezbollah Be Next?" 60.

150. Gunning, "Hizbollah," 165.

151. Lea and Stenson, "Security, Sovereignty, and Non-State Governance," 25.

152. Hamieh and Mac Ginty, "Very Political Reconstruction," 105.

153. Ibid., 106.

154. Grynkewich, "Welfare as Warfare," 362.

155. Early, "Larger Than a Party," 115, 120.

156. Sharon Behn, "U.S., Hezbollah Vie to Rebuild for Lebanese: Hope to Win Public Opinion," *Washington Times*, August 18, 2006; and Paul Richter, "Cease-Fire in the Middle East," *Los Angeles Times*, August 17, 2006.

157. Harik, *Transnational Actors in Contemporary Conflicts*, 18.

158. John Kifner, "Hezbollah Leads Work to Rebuild, Gaining Stature," *New York Times*, August 16, 2006, A1.

159. AlSayyad, "Foreword," ix.

160. Grynkewich, "Welfare as Warfare," 363; and "Poll Finds Overwhelming Majorities in Lebanon Support Hezbollah, Distrust U.S.," August 2, 2006, http://www .worldpublicopinion.org/pipa/articles/brmiddleeastnafricara/236.php?nid=&id= &pnt=236&lb=brme.

161. Hamieh and Mac Ginty, "Very Political Reconstruction," 106.

162. Sharp et al., *Lebanon*, 17.

163. AlSayyad, "Foreword," viii.

164. Hamieh and Mac Ginty, "Very Political Reconstruction," 107.

165. Ibid., 106.

166. "Aid Conference Raises $7.6 Billion for Lebanon," *New York Times*, January 26, 2007.

167. Byman, "Should Hezbollah Be Next?" 59.

168. Ibid., 59–60.

169. O'Leary, "IRA: Looking Back," 190.

170. English, *Armed Struggle*, 345.

171. Mulholland, "Irish Republican Politics," 397.

172. Ibid., 400.

173. English, *Armed Struggle*, 351.

174. O'Leary, "IRA: Looking Back," 201.

175. Ibid., 213.

176. Ibid., 211–212.

177. English, *Armed Struggle*, 355.

178. Ibid., 115, 367.

179. Ibid., 344.

180. Coogan, *IRA*, 668–669.

181. O'Leary, "Belfast Agreement and the British-Irish Agreement," 338–342.

182. English, *Armed Struggle*, 344.

183. Kushner, "Irish Republican Army," 185.

184. Patterson, *Politics of Illusion*, 14–15.

185. Lea and Stenson, "Security, Sovereignty, and Non-State Governance," 25.

186. English, *Armed Struggle*, 338.

187. Ibid., 350–351.

188. Ibid., 351.

189. Ibid., 372.

190. Ibid., 361.

191. Schanzer, "Yemen's War on Terror," 517.

192. Clark, *In the Spotlight*.

193. Ibid.

194. Clark, *Yemen*, 167.

195. Schanzer, "Yemen's War on Terror," 525.

196. Thomas and Casebeer, "Violent Systems," 36; and Bergen, *Holy War, Inc.*, 167.

197. Rabasa et al., *Ungoverned Territories*, 91.

198. Clark, *In the Spotlight*.

199. Carapico, "Yemen and the Aden-Abyan Islamic Army."

200. Schanzer, "Yemen's War on Terror," 521.

201. Margaret Coker, "Al Qaeda in Yemen Worries the West," *Wall Street Journal*, September 29, 2009, A16.

202. "Islamic Army of Aden (IAA)," March 20, 2009, http://www.aph.gov.au/house/committee/pjcis/grouped/report/appendixf.pdf.

203. Ibid.

204. Clark, *In the Spotlight*.

205. Schanzer, "Yemen's War on Terror," 522–523.

206. Ibid., 523.

207. Rabasa et al., *Ungoverned Territories*, 91.

208. Schanzer, "Yemen's War on Terror," 529.

209. Crawford and Miscik, "Rise of Mezzanine Rulers," 126.

210. Rabasa et al., *Ungoverned Territories*, 91.

211. Schanzer, "Yemen's War on Terror," 528.

212. Clark, *In the Spotlight*.

213. Rabasa et al., *Ungoverned Territories*, 24.

214. Schanzer, "Yemen's War on Terror," 518.

215. Boucek, "Yemen," 3, 14.

216. Carapico, "Yemen and the Aden-Abyan Islamic Army."

217. Schear et al., "Fragile States and Ungoverned Spaces," 104.

218. Clark, *In the Spotlight*.

219. Clark, *Yemen*, 260, 265.

220. Boucek, "Yemen," 2, 9.

221. *Foreign Policy* and the Fund for Peace, "Failed States Index 2010."

222. Boucek, "Yemen," 1.

223. Schanzer, "Yemen's War on Terror," 521.

224. Rabasa et al., *Ungoverned Territories*, 11.

225. Clark, *Yemen*, 283.

226. Van Acker, "Uganda and the Lord's Resistance Army," 336.

227. Dunn, "Uganda," 138–139.

228. Ibid., 132, 139.

229. Van Acker, "Uganda and the Lord's Resistance Army," 337.

230. Borzello, "Challenge of DDR in Northern Uganda," 144.

231. Ibid., 150–151.

232. Vinci, *Armed Groups and the Balance of Power*, 99.

233. Van Acker, "Uganda and the Lord's Resistance Army," 346.

234. Doom and Vlassenroot, "Kony's Message," 22.

235. Van Acker, "Uganda and the Lord's Resistance Army," 336.

236. Vinci, *Armed Groups and the Balance of Power*, 90.

237. Dunn, "Uganda," 134–135.

238. Cheney, "'Our Children Have Only Known War,'" 25.

239. Borzello, "Challenge of DDR in Northern Uganda," 149.

240. Van Acker, "Uganda and the Lord's Resistance Army," 336.

241. Bevan, "Myth of Madness," 347.

242. James Alfred Obita, "A Case for National Reconciliation, Peace, Democracy and Economic Prosperity for All Ugandans: The Official Presentation of the Lord's Resistance Movement/Army," http://www.km-net.org.uk/conferences/KM97/papers_htm/casefor.htm.

243. Cline, "Peeling Labels."

244. Doom and Vlassenroot, "Kony's Message," 35–36.

245. Dunn, "Uganda," 131.

246. Bevan, "Myth of Madness," 351–352.

247. Van Acker, "Uganda and the Lord's Resistance Army," 353.

248. Dunn, "Uganda," 132.

249. Vinci, *Armed Groups and the Balance of Power*, 91.

250. Ibid., 95.

251. Bevan, "Myth of Madness," 348.

252. Van Acker, "Uganda and the Lord's Resistance Army," 338–339.

253. Dunn, "Uganda," 147.

254. Vinci, *Armed Groups and the Balance of Power*, 99.

255. Bevan, "Myth of Madness," 349.

256. Berdal and Ucko, "Introduction," 3.

257. Van Acker, "Uganda and the Lord's Resistance Army," 354.

258. Dunn, "Uganda," 131.

259. Ibid., 131, 148.

260. Van Acker, "Uganda and the Lord's Resistance Army," 335–336.

261. Vinci, *Armed Groups and the Balance of Power*, 94.

262. See Hayden, *Street Wars*.

263. Bruneau, "Maras and National Security in Central America," 1.

264. Fogelbach, "Mara Salvatrucha (MS-13) and Ley Anti Mara."

265. Campo-Flores, "Most Dangerous Gang in America."

266. National Gang Intelligence Center, *National Gang Threat Assessment 2009* (January 2009), http://www.justice.gov/ndic/pubs32/32146/appb.htm.

267. Bruneau, "Maras and National Security in Central America," 3.

268. Ibid., 3–4.

269. Maggio, "Threat of Armed Street Gangs," 200–201.

270. Bruneau, "Maras and National Security in Central America," 3.

271. Maggio, "Threat of Armed Street Gangs," 201.

272. U.S. Agency for International Development, *Central America and Mexico Gangs Assessment.*

273. Bruneau, "Maras and National Security in Central America," 3.

274. Maggio, "Threat of Armed Street Gangs," 201.

275. Arana, "How the Street Gangs Took Central America," 98–110.

276. Delaney, *American Street Gangs*, 202.

277. Bruneau, "Maras and National Security in Central America," 3.

278. Maggio, "Threat of Armed Street Gangs," 201.

279. "Mara Salvatrucha: What Is It, Why Is It Here, and What Is to Be Done about It?" 3, http://www.walkingwithelsalvador.org/Karen/Mara%20Salvatrucha%20Paper.pdf.

280. Stratfor Global Intelligence, "Mara Salvatrucha Gangs and U.S. Security," August 22, 2005, http://www.drculture.com/MS13.pdf.

281. Ibid.

282. Manwaring, *Street Gangs*, 20.

283. Bruneau, "Maras and National Security in Central America," 7.

284. Ibid., 5.

285. Ibid., 6.

286. Ibid., 7.

287. Stratfor Global Intelligence, "Mara Salvatrucha Gangs and U.S. Security."

288. Bruneau, "Maras and National Security in Central America," 9.

289. Manwaring, *Contemporary Challenge to State Sovereignty*, 34.

290. Ibid., 35–36.

291. Michael Mogensen, "Corner and Area Gangs of Inner-City Jamaica," September 19, 2004, 3, http://www.coav.org.br/publique/media/Report%20Jamaica.pdf.

292. Manwaring, *Contemporary Challenge to State Sovereignty*, 35.

293. Clarke, "Politics, Violence and Drugs in Kingston, Jamaica," 420.

294. Manwaring, *Contemporary Challenge to State Sovereignty*, 37.

295. Mogensen, "Corner and Area Gangs," 3.

296. Ibid., 8.

297. Clarke, "Politics, Violence and Drugs in Kingston, Jamaica," 422–423.

298. Manwaring, *Contemporary Challenge to State Sovereignty*, 40.

299. Clarke, "Politics, Violence and Drugs in Kingston, Jamaica," 421, 433.

300. Gunst, *Born Fi' Dead*, 118.

301. Gary Brana-Shute, "Narco-Criminality in the Caribbean: Global Problems in Small Places," 7, http://www.trinitydc.edu/academics/depts/Interdisc/International/caribbean%20briefings/Caribbean%20Paper%20Series.pdf.

302. Clarke, "Politics, Violence and Drugs in Kingston, Jamaica," 435.

303. Rapley, "New Middle Ages," 95.

304. Manwaring, *Contemporary Challenge to State Sovereignty*, 33.

305. "Gangs Reign in Jamaica's Inner-City Slums," April 9, 2008, http://www.realtruth.org/news/080409-002-americas.html.

306. Brana-Shute, "Narco-Criminality in the Caribbean," 4.

307. Clarke, "Politics, Violence and Drugs in Kingston, Jamaica," 434.

308. Brana-Shute, "Narco-Criminality in the Caribbean," 5.

309. Ibid., 6.

310. Ibid., 4.

311. Clarke, "Politics, Violence and Drugs in Kingston, Jamaica," 435.

312. Ibid.

313. Brana-Shute, "Narco-Criminality in the Caribbean," 6.

314. Ibid.

315. Ibid., 7.

316. Shultz and Dew, *Insurgents, Terrorists, and Militias*, 180.

317. Ibid., 181.

318. Meshali-Ram, "Afghanistan," 477.

319. Hewitt, Wilkenfeld, and Gurr, *Peace and Conflict 2010*, 124.

320. Shultz and Dew, *Insurgents, Terrorists, and Militias*, 181.

321. Davis, "Irregular Armed Forces," 26.

322. Nojumi, *Rise of the Taliban in Afghanistan*, 186.

323. Kuite, "Drugs and Insurgencies."

324. Peters, "Crime and Insurgency in Afghanistan/Pakistan."

325. Ibid.

326. Meshali-Ram, "Afghanistan," 479.

327. Oehme, "Terrorists, Insurgents, and Criminals," 81.

328. Crawford and Miscik, "Rise of Mezzanine Rulers," 125.

329. Peters, "Crime and Insurgency in Afghanistan/Pakistan."

330. Rashid, *Taliban*, 176.

331. Schear et al., "Fragile States and Ungoverned Spaces," 100.

332. Meshali-Ram, "Afghanistan," 477.

333. Ibid., 479.

334. Ibid., 477.

335. Bruno, "Taliban in Afghanistan."

336. Shultz and Dew, *Insurgents, Terrorists, and Militias*, 186.

337. Hewitt, Wilkenfeld, and Gurr, *Peace and Conflict 2010*, 124.

338. Peters, "Crime and Insurgency in Afghanistan/Pakistan."

339. Felbab-Brown, "Rules and Regulations in Ungoverned Spaces," 180.

340. Ibid., 180–181.

341. Bruno, "Taliban in Afghanistan."

342. Meshali-Ram, "Afghanistan," 486.

343. Oehme, "Terrorists, Insurgents, and Criminals," 81.

344. Shultz and Dew, *Insurgents, Terrorists, and Militias*, 189.

345. Meshali-Ram, "Afghanistan," 481.

346. Rubin, "Who Is Responsible for the Taliban?" 11.

347. Nojumi, "Rise and Fall of the Taliban," 101.

348. Biddle, Christia, and Thier, "Defining Success in Afghanistan," 50.

349. C. Todd Lopez, "Stability Operations Now Part of Army's Core Mission," February 15, 2008, http://www.army.mil/article/7580/stability-operations-now-part-of-armys-core-mission/.

350. U.S. Government Accountability Office, *Military Operations*, 2.

351. Katzman, *Afghanistan*, 10.

352. McNerney, "Stabilization and Reconstruction in Afghanistan," 36.

353. Giustozzi, "Bureaucratic Façade," 71.

354. Coll, "U.S.-Taliban Talks."

355. Meshali-Ram, "Afghanistan," 473.

356. Ibid., 480.

357. This discussion draws from Mandel, "Security and Natural Disasters," 118–143; and Mandel, *Dark Logic*, chap. 4.

358. International Federation of Red Cross and Red Crescent Societies, *World Disaster Report 1996*, 65; and Begley and Foote, "Lessons of Kobe," 24–30.

359. Butler, "Killer Quake," 38–45; and "What the Quake Shows about Japan," *Washington Post*, February 2, 1995, A27.

360. McCormack, *Emptiness of Japanese Affluence*, 10–12.

361. Begley and Foote, "Lessons of Kobe," 24–30.

362. Hill, *Japanese Mafia*, 65.

363. Ibid., 38.

364. Jake Adelstein, "Yakuza to the Rescue," March 18, 2011, http://www.thedailybeast.com/articles/2011/03/18/japanese-yakuza-aid-earthquake-relief-efforts.html.

365. "Japanese Yakuza: History and Cultural Development," April 25, 2011, http://altman.casimirinstitute.net/yakuza.html.

366. Hill, *Japanese Mafia*, 63–64.

367. Miller, "Threat of Transnational Crime in East Asia," 12.

368. Kaplan and Dubro, *Yakuza*, 150–151.

369. McFarlane, "Transnational Crime and Asia-Pacific Security," 204.

370. Lal, "Japanese Trafficking and Smuggling," 143.

371. Miller, "Threat of Transnational Crime in East Asia," 11.

372. Delfs, "Clash of Loyalties," 30, 34.

373. Hill, *Japanese Mafia*, 37; Kaplan and Dubro, *Yakuza*, 150, 157–158, 178, 180–183, 238, 244; Adelstein, "Yakuza to the Rescue"; and Lal, "Japanese Trafficking and Smuggling," 147.

374. Eric Johnston, "Yakuza in Japan: From Rackets to Real Estate, Yakuza Multifaceted," *Japan Times*, February 14, 2007, http://search.japantimes.co.jp/cgi-bin/nn2007 0214i1.html.

375. Shelley et al., *Methods and Motives*, 60.

376. "The Yakuza," April 7, 2002, http://www.okinawan-shorinryu.com/okinawa/yakuza.html.

377. Fukishima, "Great Hanshin Earthquake."

378. Nicholas D. Kristof, "Quake That Hurt Kobe Helps Its Criminals," *New York Times*, June 6, 1995, A3.

379. Jeffrey Hays, "Yakuza and Organized Crime in Japan," http://factsanddetails.com/japan.php?itemid=811&catid=22&subcatid=147#.

380. Eric Johnston, "Police Wary as Yamaguchi-gumi Prepares to Fete Sixth Don," *Japan Times Online*, August 19, 2005, http://www.japantimes.co.jp/text/nn20050819f3.html.

381. Kristof, "Quake That Hurt Kobe Helps Its Criminals," A3.

382. Adelstein, "Yakuza to the Rescue."

383. AlternateSam, "Earthquake in Japan—Yakuza Helping Out," March 13, 2011, http://www.alternatesam.com/2011/03/13/earthquake-in-japan-yakuza-helping-out/.

384. Terril Yue Jones, "From Society's Shadows, Yakuza among First with Relief Supplies," March 25, 2011, http://uk.news.yahoo.com/22/20110325/thl-uk-japan-quake-yakuza-b2e59e8.html.

385. AlternateSam, "Earthquake in Japan."

386. Adelstein, "Yakuza to the Rescue."

Chapter 6

1. Schear et al., "Fragile States and Ungoverned Spaces," 113.

2. Mandel, *Armies without States*, 14.

3. Ibid., 16.

4. Taulbee, "Privatization of Security," 6.

5. Spearin, "Private Security Panacea?"

6. Doug Brooks, "Dogs of Peace," March 7, 1999, http://www.post-gazette.com/forum/19990307edbrooks5.asp.

7. Lea and Stenson, "Security, Sovereignty, and Non-State Governance," 13, 23.

8. Adamson, "Crossing Borders," 194.

9. Robinson, *Merger*, 17.

10. Felbab-Brown, "Drugs, Violence and Instability."

11. Galeotti, "Transnational Organized Crime," 34–35.

12. Grynkewich, "Welfare as Warfare," 353.

13. Godson and Shultz, *Adapting America's Security Paradigm*, 11.

14. Klare, "Deadly Connection," 121.

15. Williams, "Return of Barbarism."

16. Thomas and Casebeer, "Violent Systems," 12.

17. Ahram, *Proxy Warriors*, 129. See also Migdal, *Strong Societies and Weak States*, 18; and Bates, *When Things Fall Apart*, 147–148.

18. Mandel, "Fighting Fire with Fire," 69.

19. Mitton, "Engaging with Disengagement," 190.

20. Santos and Rodriguez, "Conclusion," 428.

21. Hazen, "From Social Movement to Armed Group," 96.

22. World Bank, "Fighting Poverty Key to Global Peace and Stability, Says Global Poll," June 5, 2003, http://go.worldbank.org/303UE04ZQo.

23. Vincent Ferraro, "Globalizing Weakness: Is Global Poverty a Threat to the Interests of States?" https://www.mtholyoke.edu/acad/intrel/globecon/poverty.htm.

24. Paredes, "Where Guns Rule," 228.

25. National Intelligence Council, *Mapping the Global Future*, 97.

26. Goldstone, "Population and Security," 14. See also Urdal, "Clash of Generations," 607–629.

27. National Intelligence Council, *Global Trends 2025*, iv.

28. Ssereo, "Clanpolitics, Clan-Democracy and Conflict Regulation in Africa," 25.

29. Hewitt, Wilkenfeld, and Gurr, *Peace and Conflict 2010*, 9.

30. See, for example, Victoroff, "Mind of the Terrorist," 56; Benjamin and Simon, *Next Attack*, 74, 89; and Post, "When Hatred Is Bred in the Bone," 628.

31. Davis, "Non-State Armed Actors," 230.

32. Schneckener, "Fragile Statehood," 25.

33. Kerry, *New War*, 87; and Picarelli, "Transnational Organized Crime," 457.

34. Naim, *Illicit*, 72.

35. Mandel, *Global Threat*, chap. 3.

36. Ahram, *Proxy Warriors*, 129.

Chapter 7

1. Guáqueta, "Way Back In," 37.

2. Krahmann, *States, Citizens and the Privatization of Security*, 49.

3. Cutler, Haufler, and Porter, "Contours and Significance of Private Authority," 369.

4. Schneckener, "State Building or New Modes of Governance?" 250.

5. Schear et al., "Fragile States and Ungoverned Spaces," 112–113.

6. For a parallel but different discussion focusing just on transnational organized crime, see Mandel, *Dark Logic*, chap. 8.

7. Thomas, Kiser, and Casebeer, *Warlords Rising*, 5. See also Herz, *Nation-State*.

8. Andreas and Nadelmann, *Policing the Globe*, 246.

9. Andreas, "Redrawing the Line," 95–96.

10. Mandel, *Changing Face of National Security*, 135.

11. Freedman, "Order and Disorder in the New World," 37.

12. Ahram, *Proxy Warriors*, 139.

13. Berdal and Ucko, "Introduction," 4.

14. See Diamond, "What Went Wrong in Iraq," 36; "Iraq at War with Itself," *Economist*, March 4, 2006, 9; and Mandel, *Global Threat*, 71–72.

15. Mandel, *Armies without States*, 7.

16. Paul Lewis, "It's Not Just Governments That Make War and Peace Now," *New York Times*, November 28, 1998, B9, B11.

17. Anthony Burke, "Paradoxes of Force and Security: Postmodern Conflict," December 9, 2010, http://worldthoughtworldpolitics.wordpress.com/2010/12/09/paradoxes-of-force-and-security/.

18. See Mandel, *Meaning of Military Victory*, chaps. 1–2 and 5–7.

19. Gray, *Hard and Soft Power*, vi–vii.

20. Schear et al., "Fragile States and Ungoverned Spaces," 103–104.

21. See Mandel, *Global Threat*, 108–110.

22. Cunningham, "What Is So Extreme about Extreme Violence?"

23. Hazen, "From Social Movement to Armed Group," 96.

24. Schneckener, "Fragile Statehood," 35.

25. Diane E. Davis, "Irregular Armed Forces, Shifting Patterns of Commitment, and Fragmented Sovereignty in the Developing World" (September 2009), 22, http://hdl.handle.net/1721.1/51817.

26. Clunan, "Ungoverned Spaces?" 4.

27. Rapley, "New Middle Ages," 96.

28. Clunan and Trinkunas, "Conceptualizing Ungoverned Spaces," 27.

29. Williams, *From the New Middle Ages to a New Dark Age*, 6.

30. Steinhoff, "Talking to the Enemy," 308, 310.

31. Program on Humanitarian Policy and Conflict Research, *Empowered Groups*, 38.

32. Ibid., 38–39.

33. Steinhoff, "Talking to the Enemy," 308, 319.

34. Schneckener, "State Building or New Modes of Governance?" 250.

35. Steinhoff, "Talking to the Enemy," 302; and Claude Bruderlein, "The Role of Non-State Actors in Building Human Security: The Case of Armed Groups in Intra-State Wars," May 2000, http://reliefweb.int/sites/reliefweb.int/files/resources/60D788FF A78FBC23C1256C3E0029C598-hd-security-may00.pdf.

36. Reno, "Explaining Patterns of Violence in Collapsed States," 165.

37. Crawford and Miscik, "Rise of Mezzanine Rulers," 123.

38. Holmqvist, "Engaging Armed Non-State Actors," 49.

39. Steinhoff, "Talking to the Enemy," 320.

40. Schneckener, "Spoilers or Governance Actors?" 18.

41. Ahram, *Proxy Warriors*, 137.

42. Karp, "Changing Ownership of War," 187.

43. Schneckener, "State Building or New Modes of Governance?" 249–250.

44. Davis, "Non-State Armed Actors," 223–224.

45. Godson and Shultz, *Adapting America's Security Paradigm*, 6; see also Schneckener, "Spoilers or Governance Actors?" 10.

46. Davis, "Non-State Armed Actors," 239.

47. Clunan and Trinkunas, "Alternative Governance and Security," 276.

48. See Mandel, *Deadly Transfers*; and Rapley, "New Middle Ages," 102.

49. Patrick, "Weak States and Global Threats," 44.

50. Rapley, "New Middle Ages," 96.

51. Clunan and Trinkunas, "Alternative Governance and Security," 284–286.

52. Lea and Stenson, "Security, Sovereignty, and Non-State Governance," 24.

53. Thomson, *Mercenaries, Pirates, and Sovereigns*, 21.

54. Bryden, "Shaping the Security Governance Agenda," 255.

55. Crawford and Miscik, "Rise of Mezzanine Rulers," 128.

56. Ahram, *Proxy Warriors*, 120. See also Mitchell, *Agents of Atrocity*; and Cohen, *States of Denial*, 108–109.

57. Sterling, *Thieves' World*, 21.

58. Harris, *Political Corruption*, 168.

59. Ibid., 169.

60. Naim, "Mafia States," 101.

61. Makarenko, "Crime–Terror Continuum," 138.

62. Lea and Stenson, "Security, Sovereignty, and Non-State Governance," 18.

63. Harris, *Political Corruption*, 173.

64. Kalyvas, *Logic of Violence in Civil War*, 150.

65. See, for example, Gray, *Another Bloody Century*, chap. 9.

66. Murtazashvili, "State of the State in Afghanistan."

Chapter 8

1. Ahram, *Proxy Warriors*, 133; and Kaldor, *New and Old Wars*, x.

2. Clunan and Trinkunas, "Conceptualizing Ungoverned Spaces," 21.

3. Mueller, *Remnants of War*, 176.

4. Risse, "Governance in Areas of Limited Statehood," 1.

5. Godson and Shultz, *Adapting America's Security Paradigm*, 1.

6. Patrick, "Weak States and Global Threats," 27–28.

7. Rabasa et al., *Ungoverned Territories*, 39.

8. Ahram, *Proxy Warriors*, 133.

9. North, Wallis, and Weingast, *Violence and Social Orders*, 258.

10. Davis, "Non-State Armed Actors," 221.

11. Nagle, "Criminal Gangs in Latin America," 19.

12. Rabasa et al., *Ungoverned Territories*, 31.

13. Clunan, "Ungoverned Spaces?" 6.

14. Holmqvist, "Engaging Armed Non-State Actors," 49.

15. Kaldor, *New and Old Wars*, 178.

16. Mohamed El Baradei, "Egypt's Real State of Emergency Is Its Repressed Democracy," *Washington Post*, December 26, 2010, http://www.washingtonpost.com/wp-dyn/content/article/2010/12/26/AR2010122601699.html.

17. Brauer and Haywood, "Non-State Sovereign Entrepreneurs," 7.

18. Naim, "Mafia States," 108–109.

19. Grynkewich, "Welfare as Warfare," 350.

20. Ibid., 355.

21. Santos, "Terrorism and Philippine Armed Groups," 109.

22. Ahram, *Proxy Warriors*, 138.

23. Krause and Milliken, "Introduction," 1.

24. Kaldor, *New and Old Wars*, 186–187.

25. This study fully recognizes that difficulties exist in making a black-and-white distinction between public and private across times periods and cultures.

26. Santos and Rodriguez, "Conclusion," 421.

27. Risse, "Governance in Areas of Limited Statehood," 9.

28. Conrad and Stange, "Governance and Colonial Rule," 48.

29. Guáqueta, "Way Back In," 11.

30. Holmqvist, "Engaging Armed Non-State Actors," 48.

31. Krahmann, "Conceptualizing Security Governance," 6.

32. Berdal and Ucko, "Introduction," 6.

33. Shultz, Farah, and Lochard, "Armed Groups," 74.

34. Williams, *From the New Middle Ages to a New Dark Age*, 49.

35. Steinhoff, "Talking to the Enemy," 319.

36. Ahram, *Proxy Warriors*, 135.

37. Linklater, *Transformation of Political Community*, 194–195; and Bull, *Anarchical Society*, 266.

38. Schear et al., "Fragile States and Ungoverned Spaces," 99.

39. Ibid.

40. Godson and Shultz, *Adapting America's Security Paradigm*, 24.

41. Davis, "Non-State Armed Actors," 223.

42. Ibid., 241–242.

43. Giustozzi, "Bureaucratic Façade," 67.

44. Berdal and Ucko, "Introduction," 5.

45. Godson and Shultz, *Adapting America's Security Paradigm*, 24.

46. Steinhoff, "Talking to the Enemy," 305.

47. Lea and Stenson, "Security, Sovereignty, and Non-State Governance," 23.

48. Program on Humanitarian Policy and Conflict Research, *Empowered Groups*, 40.

49. Ahram, *Proxy Warriors*, 138.

50. Schneckener, "Fragile Statehood," 36–37.

51. Torjesen and MacFarlane, "Reintegration before Disarmament," 61.

52. Ibid., 62.

53. Cunningham, "What Is So Extreme about Extreme Violence?"

54. Nadelmann, *Cops across Borders*, 475–476.

55. Program on Humanitarian Policy and Conflict Research, *Empowered Groups*, 23–24.

56. Mandel, "Distortions," 79.

57. Motley, "Coping with the Terrorist Threat," 169.

58. Bond, "Hybrid War," 2.

59. Karp, "Changing Ownership of War," 181.

60. Thomas, Kiser, and Casebeer, *Warlords Rising*, 199.

61. Thaler, "Stabilizing States in Crisis," 50–52.

62. Andreas, "Redrawing the Line," 95–99.

63. Perl, *International Terrorism*, 11–14.

64. Torjesen and MacFarlane, "Reintegration before Disarmament," 61.

65. McLean, "Colombia," 133.

66. Thomas and Casebeer, "Violent Systems," ix.

67. Luna, "Dismantling Illicit Networks," 7.

68. Program on Humanitarian Policy and Conflict Research, *Empowered Groups*, 25.

69. McLean, "Colombia," 133.

70. Thomas, Kiser, and Casebeer, *Warlords Rising*, 218.

71. Shaw, "Crime, Police and Public in Transitional Societies," 14–15.

72. Thomas and Casebeer, "Violent Systems," 11; and Snow, *Uncivil Wars*, 35.

73. Tilly, *From Mobilization to Revolution*, 177; Goodwin, *No Other Way Out*, and Lawrence, "Driven to Arms?" 149.

74. Ucko, "Militias, Tribes, and Insurgents," 90.

75. Program on Humanitarian Policy and Conflict Research, *Empowered Groups*, 18.

76. Cline, "Peeling Labels."

77. Program on Humanitarian Policy and Conflict Research, *Empowered Groups*, 40.

78. "Brigands Seeking Harbours—Piracy: Why Pirates Like a Little Law and Order," *Economist*, April 23, 2011, 80.

79. Frank and Melville, "Image of the Enemy," 203–204.

80. Naim, "Mafia States," 111.

81. See Flynn, "Brittle Superpower," 32.

82. See Kay, *Global Security in the Twenty-First Century*, 249.

83. Garrison, "Grand Strategic Implications."

84. See Mandel, *Global Threat*, chap. 5. Target-centered threat management would require radical shifts from the standard threat assessment and management systems currently being used in most countries.

85. Naim, "Mafia States," 110.

86. Grynkewich, "Welfare as Warfare," 351.

87. Hutchful, "Understanding the African Security Crisis," 222.

88. For a detailed discussion of competing security protection priorities, see Mandel, "What Are We Protecting?" 335–355; and Caldwell and Williams, *Seeking Security in an Insecure World*, 4.

89. Krahmann, "Conceptualizing Security Governance," 20.

90. Godson and Shultz, *Adapting America's Security Paradigm*, 16–17.

91. Vinci, *Armed Groups and the Balance of Power*, 140.

92. Schneckener, "Spoilers or Governance Actors?" 7, 18.

93. Williams, *From the New Middle Ages to a New Dark Age*, 30–31.

94. Ahram, *Proxy Warriors*, 140.

95. Rodriguez and Santos, "Introduction," 10.

96. Karp, "Changing Ownership of War," 190.

BIBLIOGRAPHY

Adamson, Fiona B. "Crossing Borders: International Migration and National Security." *International Security* 31 (Summer 2006): 165–199.

Ahram, Ariel I. *Proxy Warriors: The Rise and Fall of State-Sponsored Militias.* Stanford, CA: Stanford University Press, 2011.

AlSayyad, Nezar. "Foreword." In *Lessons in Post-War Reconstruction: Case Studies from Lebanon in the Aftermath of the 2006 War*, edited by Howayda Al-Harithy, vii–ix. London: Routledge, 2010.

Andreas, Peter. "Redrawing the Line: Borders and Security in the Twenty-First Century." *International Security* 28 (Fall 2003): 78–111.

Andreas, Peter, and Ethan Nadelmann. *Policing the Globe: Criminalization and Crime Control in International Relations.* Oxford: Oxford University Press, 2006.

Arana, Ana. "How the Street Gangs Took Central America." *Foreign Affairs* 98 (2005): 98–110.

Bakke, Kristin M. "The Turn to Violence in Self-Determination Struggles in Chechnya and Punjab." In *Rethinking Violence: States and Non-State Actors in Conflict*, edited by Adria Lawrence and Erica Chenoweth, 221–247. Cambridge, MA: MIT Press, 2010.

Bakonyi, Jutta, and Kirsti Stuvøy. "Violence and Social Order beyond the State: Somalia and Angola." *Review of African Political Economy* 32 (June/September 2005): 359–382.

Bates, Robert. *When Things Fall Apart: State Failure in Late-Century Africa.* New York: Cambridge University Press, 2008.

Begley, Sharon, and Donna Foote. "Lessons of Kobe." *Newsweek*, January 30, 1995.

Benjamin, Daniel, and Steven Simon. *The Next Attack: The Failure of the War on Terror and a Strategy for Getting It Right.* New York: Times Books, 2005.

Berdal, Mats, and Monica Serrano, eds. *Transnational Organized Crime and International Security: Business as Usual?* Boulder, CO: Lynne Rienner, 2002.

Berdal, Mats, and David H. Ucko. "Introduction: The Political Reintegration of Armed Groups after War." In *Reintegrating Armed Groups after Conflict: Politics, Violence and Transition*, edited by Mats Berdal and David H. Ucko, 1–9. New York: Routledge, 2009.

———, eds. *Reintegrating Armed Groups after Conflict: Politics, Violence and Transition.* New York: Routledge, 2009.

Bergen, Peter L. *Holy War, Inc.: Inside the Secret World of Osama bin Laden.* New York: Free Press, 2001.

Bevan, James. "The Myth of Madness: Cold Rationality and 'Resource' Plunder by the Lord's Resistance Army." *Civil Wars* 9 (December 2007): 343–358.

Biddle, Stephen, Fotini Christia, and J. Alexander Thier. "Defining Success in Afghanistan: What Can the United States Accept?" *Foreign Affairs* 89 (July/August 2010): 48–60.

Binnendijk, Hans, and Stuart E. Johnson. *Transforming for Stabilization and Reconstruction Operations.* Washington, DC: National Defense University Press, 2004.

Bolivar, Ingrid. "Local Dimensions of the Colombian Conflict: Order and Security in Drug Trafficking." Working Paper 15, Clingendael Institute, The Hague, Netherlands, July 2003. http://www.clingendael.nl/publications/2003/20030700_cru_working_paper_15.pdf.

Bond, Margaret S. "Hybrid War: A New Paradigm for Stability Operations in Failing States." Strategy Research Project, U.S. Army War College, Carlisle, PA, March 30, 2007.

Bonner, Robert C. "The New Cocaine Cowboys: How to Defeat Mexico's Drug Cartels." *Foreign Affairs* 89 (July/August 2010): 35–37.

Boot, Max. "Pirates, Then and Now: How Piracy Was Defeated in the Past and Can Be Again." *Foreign Affairs* 88 (July/August 2009): 94–107.

Borzello, Anna. "The Challenge of DDR in Northern Uganda: The Lord's Resistance Army." In *Reintegrating Armed Groups after Conflict: Politics, Violence and Transition*, edited by Mats Berdal and David H. Ucko, 144–171. New York: Routledge, 2009.

Boucek, Christopher. "Yemen: Avoiding a Downward Spiral." Working Paper 102, Carnegie Endowment for International Peace, Washington, DC, September 2009.

Boudon, Lawrence. "Guerrillas and the State: The Role of the State in the Colombian Peace Process." *Journal of Latin American Studies* 28 (May 1996): 279–297.

Branscomb, Lewis M. "A Nation Forewarned: Vulnerability of Critical Infrastructure in the Twenty-First Century." In *Seeds of Disaster, Roots of Response: How Private Action Can Reduce Public Vulnerability*, edited by Philip E. Auerswald, Lewis M. Branscomb, Todd M. La Porte, and Erwann O. Michel-Kerjan, 19–25. Cambridge: Cambridge University Press, 2006.

Brauer, Jurgen. "An Economic Perspective on Mercenaries, Military Companies, and the Privatization of Force." *Cambridge Review of International Affairs* 13 (Autumn/Winter 1999): 130–146.

Brauer, Jurgen, and Robert Haywood. "Non-State Sovereign Entrepreneurs and Non-Territorial Sovereign Organizations." Working Paper 2010/09, United Nations University, New York, February 2010. http://www.wider.unu.edu/publications/working-papers/2010/en_GB/wp2010-09/_files/82967192285675604/default/2010-09.pdf.

Bruderlein, Claude. "People's Security as a New Measure of Global Stability." *International Review of the Red Cross* 83 (June 2001): 353–366. http://www.icrc.org/web/eng/siteengo.nsf/html/57JR5Q.

Bruneau, Thomas. "The Maras and National Security in Central America." *Strategic Insights* 4 (May 2005): 1–12.

Bruno, Gregg. "The Taliban in Afghanistan." *Council on Foreign Relations Online*, August 3, 2009. http://www.cfr.org/publication/10551/taliban_in_afghanistan.html.

Bryden, Alan. "Shaping the Security Governance Agenda in Post-Conflict Peacebuilding." In *Security Governance in Post-Conflict Peacebuilding*, edited by Alan Bryden and Heiner Hänggi, 253–268. Geneva: Geneva Centre for the Democratic Control of Armed Forces, 2005.

Bryden, Alan, and Marina Caparini, eds. *Private Actors and Security Governance.* Geneva: Geneva Centre for the Democratic Control of Armed Forces, 2006.

Bryden, Alan, and Heiner Hänggi, eds. *Security Governance in Post-Conflict Peacebuilding.* Geneva: Geneva Centre for the Democratic Control of Armed Forces, 2005.

Bull, Hedley. *The Anarchical Society: A Study of Order in World Politics.* London: Macmillan, 1977.

Butler, Steven. "Killer Quake." *U.S. News & World Report*, January 30, 1995.

Byman, Daniel. "Should Hezbollah Be Next?" *Foreign Affairs* 54 (November/December 2003): 54–66.

Caldwell, Dan, and Robert E. Williams Jr. *Seeking Security in an Insecure World.* Lanham, MD: Rowman & Littlefield, 2006.

———. *Seeking Security in an Insecure World.* 2nd ed. Lanham, MD: Rowman & Littlefield, 2012.

Campo-Flores, Arian. "The Most Dangerous Gang in America." *Newsweek*, March 28, 2006.

Carafano, James Jay. "Contracting in Combat: Advice for the Commission on Wartime Contracting." Backgrounder 2228, Heritage Foundation, Washington, DC, January 13, 2009. http://www.heritage.org/research/NationalSecurity/upload/bg_2228.pdf.

Carapico, Sheila. "Yemen and the Aden-Abyan Islamic Army." *Middle East Report Online*, October 18, 2000.

Casebeer, William. "Stories, Identities, and Conflict." Paper presented at the Conference on Violent Armed Groups: A Global Challenge, Pittsburgh, September 16–17, 2010.

Cederman, Lars-Erik. *Emergent Actors in World Politics: How States and Nations Develop and Dissolve.* Princeton, NJ: Princeton University Press, 1997.

Cheney, Kristen. "'Our Children Have Only Known War': Children's Experiences and the Use of Childhood in Northern Uganda." *Children's Geographies* 3 (April 2005): 23–45.

Chernick, Marc. "FARC-EP: From Liberal Guerrillas to Marxist Rebels to Post–Cold War Insurgents." In *Terror, Insurgency, and the State: Ending Protracted Conflicts,* edited by Marianne Heiberg, Brendan O'Leary, and John Tirman, 51–82. Philadelphia: University of Pennsylvania Press, 2007.

Chesterman, Simon, and Chia Lehnardt. *From Mercenaries to Market: The Rise and Regulation of Private Security Companies.* New York: Oxford University Press, 2007.

Clark, Michael. *In the Spotlight: The Islamic Army of Aden (IAA).* Washington, DC: Center for Defense Information, 2004. http://www.cdi.org/program/document.cfm?DocumentID=2679&from_page=./index.cfm.

Clark, Victoria. *Yemen: Dancing on the Heads of Snakes.* New Haven, CT: Yale University Press, 2010.

Clarke, Colin. "Politics, Violence and Drugs in Kingston, Jamaica." *Bulletin of Latin American Research* 25 (2006): 420–440.

Cleaver, Gerry. "Subcontracting Military Power: The Privatisation of Security in Sub-Saharan Africa." *Crime, Law and Social Change* 33 (2000): 131–149.

Cline, Lawrence. "Peeling Labels: Categorizing Armed Groups over Time." Paper presented at the Conference on Violent Armed Groups: A Global Challenge, Pittsburgh, September 16–17, 2010.

Clunan, Anne L. "Ungoverned Spaces? The Need for Reevaluation." In *Ungoverned Spaces: Alternatives to State Authority in an Era of Softened Sovereignty,* edited by Anne L. Clunan and Harold A. Trinkunas, 3–13. Stanford, CA: Stanford University Press, 2010.

Clunan, Anne L., and Harold A. Trinkunas. "Alternative Governance and Security." In *Ungoverned Spaces: Alternatives to State Authority in an Era of Softened Sovereignty,* edited by Anne L. Clunan and Harold A. Trinkunas, 275–293. Stanford, CA: Stanford University Press, 2010.

———. "Conceptualizing Ungoverned Spaces: Territorial Statehood, Contested Authority, and Softened Sovereignty." In *Ungoverned Spaces: Alternatives to State Authority in an Era of Softened Sovereignty,* edited by Anne L. Clunan and Harold A. Trinkunas, 17–33. Stanford, CA: Stanford University Press, 2010.

———, eds. *Ungoverned Spaces: Alternatives to State Authority in an Era of Softened Sovereignty.* Stanford, CA: Stanford University Press, 2010.

Cockayne, James, and Christoph Mikulaschek. *Transnational Security Challenges and the United Nations: Overcoming Sovereign Walls and Institutional Silos.* New York: International Peace Academy, 2008. http://www.ipacademy.org/asset/file/253/west point.pdf.

Cohen, Stanley. *States of Denial: Knowing about Atrocities and Suffering*. Malden, MA: Polity Press, 2001.

Coll, Steve. "U.S.-Taliban Talks." *New Yorker*, February 28, 2011. http://www.newyorker .com/talk/comment/2011/02/28/110228taco_talk_coll.

Conrad, Sebastian, and Marion Stange. "Governance and Colonial Rule." In *Governance without a State? Policies and Politics in Areas of Limited Statehood*, edited by Thomas Risse, 39–64. New York: Columbia University Press, 2011.

Coogan, Tim Pat. *The IRA*. New York: Palgrave, 2000.

Council on Foreign Relations. "Hezbollah (a.k.a. Hizbollah, Hizbu'llah)." *Council on Foreign Relations Online*, June 8, 2009. http://www.cfr.org/publication/9155/hezbol lah.html?breadcrumb=%2F.

Crawford, Michael, and Jami Miscik, "The Rise of Mezzanine Rulers: The New Frontier for International Law." *Foreign Affairs* 89 (November/December 2010): 123–132.

Cunningham, Karla. "What Is So Extreme about Extreme Violence? Explaining the Escalation in Extreme Violence by Non-State Actors." Paper presented at the Conference on Violent Armed Groups: A Global Challenge, Pittsburgh, September 16–17, 2010.

Curtis, Glenn E., and Tara Karacan. *The Nexus among Terrorists, Narcotics Traffickers, Weapons Proliferators, and Organized Crime Networks in Western Europe*. Washington, DC: Federal Research Division of the Library of Congress, 2002. https://www .hsdl.org/homesec/docs/justice/nps10-071306-02.pdf&code=c2ccd3f559c7e727d5c7f8 52ff0ab93c.

Cutler, A. Claire, Virginia Haufler, and Tony Porter. "The Contours and Significance of Private Authority and International Affairs." In *Private Authority and International Affairs*, edited by A. Claire Cutler, Virginia Haufler, and Tony Porter, 333–376. Albany: State University of New York Press, 1999.

———. "Private Authority and International Affairs." In *Private Authority and International Affairs*, edited by A. Claire Cutler, Virginia Haufler, and Tony Porter, 3–38. Albany: State University of New York Press, 1999.

———, eds. *Private Authority and International Affairs*. Albany: State University of New York Press, 1999.

Davis, Diane E. "Non-State Armed Actors, New Imagined Communities, and Shifting Patterns of Sovereignty and Insecurity in the Modern World." *Contemporary Security Policy* 30 (August 2009): 221–245.

Davis, Diane E., and Anthony W. Pereira. *Irregular Armed Forces and Their Role in Politics and State Formation*. Cambridge: Cambridge University Press, 2003.

Davis, R. C., C. Ortiz, S. Dadush, J. Irish, A. Alvarado, and Diane E. Davis. "The Public Accountability of Private Police: Lessons from New York, Johannesburg, and Mexico City." *Policing and Society* 13 (June 2003): 197–210.

Dekmejian, R. Hrair. *Spectrum of Terror*. Washington, DC: CQ Press, 2007.

Delaney, Tim. *American Street Gangs.* Upper Saddle River, NJ: Prentice Hall, 2006.

Delfs, Robert. "Clash of Loyalties." *Far Eastern Economic Review,* November 21, 1991.

Diamond, Larry. "What Went Wrong in Iraq." *Foreign Affairs* 83 (September/October 2004): 34–56.

Doom, Rudy, and Koen Vlassenroot. "Kony's Message: A New Koine? The Lord's Resistance Army in Northern Uganda." *African Affairs* 98 (1999): 5–36.

Duffield, Mark. "Post-Modern Conflict: Warlords, Post-Adjustment States and Private Protection." *Civil Wars* 1 (Spring 1998): 65–102.

Dunn, Kevin C. "Uganda: The Lord's Resistance Army." In *African Guerrillas: Raging against the Machine,* edited by Morten Bøås and Kevin C. Dunn, 131–149. Boulder, CO: Lynne Rienner, 2007.

Early, Bryan R. "Larger Than a Party, Yet Smaller Than a State: Locating Hezbollah's Place within Lebanon's State and Society." *World Affairs* 168 (Winter 2006): 115–129.

Edwards, Adam, and Peter Gill. "After Transnational Organized Crime? The Politics of Public Safety." In *Transnational Organized Crime: Perspectives on Global Security,* edited by Adam Edwards and Peter Gill, 264–281. New York: Routledge, 2003.

English, Richard. *Armed Struggle: The History of the IRA.* New York: Oxford University Press, 2003.

Ervin, Clark Kent. *Open Target: Where America Is Vulnerable to Attack.* New York: Palgrave Macmillan, 2006.

Felbab-Brown, Vanda. "Drugs, Violence and Instability: A Global Perspective." Paper presented at the Conference on Drug Trafficking, Violence and Instability in Mexico, Colombia and the Caribbean: Implications for US National Security, Pittsburgh, October 29–30, 2009.

———. "Rules and Regulations in Ungoverned Spaces: Illicit Economies, Criminals, and Belligerents." In *Ungoverned Spaces: Alternatives to State Authority in an Era of Softened Sovereignty,* edited by Anne L. Clunan and Harold A. Trinkunas, 175–192. Stanford, CA: Stanford University Press, 2010.

Feldman, Stacy, and Brian Slattery. "Living without a Government in Somalia: An Interview with Mark Bradbury." *Journal of International Affairs* 57 (Fall 2003): 201–217.

Fisman, Raymond, and Edward Miguel. *Economic Gangsters: Corruption, Violence, and the Poverty of Nations.* Princeton, NJ: Princeton University Press, 2008.

Flynn, Stephen E. "The Brittle Superpower." In *Seeds of Disaster, Roots of Response: How Private Action Can Reduce Public Vulnerability,* edited by Philip E. Auerswald, Lewis M. Branscomb, Todd M. La Porte, and Erwann O. Michel-Kerjan, 26–36. Cambridge: Cambridge University Press, 2006.

Fogelbach, Juan. "Mara Salvatrucha (MS-13) and Ley Anti Mara: El Salvador's Struggle to Reclaim Social Order." *San Diego International Law Journal* 223 (2005/2006): 223–258.

Frank, Jerome D., and Andrei Y. Melville. "The Image of the Enemy and the Process of Change." In *Breakthrough—Emerging New Thinking: Soviet and Western Scholars Issue a Challenge to Build a World Beyond War*, edited by Anatoly Gromyko and Martin Hellman, 199–208. New York: Walker, 1988.

Freedman, Lawrence. "Order and Disorder in the New World." *Foreign Affairs* 71 (1991/1992): 20–37.

Fukishima, Glen S. "The Great Hanshin Earthquake." Occasional Paper 2, Japan Policy Research Institute, University of San Francisco Center for the Pacific Rim, San Francisco, March 1995. http://www.jpri.org/publications/occasionalpapers/op2.html.

Galeotti, Mark. "Transnational Organized Crime: Law Enforcement as a Global Battlespace." In *Non-State Threats and Future Wars*, edited by Robert J. Bunker, 29–39. London: Frank Cass, 2003.

Garrison, Joel. "Grand Strategic Implications of Violent Armed Groups." Paper presented at the Conference on Violent Armed Groups: A Global Challenge, Pittsburgh, September 16–17, 2010.

Ghani, Ashraf, and Clare Lockhart. *Fixing Failed States: A Framework for Rebuilding a Fractured World*. New York: Oxford University Press, 2008.

Ghani, Ashraf, Clare Lockhart, and Michael Carnahan. *Closing the Sovereignty Gap: An Approach to State-Building*. London: Overseas Development Institute, 2005.

Giustozzi, Antonio. "Bureaucratic Façade and Political Realities of Disarmament and Demobilization in Afghanistan." In *Reintegrating Armed Groups after Conflict: Politics, Violence and Transition*, edited by Mats Berdal and David H. Ucko, 67–88. New York: Routledge, 2009.

Godson, Roy, and Richard Shultz. *Adapting America's Security Paradigm and Security Agenda*. Washington, DC: National Strategy Information Center, 2010.

Goldstone, Jack A. "Population and Security: How Demographics Change Can Lead to Violent Conflict." *Journal of International Affairs* 56 (Fall 2002): 3–22.

Goldstone, Jack A., Robert H. Bates, David L. Epstein, Ted Robert Gurr, Michael B. Lustik, Monty G. Marshall, Jay Ulfelder, and Mark Woodward. "A Global Model for Forecasting Political Instability." *American Journal of Political Science* 54 (January 2010): 190–208.

Goodwin, Jeff. *No Other Way Out: States and Revolutionary Movements, 1945–1991*. Cambridge: Cambridge University Press, 2001.

Gorenburg, Dmitry. "Russia Confronts Radical Islam." *Foreign Service Journal* (April 2007): 39–48.

Gray, Colin. *Another Bloody Century: Future Warfare*. London: Weidenfeld & Nicolson, 2005.

———. "Stability Operations in Strategic Perspective: A Skeptical View." *Parameters* (Summer 2006): 4–14.

————. *Hard and Soft Power: The Utility of Military Force as an Instrument of Policy in the 21st Century.* Carlisle, PA: Strategic Studies Institute, 2011.

Grynkewich, Alexus G. "Welfare as Warfare: How Violent Non-State Groups Use Social Services to Attack the State." *Studies in Conflict and Terrorism* 31 (April 2008): 350–370.

Guáqueta, Alexandra. "The Colombian Conflict: Political and Economic Dimensions." In *The Political Economy of Armed Conflict: Beyond Greed and Grievance,* edited by Karen Ballentine and Jake Sherman, 73–106. Boulder, CO: Lynne Rienner, 2003.

————. "The Way Back In: Reintegrating Illegal Armed Groups in Colombia Then and Now." In *Reintegrating Armed Groups after Conflict: Politics, Violence and Transition,* edited by Mats Berdal and David H. Ucko, 10–46. New York: Routledge, 2009.

Gunning, Jeroen. "Hizbollah and the Logic of Political Participation." In *Terror, Insurgency, and the State: Ending Protracted Conflicts,* edited by Marianne Heiberg, Brendan O'Leary, and John Tirman, 157–186. Philadelphia: University of Pennsylvania Press, 2007.

Gunst, Laurie. *Born Fi' Dead: A Journey through the Jamaican Posse Underground.* New York: Henry Holt, 1995.

Hall, Rodney Bruce, and Thomas J. Biersteker. "The Emergence of Private Authority in the International System." In *The Emergence of Private Authority in Global Governance,* edited by Rodney Bruce Hall and Thomas J. Biersteker, 3–22. Cambridge: Cambridge University Press, 2002.

————, eds. *The Emergence of Private Authority in Global Governance.* Cambridge: Cambridge University Press, 2002.

Hamieh, Christine, and Roger Mac Ginty. "A Very Political Reconstruction: Governance and Reconstruction in Lebanon after the 2006 War." *Disasters* 33 (March 2009): S103–S123.

Hammes, Thomas X. *The Sling and the Stone: On War in the 21st Century.* St. Paul, MN: Zenith Press, 2004.

————. "Armed Groups: Changing the Rules." In *Pirates, Terrorists, and Warlords: The History, Influence, and Future of Armed Groups around the World,* edited by Jeffrey H. Norwitz, 441–449. New York: Skyhorse, 2009.

Hanson, Stephanie. "Combating Maritime Piracy." Backgrounder, Council on Foreign Relations, New York, January 7, 2010. http://www.cfr.org/publication/18376/.

Harik, Judith Palmer. *Transnational Actors in Contemporary Conflicts: Hizbullah and Its 2006 War with Israel.* Cambridge, MA: Program on Humanitarian Policy and Conflict Research, Harvard University, 2007. http://www.tagsproject.org/publications.

Harris, Robert. *Political Corruption: In and Beyond the Nation State.* London: Routledge, 2003.

Hayden, Tom. *Street Wars: Gangs and the Future of Violence.* New York: New Press, 2004.

Haywood, Robert, and Jeffrey French. "Potential Roles for Nonstate Actors and Nonterritorial Sovereign Organizations in Reducing Armed Violence." White paper, One Earth Future Foundation, Louisville, CO, November 30, 2009. http://www.oneearth future.org/siteadmin/images/files/file_55.pdf.

Hazen, Jennifer M. "From Social Movement to Armed Group: A Case Study from Nigeria." In *Armed Groups and Contemporary Conflicts: Challenging the Weberian State*, edited by Keith Krause, 80–99. New York: Routledge, 2010.

Herbst, Jeff. "The Regulation of Private Security Forces." In *The Privatisation of Security in Africa*, edited by Greg Mills and John Stremlau, 107–127. Johannesburg: South African Institute of International Affairs, 1999.

Herz, John H. "Rise and Demise of the Territorial State." *World Politics* 9 (July 1957): 473–493.

———. *The Nation-State and the Crisis of World Politics*. Philadelphia: David McKay, 1976.

Hewitt, J. Joseph, Jonathan Wilkenfeld, and Ted Robert Gurr. *Peace and Conflict 2010*. Boulder, CO: Paradigm, 2010.

———. *Peace and Conflict 2012*. Boulder, CO: Paradigm, 2012.

Higgott, Richard A., Geoffrey R. D. Underhill, and Andreas Bieler, eds. *Non-State Actors and Authority in the Global System*. New York: Routledge, 2000.

Hill, Peter B. E. *The Japanese Mafia: Yakuza, Law, and the State*. New York: Oxford University Press, 2003.

Hills, Alice. "Warlords, Militia, and Conflict in Contemporary Africa: A Re-examination of Terms." *Small Wars and Insurgencies* 8 (Spring 1997): 35–51.

Holmqvist, Caroline. "Engaging Armed Non-State Actors in Post-Conflict Settings." In *Security Governance in Post-Conflict Peacebuilding*, edited by Alan Bryden and Heiner Hänggi, 45–68. Geneva: Geneva Centre for the Democratic Control of Armed Forces, 2005.

Holt, Cameron G. *Against All Enemies, Foreign and Domestic: Future Scenarios of National Security and the Constitution*. Maxwell Air Force Base, AL: Air Command and Staff College, 2005. http://www.dtic.mil/cgi-bin/GetTRDoc?AD=ADA475903&Loca tion=U2&doc=GetTRDoc.pdf.

Howe, Herbert M. "Global Order and the Privatization of Security." *Fletcher Forum of World Affairs* 22 (Summer/Fall 1998): 1–9.

———. "Private Security Forces and African Stability: The Case of Executive Outcomes." *Journal of Modern African Studies* 36 (June 1998): 307–331.

Hughes, James. "Chechnya: The Causes of Protracted Post-Soviet Conflict." *Civil Wars* 4 (Winter 2001): 11–48.

Hutchful, Eboe. "Understanding the African Security Crisis." In *Mercenaries: An African Security Dilemma*, edited by Abdel-Fatau Musah and J. 'Kayode Fayemi, 210–232. London: Pluto Press, 2000.

Industrial College of the Armed Forces. *Privatized Military Operations.* Washington, DC: National Defense University, 2009. http://www.ndu.edu/icaf/industry/reports/2009/pdf/icaf-is-report-private-mil-ops-2009.pdf.

Institute for Economics and Peace. *Peace, Wealth, and Human Potential: Global Peace Index.* Sydney, Australia: Institute for Economics and Peace, 2010.

International Alert. "An Assessment of the Mercenary Issue at the Fifty-Fifth Session of the UN Commission on Human Rights." Unpublished manuscript, May 1999.

International Federation of Red Cross and Red Crescent Societies. *World Disaster Report 1996.* New York: Oxford University Press, 1996.

Isenberg, David. *Soldiers of Fortune Ltd.: A Profile of Today's Private Sector Corporate Mercenary Firms.* Washington, DC: Center for Defense Information, 1997.

Janus, Annie, and Kendall Lawrence. *Al Shabaab and the Somalia Food Crisis.* Washington, DC: Fund for Peace, 2011.

Jojarth, Christine. *Crime, War, and Global Trafficking: Designing International Cooperation.* Cambridge: Cambridge University Press, 2009.

Kaldor, Mary. *New and Old Wars: Organizing Violence in a Global Era.* 2nd ed. Stanford, CA: Stanford University Press, 2007.

Kalyvas, Stathis N. *The Logic of Violence in Civil War.* Cambridge: Cambridge University Press, 2006.

Kaplan, David E., and Alex Dubro. *Yakuza: Japan's Criminal Underworld.* Berkeley: University of California Press, 2003.

Kaplan, Robert D. "The Coming Anarchy." *Atlantic Monthly* 273 (February 1994): 44–76.

Karp, Aaron. "The Changing Ownership of War: States, Insurgencies and Technology." In *Armed Groups and Contemporary Conflicts: Challenging the Weberian State,* edited by Keith Krause, 174–194. New York: Routledge, 2010.

Katzman, Kenneth. *Afghanistan: Post-War Governance, Security, and U.S. Policy.* Washington, DC: Congressional Research Service, 2006. http://fpc.state.gov/documents/organization/71863.pdf.

Kaufmann, Daniel, Aart Kraay, and Massimo Mastruzzi. "Governance Matters VIII: Aggregate and Individual Governance Indicators, 1996–2008." Policy Research Working Paper 4978, World Bank, Washington, DC, June 29, 2009. http://papers.ssrn.com/sol3/papers.cfm?abstract_id=1424591.

Kay, Sean. *Global Security in the Twenty-First Century: The Quest for Power and the Search for Peace.* Lanham, MD: Rowman & Littlefield, 2006.

Kelly, Robert J. "Criminal Underworlds: Looking Down on Society from Below." In *Organized Crime: A Global Perspective,* edited by Robert J. Kelly, 10–31. Totowa, NJ: Rowman & Littlefield, 1986.

Keohane, Robert O., and Joseph S. Nye. "Introduction." In *Governance in a Globalizing World,* edited by Joseph S. Nye and John D. Donahue, 1–41. Washington, DC: Brookings Institution Press, 2000.

Kerry, John. *The New War: The Web of Crime That Threatens America's Security.* New York: Simon & Schuster, 1997.

King, Charles, and Rajon Menon. "Prisoners of the Caucasus: Russia's Invisible Civil War." *Foreign Affairs* 89 (July/August 2010): 20–34.

Kirchner, Emil J. "Regional and Global Security: Changing Threats and Institutional Responses." In *Global Security Governance: Competing Perceptions of Security in the 21st Century*, edited by Emil J. Kirchner and James Sperling, 3–22. New York: Routledge, 2007.

Kirchner, Emil J., and James Sperling, eds. *Global Security Governance: Competing Perceptions of Security in the 21st Century.* New York: Routledge, 2007.

Klare, Michael T. "The Deadly Connection: Paramilitary Bands, Small Arms Diffusion, and State Failure." In *When States Fail: Causes and Consequences*, edited by Robert I. Rotberg, 116–134. Princeton, NJ: Princeton University Press, 2004.

Kraft, Herman Joseph S. "The Foibles of an Armed Citizenry: Armed Auxiliaries of the State and Private Armed Groups in the Philippines." In *Primed and Purposeful: Armed Groups and Human Security Efforts in the Philippines*, edited by Soliman M. Santos Jr. and Paz Verdades M. Santos, 185–215. Geneva: Small Arms Survey, Graduate Institute of International and Development Studies, 2010.

Krahmann, Elke. "Conceptualizing Security Governance." *Cooperation and Conflict* 38 (March 2003): 5–26.

———. *States, Citizens and the Privatization of Security.* Cambridge: Cambridge University Press, 2010.

Kramer, Mark. "The Perils of Counterinsurgency: Russia's War in Chechnya." *International Security* 29 (Winter 2004/2005): 5–63.

Kraska, Peter B. "Militarization and Policing—Its Relevance to 21st Century Police." *Policing* 1 (2007): 501–513.

Krause, Keith. "Armed Groups and Contemporary Conflict Dynamics." Paper presented at the Conference on Violent Armed Groups: A Global Challenge, Pittsburgh, September 16–17, 2010.

———, ed. *Armed Groups and Contemporary Conflicts: Challenging the Weberian State.* New York: Routledge, 2010.

Krause, Keith, and Jennifer Milliken. "Introduction: The Challenge of Non-State Armed Groups." In *Armed Groups and Contemporary Conflicts: Challenging the Weberian State*, edited by Keith Krause, 1–19. New York: Routledge, 2010.

Kuite, Mark. "Drugs and Insurgencies." Paper presented at the Conference on Violent Armed Groups: A Global Challenge, Pittsburgh, September 16–17, 2010.

Kushner, Harvey W. "Irish Republican Army." In *Encyclopedia of Terrorism.* Thousand Oaks, CA: Sage, 2003.

Lal, Rollie, "Japanese Trafficking and Smuggling." In *Transnational Threats: Smuggling and Trafficking in Arms, Drugs, and Human Life*, edited by Kimberley L. Thachuk, 143–149. Westport, CT: Praeger Security International, 2007.

Lamb, Robert D. *Ungoverned Areas and Threats from Safe Havens.* Washington, DC: Office of the Under Secretary of Defense for Policy, 2007.

Lapidus, Gail. "Contested Sovereignty: The Tragedy of Chechnya." *International Security* 23 (Summer 1998): 5–49.

Lawrence, Adria. "Driven to Arms? The Escalation of Violence in Nationalist Conflicts." In *Rethinking Violence: States and Non-State Actors in Conflict,* edited by Adria Lawrence and Erica Chenoweth, 143–171. Cambridge, MA: MIT Press, 2010.

Lawrence, Adria, and Erica Chenoweth. "Introduction." In *Rethinking Violence: States and Non-State Actors in Conflict,* edited by Adria Lawrence and Erica Chenoweth, 1–19. Cambridge, MA: MIT Press, 2010.

————, eds. *Rethinking Violence: States and Non-State Actors in Conflict.* Cambridge, MA: MIT Press, 2010.

Lea, John, and Kevin Stenson. "Security, Sovereignty, and Non-State Governance 'From Below.'" *Canadian Journal of Law and Society* 22 (2007): 9–27.

Linklater, Andrew. *The Transformation of Political Community: Ethical Foundations of the Post-Westphalian Era.* Columbia: University of South Carolina Press, 1998.

Luna, David M. "Dismantling Illicit Networks and Corruption Nodes." Paper presented at the 13th International Anti-Corruption Conference, Athens, November 2, 2008. http://www.13iacc.org/IACC_Workshops/Workshop_6.2.

Lutterbeck, Derek. "Between Police and Military: The New Security Agenda and the Rise of the Gendarmeries." *Cooperation and Conflict* 39 (March 2004): 45–68.

————. "Blurring the Dividing Line: The Convergence of Internal and External Security in Western Europe." *European Security* 14 (June 2005): 231–253.

Lynch, Tony, and A. J. Walsh. "The Good Mercenary." *Journal of Political Philosophy* 8 (June 2000): 133–153.

Mabry, Marcus. "Soldiers of Misfortune." *Newsweek,* February 24, 1997.

MacDonald, Scott B. *Dancing on a Volcano: The Latin American Drug Trade.* Westport, CT: Praeger, 1988.

Mac Ginty, Roger. "Reconstructing Post-War Lebanon: A Challenge to the Liberal Peace?" *Conflict, Security and Development* 7 (2007): 457–482.

Maggio, Edward J. "The Threat of Armed Street Gangs in America." In *Pirates, Terrorists, and Warlords: The History, Influence, and Future of Armed Groups around the World,* edited by Jeffrey H. Norwitz, 193–204. New York: Skyhorse, 2009.

Mair, Stephan. "The New World of Privatized Violence." In *Challenges of Globalization: New Trends in International Politics and Society,* edited by Alfred Pfaller and Marika Lerch, 47–61. New Brunswick, NJ: Transaction, 2005.

Makarenko, Tamara. "The Crime–Terror Continuum: Tracing the Interplay between Transnational Organised Crime and Terrorism." *Global Crime* 6 (February 2004): 129–145.

Mandel, Robert. "Distortions in the Intelligence Decision-Making Process." In *Intelligence and Intelligence Policy in a Democratic Society*, edited by Stephen J. Cimbala, 69–83. Dobbs Ferry, NY: Transnational, 1987.

———. *The Changing Face of National Security: A Conceptual Analysis.* Westport, CT: Greenwood Press, 1994.

———. "What Are We Protecting?" *Armed Forces and Society* 22 (Spring 1996): 335–355.

———. *Deadly Transfers and the Global Playground: Transnational Security Threats in a Disorderly World.* Westport, CT: Greenwood Press, 1999.

———. *Armies without States: The Privatization of Security.* Boulder, CO: Lynne Rienner, 2002.

———. "Security and Natural Disasters." *Journal of Conflict Studies* 32 (Fall 2002): 118–143.

———. "Fighting Fire with Fire: Privatizing Counterterrorism." In *Defeating Terrorism: Shaping the New Security Environment*, edited by Russell D. Howard and Reid L. Sawyer, 62–73. New York: McGraw-Hill, 2003.

———. *Security, Strategy, and the Quest for Bloodless War.* Boulder, CO: Lynne Rienner, 2004.

———. *The Meaning of Military Victory.* Boulder, CO: Lynne Rienner, 2006.

———. *Global Threat: Target-Centered Assessment and Management.* Westport, CT: Praeger Security International, 2008.

———. *Dark Logic: Transnational Criminal Tactics and Global Security.* Stanford, CA: Stanford University Press, 2011.

———. "Overview of American Expeditionary Operations Using Private Contractors." In *Contractors and War: The Transformation of United States' Military and Stabilization Operations*, edited by Christopher Kinsey and Malcolm Patterson, 13–35. Stanford, CA: Stanford University Press, 2012.

Manwaring, Max G. *Street Gangs: The New Urban Insurgency.* Carlisle, PA: Strategic Studies Institute, 2005.

———. *A Contemporary Challenge to State Sovereignty: Gangs and Other Illicit Transnational Criminal Organizations in Central America, El Salvador, Mexico, Jamaica, and Brazil.* Carlisle, PA: Strategic Studies Institute, 2007.

Matveeva, Anna. "Chechnya: Dynamics of War and Peace." *Problems of Post-Communism* 54 (May/June 2007): 3–17.

McCormack, Gavan. *The Emptiness of Japanese Affluence.* Armonk, NY: Sharpe, 1996.

McDougall, Alex. "State Power and Its Implications for Civil War in Colombia." *Studies in Conflict and Terrorism* 32 (2009): 322–345.

McFarlane, John. "Transnational Crime and Asia-Pacific Security." In *The Many Faces of Asian Security*, edited by Sheldon W. Simon, 197–229. Lanham, MD: Rowman & Littlefield, 2001.

McGhie, Stuart. "Private Military Companies: Soldiers, Inc." *Jane's Defence Weekly*, May 22, 2002. http://www.sandline.com/hotlinks/20020518-janes/default.html.

McLean, Phillip. "Colombia: Failed, Failing, or Just Weak?" *Washington Quarterly* 25 (Summer 2002): 123–134.

McNerney, Michael J. "Stabilization and Reconstruction in Afghanistan: Are PRTs a Model or a Muddle?" *Parameters* (Winter 2005/2006): 32–46.

Melvin, Neil J. "Building Stability in the North Caucasus." Policy Paper 16, International Peace Research Institute, Stockholm, May 2007.

Menkhaus, Ken. *Somalia: State Collapse and the Threat of Terrorism*. London: International Institute for Strategic Studies, 2004.

———. "Governance without Government in Somalia: Spoilers, State Building, and the Politics of Coping." *International Security* 31 (Winter 2006/2007): 74–106.

Menkhaus, Ken, and Jacob N. Shapiro. "Non-State Actors and Failed States: Lessons from Al-Qa'ida's Experiences in the Horn of Africa." In *Ungoverned Spaces: Alternatives to State Authority in an Era of Softened Sovereignty*, edited by Anne L. Clunan and Harold A. Trinkunas, 77–94. Stanford, CA: Stanford University Press, 2010.

Meshali-Ram, Meirav. "Afghanistan: A Legacy of Violence? Internal and External Factors of the Enduring Violent Conflict." *Comparative Studies of South Asia, Africa and the Middle East* 28 (2008): 473–486.

Migdal, Joel. *Strong Societies and Weak States: State-Society Relations and State Capabilities in the Third World*. Princeton, NJ: Princeton University Press, 1988.

Miller, Rose M. "The Threat of Transnational Crime in East Asia." Strategy Research Project, U.S. Army War College, Carlisle, PA, March 19, 2002. http://www.dtic.mil/cgi-bin/GetTRDoc?AD=ADA402060&Location=U2&doc=GetTRDoc.pdf.

Mitchell, Neil J. *Agents of Atrocity: Leaders, Followers, and the Violation of Human Rights in Civil War*. New York: Palgrave Macmillan, 2004.

Mitton, Kieran. "Engaging with Disengagement: The Political Reintegration of Sierra Leone's Revolutionary United Front." In *Reintegrating Armed Groups after Conflict: Politics, Violence and Transition*, edited by Mats Berdal and David H. Ucko, 172–198. New York: Routledge, 2009.

Motley, James B. "Coping with the Terrorist Threat: The U.S. Intelligence Dilemma." In *Intelligence and Intelligence Policy in a Democratic Society*, edited by Stephen J. Cimbala, 165–175. Dobbs Ferry, NY: Transnational, 1987.

Mueller, John. *The Remnants of War*. Ithaca, NY: Cornell University Press, 2004.

Mulholland, Marc. "Irish Republican Politics and Violence before the Peace Process, 1968–1994." *European Review of History* 14 (September 2007): 397–421.

Murtazashvili, Jennifer Brick. "The State of the State in Afghanistan." Paper presented at the Conference on Violent Armed Groups: A Global Challenge, Pittsburgh, September 16–17, 2010.

Musah, Abdel-Fatau, and J. 'Kayode Fayemi, eds. *Mercenaries: An African Security Dilemma.* London: Pluto Press, 2000.

Nadelmann, Ethan A. *Cops across Borders: The Internationalization of U.S. Criminal Law Enforcement.* University Park: Pennsylvania State University Press, 1995.

Nagle, Luz E. "Criminal Gangs in Latin America: The Next Great Threat to Regional Security and Stability." *Texas Hispanic Journal of Law and Policy* 14 (2008): 7–27.

Naim, Moisés. *Illicit: How Smugglers, Traffickers, and Copycats Are Hijacking the Global Economy.* New York: Doubleday, 2005.

———. "Mafia States: Organized Crime Takes Office." *Foreign Affairs* 91 (May/June 2012): 100–111.

National Intelligence Council. *Mapping the Global Future: Report of the National Intelligence Council's 2020 Project.* Washington, DC: U.S. Government Printing Office, 2004.

———. *Global Trends 2025: A Transformed World.* Washington, DC: U.S. Government Printing Office, 2008. http://www.dni.gov/nic/NIC_2025_project.html.

Nichol, Jim. *Stability in Russia's Chechnya and Other Regions of the North Caucasus: Recent Developments.* Washington, DC: Congressional Research Service, 2009. http://www.fas.org/sgp/crs/row/RL34613.pdf.

Nojumi, Neamatollah. *The Rise of the Taliban in Afghanistan: Mass Mobilization, Civil War and the Future of the Region.* New York: St. Martin's Press, 2002.

———. "The Rise and Fall of the Taliban." In *The Taliban and the Crises of Afghanistan*, edited by Robert D. Crews and Amin Tarzi, 90–117. Cambridge, MA: Harvard University Press, 2008.

North, Douglass C., John Joseph Wallis, and Barry R. Weingast. *Violence and Social Orders: A Conceptual Framework for Interpreting Recorded Human History.* Cambridge: Cambridge University Press, 2009.

Norton, Augustus Richard. *Hezbollah.* Princeton, NJ: Princeton University Press, 2007.

Norwitz, Jeffrey H., ed. *Pirates, Terrorists, and Warlords: The History, Influence, and Future of Armed Groups around the World.* New York: Skyhorse, 2009.

O'Brien, Kevin. "Freelance Forces: Exploiters of Old or New-Age Peacebrokers?" *Jane's Intelligence Review* 10 (August 1998): 42–46.

Oehme, Chester G., III. "Terrorists, Insurgents, and Criminals—Growing Nexus?" *Studies in Conflict and Terrorism* 31 (January 2008): 80–93.

Office of Conflict Management and Mitigation, U.S. Agency for International Development. *2010 Alert Lists—Fragility and Risk for Instability: Worldwide Rankings.* Washington, DC: U.S. Government Printing Office, 2010.

O'Leary, Brendan. "The Belfast Agreement and the British-Irish Agreement: Consociation, Confederal Institutions, a Federacy, and a Peace Process." In *The Architecture of Democracy: Constitutional Design, Conflict Management, and Democracy*, edited by Andrew Reynolds, 293–356. New York: Oxford University Press, 2002.

————. "The IRA: Looking Back: Mission Accomplished?" In *Terror, Insurgency, and the State: Ending Protracted Conflicts*, edited by Marianne Heiberg, Brendan O'Leary, and John Tirman, 189–227. Philadelphia: University of Pennsylvania Press, 2007.

Paredes, Artha Kira R. "Where Guns Rule: Private Armies in Abra." In *Primed and Purposeful: Armed Groups and Human Security Efforts in the Philippines*, edited by Soliman M. Santos Jr. and Paz Verdades M. Santos, 216–230. Geneva: Small Arms Survey, Graduate Institute of International and Development Studies, 2010.

Patrick, Stewart. "Weak States and Global Threats: Fact or Fiction?" *Washington Quarterly* 29 (Spring 2006): 27–53.

————. *Weak Links: Fragile States, Global Threats, and International Security.* New York: Oxford University Press, 2011.

Patterson, Henry. *The Politics of Illusion: A Political History of the IRA.* London: Serif, 1997.

Patterson, Malcolm Hugh. *Privatising Peace: A Corporate Adjunct to United Nations Peacekeeping and Humanitarian Operations.* New York: Palgrave Macmillan, 2009.

Pauly, Louis W., and Edgar Grande. "Reconstituting Political Authority: Sovereignty, Effectiveness, and Legitimacy in a Transnational Order." In *Complex Sovereignty: Reconstituting Political Authority in the Twenty-First Century*, edited by Edgar Grande and Louis W. Pauly, 3–21. Toronto: University of Toronto Press, 2005.

Pearlman, Wendy. "A Composite-Actor Approach to Conflict Behavior." In *Rethinking Violence: States and Non-State Actors in Conflict*, edited by Adria Lawrence and Erica Chenoweth, 197–219. Cambridge, MA: MIT Press, 2010.

Pereira, Anthony W. "Armed Forces, Coercive Monopolies, and Changing Patterns of State Formation and Violence." In *Irregular Armed Forces and Their Role in Politics and State Formation*, edited by Diane E. Davis and Anthony W. Pereira, 387–407. Cambridge: Cambridge University Press, 2003.

Perl, Raphael F. *International Terrorism: Threat, Policy, and Response.* Washington, DC: Congressional Research Service, 2007.

Peters, Gretchen. "Crime and Insurgency in Afghanistan/Pakistan: Assessing Motives of Conflict Actors." Paper presented at the Conference on Violent Armed Groups: A Global Challenge, Pittsburgh, September 16–17, 2010.

Phillips, James. "Somalia and al-Qaeda: Implications for the War on Terrorism." Backgrounder 1526, Heritage Foundation, Washington, DC, 2002.

Picarelli, John T. "Transnational Organized Crime." In *Security Studies: An Introduction*, edited by Paul D. Williams, 453–467. London: Routledge, 2008.

Posner, Richard A. *Catastrophe: Risk and Response.* Oxford: Oxford University Press, 2004.

Post, Jerrold M. "When Hatred Is Bred in the Bone: Psycho-Cultural Foundations of Contemporary Terrorism." *Political Psychology* 26 (August 2005): 615–636.

Program on Humanitarian Policy and Conflict Research. *Empowered Groups, Tested Laws, and Policy Options.* Cambridge, MA: Program on Humanitarian Policy and Conflict Research, Harvard University, 2007. http://www.tagsproject.org/publications.

Rabasa, Angel, Steven Boraz, Peter Chalk, Kim Cragin, Theodore W. Karasik, Jennifer D. P. Moroney, Kevin A. O'Brien, and John E. Peters. *Ungoverned Territories: Understanding and Reducing Terrorism Risks.* Santa Monica, CA: RAND Corporation, 2007.

Rapley, John. "The New Middle Ages." *Foreign Affairs* 85 (May/June 2006), 95–103.

Rashid, Ahmed. *Taliban: Militant Islam, Oil and Fundamentalism in Central Asia.* New Haven, CT: Yale University Press, 2000.

Reese, Shawn. *Homeland Security Advisory System: Possible Issues for Congressional Oversight.* Washington, DC: Congressional Research Service, 2007.

Reno, William. "Privatizing War in Sierra Leone." *Current History* 96 (May 1997): 227–230.

———. "African Warlords: Are They a Distinct Type?" Paper presented at the Conference on Violent Armed Groups: A Global Challenge, Pittsburgh, September 16–17, 2010.

———. "Explaining Patterns of Violence in Collapsed States." In *Armed Groups and Contemporary Conflicts: Challenging the Weberian State*, edited by Keith Krause, 155–173. New York: Routledge, 2010.

Reppert, John, and Alexei Shevchenko. "The Failure of Chechen Separatism." In *No More States? Globalization, National Self-Determination, and Terrorism*, edited by Richard N. Rosecrance and Arthur A. Stein, 131–143. Lanham, MD: Rowman & Littlefield, 2006.

Rice, Susan E., and Stewart Patrick. *Index of State Weakness in the Developing World.* Washington, DC: Brookings Institution Press, 2008.

Rich, Paul B., ed. *Warlords in International Relations.* New York: St. Martin's Press, 1999.

Ricks, Thomas E. "FM-3-XX: Revolutionary Operations." *Foreign Policy*, March 24, 2009. http://ricks.foreignpolicy.com/posts/2009/03/24/fm_3_xx_revolutionary_operations.

Risse, Thomas. "Governance in Areas of Limited Statehood: Introduction and Overview." In *Governance without a State? Policies and Politics in Areas of Limited Statehood*, edited by Thomas Risse, 1–35. New York: Columbia University Press, 2011.

———, ed. *Governance without a State? Policies and Politics in Areas of Limited Statehood.* New York: Columbia University Press, 2011.

Robinson, Jeffrey. *The Merger: The Conglomeration of International Organized Crime.* New York: Overlook Press, 2000.

Rodriguez, Diana, and Soliman M. Santos Jr. "Introduction." In *Primed and Purposeful: Armed Groups and Human Security Efforts in the Philippines*, edited by Soliman M. Santos Jr. and Paz Verdades M. Santos, 1–13. Geneva: Small Arms Survey, Graduate Institute of International and Development Studies, 2010.

Rosecrance, Richard N., Etel Solingen, and Arthur A. Stein. "Globalization and Its Effects: Introduction and Overview." In *No More States? Globalization, National Self-Determination, and Terrorism*, edited by Richard N. Rosecrance and Arthur A. Stein, 3–22. Lanham, MD: Rowman & Littlefield, 2006.

Rotberg, Robert I. "The Failure and Collapse of Nation-States: Breakdown, Prevention, and Repair." In *When States Fail: Causes and Consequences*, edited by Robert I. Rotberg, 1–50. Princeton, NJ: Princeton University Press, 2004.

Rubin, Michael. "Who Is Responsible for the Taliban?" *Middle East Review of International Affairs* 6 (March 2006): 1–16.

Ruggie, John Gerard. "Territoriality and Beyond: Problematizing Modernity in International Relations." *International Organization* 47 (Winter 1993): 139–174.

Sanín, Francisco Gutiérrez. "Internal Conflict, Terrorism and Crime in Colombia." *Journal of International Development* 18 (January 2006): 137–150.

Santos, Soliman M., Jr. "Terrorism and Philippine Armed Groups: Networks, Lists, and the Peace Process." In *Primed and Purposeful: Armed Groups and Human Security Efforts in the Philippines*, edited by Soliman M. Santos Jr. and Paz Verdades M. Santos, 91–114. Geneva: Small Arms Survey, Graduate Institute of International and Development Studies, 2010.

Santos, Soliman M., Jr., and Diana Rodriguez. "Conclusion." In *Primed and Purposeful: Armed Groups and Human Security Efforts in the Philippines*, edited by Soliman M. Santos Jr. and Paz Verdades M. Santos, 419–432. Geneva: Small Arms Survey, Graduate Institute of International and Development Studies, 2010.

Schanzer, Jonathan. "Yemen's War on Terror." *Orbis* 48 (Summer 2004): 517–531.

Schear, James A., Frederick M. Burkle Jr., Michael T. Klare, Joseph McMillan, and Anthony S. Naitsios. "Fragile States and Ungoverned Spaces." In *Global Strategic Assessment 2009: America's Security Role in a Changing World*, edited by Patrick M. Cronin. Washington, DC: Institute for National Strategic Studies, National Defense University, 2009. http://www.ndu.edu/inss/index.cfm?secID=8&pageID=126&type=section.

Schlichte, Klaus. "With the State against the State? The Formation of Armed Groups." In *Armed Groups and Contemporary Conflicts: Challenging the Weberian State*, edited by Keith Krause, 45–63. New York: Routledge, 2010.

Schneckener, Ulrich. "Fragile Statehood, Armed Non-State Actors and Security Governance." In *Private Actors and Security Governance*, edited by Alan Bryden and Marina Caparini, 23–40. Geneva: Geneva Centre for the Democratic Control of Armed Forces, 2006.

———. "Spoilers or Governance Actors? Engaging Armed Non-State Groups in Areas of Limited Statehood." SFB-Governance Working Paper Series 21, Berlin, October 2009. http://www.sfb-governance.de/publikationen/sfbgov_wp/wp21_en/SFB-Governance_Working_Paper_No21.pdf.

———. "State Building or New Modes of Governance? The Effects of International Involvement in Areas of Limited Statehood." In *Governance without a State? Policies and Politics in Areas of Limited Statehood*, edited by Thomas Risse, 232–261. New York: Columbia University Press, 2011.

Scott, James C. *The Art of Not Being Governed: An Anarchist History of Upland Southeast Asia*. New Haven, CT: Yale University Press, 2009.

Serafino, Nina M. *Peacekeeping and Related Stability Operations: Issues of U.S. Military Involvement*. Washington, DC: Congressional Research Service, 2006.

Sharp, Jeremy M., et al. *Lebanon: The Israel-Hamas-Hezbollah Conflict*. Washington, DC: Congressional Research Service, 2006.

Shaw, Mark. "Crime, Police and Public in Transitional Societies." *Transformation* 49 (2002): 1–24.

Shearer, David. *Private Armies and Military Intervention*. London: Oxford University Press, International Institute for Strategic Studies, 1998.

Shelley, Louise I., et al. *Methods and Motives: Exploring Links between Transnational Organized Crime and International Terrorism*. Washington, DC: U.S. Department of Justice, 2005.

Shin, David W. "Narrowing the Gap: DOD and Stability Operations." *Military Review* 89 (March/April 2009): 23–32.

Shultz, Richard H., and Andrea J. Dew. *Insurgents, Terrorists, and Militias: The Warriors of Contemporary Combat*. New York: Columbia University Press, 2006.

Shultz, Richard H., Douglas Farah, and Itamara V. Lochard. "Armed Groups: A Tier-One Security Priority." Occasional Paper 57, Institute for National Security Studies, U.S. Air Force, Colorado Springs, CO, September 2004.

Silverstein, Ken. "Privatizing War." *Nation*, July 28/August 4, 1997.

Smith, Dan. *The Penguin Atlas of War and Peace*. rev. ed. New York: Penguin Books, 2003.

———. *The Penguin State of the World Atlas*. 6th ed. New York: Penguin Books, 2008.

Snow, Donald. *Uncivil Wars: International Security and the New Internal Conflicts*. Boulder, CO: Lynne Rienner, 1996.

Spearin, Christopher. "A Private Security Panacea? A Response to Mean Times on Securing the Humanitarian Space." Annual Graduate Student Seminar, Canadian Centre for Foreign Policy, Vancouver, BC, April 30–May 5, 2000.

Ssereo, Florence. "Clanpolitics, Clan-Democracy and Conflict Regulation in Africa: The Experience of Somalia." *Global Review of Ethnopolitics* 2 (March/June 2003): 25–40.

Stedman, Stephen John. "Spoiler Problems in Peace Processes." *International Security* 22 (Fall 1997): 5–53.

Steinhoff, Dawn. "Talking to the Enemy: State Legitimacy Concerns with Engaging Non-State Armed Groups." *Texas International Law Journal* 45 (Fall 2009), 297–322.

Sterling, Claire. *Thieves' World: The Threat of the New Global Network of Organized Crime*. New York: Simon & Schuster, 1994.

Stillman, Peter G. "The Concept of Legitimacy." *Polity* 7 (Autumn 1974): 32–56.

Sweeney, John P. "Colombia's Narco-Democracy Threatens Hemispheric Security." Backgrounder 1028, Heritage Foundation, Washington, DC, March 21, 1995. http://www.heritage.org/Research/PoliticalPhilosophy/BG1028.cfm.

Szayna, Thomas S., Derek Eaton, James E. Barnett II, Brooke Stearns Lawson, Terrence K. Kelly, and Zachary Haldeman. *Integrating Civilian Agencies in Stability Operations*. Santa Monica, CA: RAND Corporation, 2009.

Taulbee, James Larry. "The Privatization of Security: Modern Conflict, Globalization and Weak States." *Civil Wars* 5 (Summer 2002): 1–24.

Thaler, Farah Faisal. "Stabilizing States in Crisis: Leveraging International Capacity." In *The Challenges of State Fragility for US and Global Security in an Interdependent World*. Warrenton, VA: Stanley Foundation, 2009.

Thomas, Troy S., and William D. Casebeer. "Violent Systems: Defeating Terrorists, Insurgents, and Other Non-State Adversaries." Occasional Paper 52, Institute for National Security Studies, U.S. Air Force, Colorado Springs, CO, March 2004.

———. "Turbulent Arena: Global Effects against Non-State Adversaries." Occasional Paper 58, Institute for National Security Studies, U.S. Air Force, Colorado Springs, CO, June 2005.

Thomas, Troy S., and Stephen D. Kiser. *Lords of the Silk Route: Violent Non-State Actors in Central Asia*. Washington, DC: Institute for National Security Studies, 2002.

Thomas, Troy S., Stephen D. Kiser, and William D. Casebeer. *Warlords Rising: Confronting Violent Non-State Actors*. Lanham, MD: Lexington Books, 2005.

Thomson, Janice E. *Mercenaries, Pirates, and Sovereigns: State-Building and Extraterritorial Violence in Early Modern Europe*. Princeton, NJ: Princeton University Press, 1994.

Thornton, Rod. *Asymmetric Warfare: Threat and Response in the Twenty-First Century*. Cambridge: Polity Press, 2007.

Tilly, Charles. *From Mobilization to Revolution*. New York: McGraw-Hill, 1978.

———. "War Making and State Making as Organized Crime." In *Bringing the State Back In*, edited by Peter Evans, Dietrich Rueschmeyer, and Theda Skocpol, 169–191. Cambridge: Cambridge University Press, 1985.

Toffler, Alvin, and Heidi Toffler. *War and Anti-War*. New York: Warner Books, 1993.

Torjesen, Stina, and S. Neil MacFarlane. "Reintegration before Disarmament: The Case of Post-Conflict Reintegration in Tajikistan." In *Reintegrating Armed Groups after Conflict: Politics, Violence and Transition*, edited by Mats Berdal and David H. Ucko, 47–66. New York: Routledge, 2009.

Ucko, David H. "Militias, Tribes, and Insurgents: The Challenge of Political Reintegration in Iraq." In *Reintegrating Armed Groups after Conflict: Politics, Violence and Transition*, edited by Mats Berdal and David H. Ucko, 89–118. New York: Routledge, 2009.

U.K. Department for International Development. *Why We Need to Work More Effectively in Fragile States*. London: U.K. Department for International Development, 2005.

Urdal, Henrik. "A Clash of Generations: Youth Bulges and Political Violence." *International Studies Quarterly* 50 (2006): 607–629.

U.S. Agency for International Development. *Fragile States Strategy.* Washington, DC: U.S. Government Printing Office, 2005.

———. *Central America and Mexico Gangs Assessment.* Washington, DC: USAID, 2006. http://www.usaid.gov/locations/latin_america_caribbean/democracy/gangs_cam .pdf.

U.S. Department of Defense. *Military Support for Stability, Security, Transition, and Reconstruction (SSTR) Operations.* Directive 3000.05. Washington, DC: U.S. Government Printing Office, 2005.

U.S. Department of the Army. Field Manual 3-07 *Stability Operations.* Washington, DC: U.S. Government Printing Office, 2008.

U.S. Government Accountability Office. *Military Operations: Actions Needed to Improve DOD's Stability Operations Approach and Enhance Interagency Planning.* Washington, DC: U.S. Government Printing Office, 2007.

Van Acker, Frank. "Uganda and the Lord's Resistance Army: The New Order No One Ordered." *African Affairs* 103 (2004): 335–357.

Van Creveld, Martin. *The Transformation of War.* New York: Free Press, 1991.

Victoroff, Jeff. "The Mind of the Terrorist." *Journal of Conflict Resolution* 49 (February 2005): 3–42.

Vinci, Anthony. *Armed Groups and the Balance of Power: The International Relations of Terrorists, Warlords and Insurgents.* New York: Routledge, 2008.

Volkov, Vadim. *Violent Entrepreneurs: The Use of Force in the Making of Russian Capitalism.* Ithaca, NY: Cornell University Press, 2002.

Weber, Max. "Politics as a Vocation." In *From Max Weber: Essays in Sociology*, edited by H. H. Gerth and C. Wright Mills, 77–128. London: Routledge & Kegan Paul, 1948.

Whitelaw, Kevin. "Have Gun, Will Prop Up Regime." *U.S. News & World Report*, January 20, 1997.

Williams, Phil. *From the New Middle Ages to a New Dark Age: The Decline of the State and U.S. Strategy.* Carlisle, PA: Strategic Studies Institute, 2008.

———. *Violent Non-State Actors and National and International Security.* Zurich: Swiss Federal Institute of Technology, 2008.

———. "The Return of Barbarism." Paper presented at the Conference on Violent Armed Groups: A Global Challenge, Pittsburgh, September 16–17, 2010.

INDEX

accountability, of authority, 5, 20, 30, 32–33, 78, 83, 86, 189, 221, 228

action-reaction cycle, 33, 177, 180, 193, 226, 227

Afghanistan, 52, 56, 60, 82, 135–141, 163–164, 171, 201, 223

al-Qaeda, 59, 91–94, 97, 108, 111, 120–123, 132, 135–141

anarchy, 3, 23, 30, 62–63, 167–168, 183, 194, 202, 209, 230

"Arab Spring," 199

armed nonstate groups, 37–64; case studies, 89–146; coercive capabilities, 44, 54, 57–58, 81, 225; common assumptions about, 7, 60, 80–81, 200; conditions when they enhance stability, 155–160, 232; cooperative versus uncooperative, 4, 6, 12, 196, 209–219, 219–231; definition, 42–44; facilitating cooperative groups, 209–219; funding and support, 53, 58, 97, 108, 114, 121, 143, 157–158, 165–166, 221–222; impeding uncooperative groups, 219–231; motivations, 187; mutating identity, 8, 51–52; potential as stability enhancers, 2, 3, 5, 6, 10, 37, 71–76, 174–175; rationality, 43, 44; reasons for rise, 72–73, 80–81; relationships among, 51–52, 60; role as "spoilers," 1, 2, 200, 215, 225, 227; secrecy, 7; success of, 147–151; success of control attempts, 151–155; "tipping points" for shifting behavior, 227; types of, 47–52; types of control attempts, 52–60

arms. *See* weapons

Aruba, 189

asymmetric warfare, 45, 226

authority, 1, 4–5, 18–22, 24–26, 170–175, 188–192, 197–199, 202–210, 215–216, 218–219; erosion of state security authority, 63–68, 86; transformation of, 170, 173–174, 218–219

autonomy, 18–19, 23, 50, 81–83, 95–96, 139, 157–158, 171, 215–216

basic needs. *See* survival needs

"Big Brother" societal control, 174

"black hole syndrome," 190

Brazil, 182

brute force. *See* coercion/force

bureaucratic inertia, 39–40, 58, 89, 116, 141, 199, 207, 212, 222

Central Intelligence Agency (CIA), 14

Chechens, 82, 91–94, 163, 164, 165, 166, 172

civil society, 21, 26, 39, 86, 179–182, 192, 202, 207, 226, 228–229

coercion/force, 29, 53, 60, 65–67, 75, 152, 176–180, 218, 219, 225–228

coercion-stability tensions, 11, 176–180, 193–194

coercive capabilities, 44, 54, 57–58, 81, 225

Colombia, 91–94, 103–107, 162, 164, 166, 182, 200

combatant/noncombatant distinction, 45

conflict contagion/regional instability, 27, 32–34, 80, 94, 98, 103, 107, 111–112, 123, 130–132

conventional security/stability mode, 1–2